TARNISHED ARMOUR

TARNISHED ARMOUR

Hopes and Fears in Heavyweight Boxing

DOMINIC CALDER-SMITH

MAINSTREAM
PUBLISHING

EDINBURGH AND LONDON

First published in Great Britain in 2000 by
MAINSTREAM PUBLISHING COMPANY (EDINBURGH) LTD
7 Albany Street
Edinburgh EH1 3UG

ISBN 1 84018 363 2

A catalogue record for this book is available
from the British Library

Typeset in 10.5 on 14pt Bembo
Printed and bound in Great Britain by
Butler and Tanner Ltd, Frome and London

Contents

Acknowledgements

It seems that for each day I spent writing *Tarnished Armour* there are several people to whom I am indebted to one degree or another, whether it be for their help, generosity, time, support or encouragement.

I would like to start by thanking Donald McRae, author of *Dark Trade*, and Claude Abrams, editor of the weekly *Boxing News*.

It was over a pint at a Wimbledon pub, more than three years ago, that Donald indirectly persuaded me that the following pages would be worth putting together. During the time since, his advice and direction have been valuable and selfless. It will be a hard task repaying his kindnesses.

To Claude I am equally indebted, for my savings only went so far during my time in America, and his willingness to use sporadic articles of mine in *Boxing News* helped me enormously. He too has been a great source of encouragement over the course of the last thirty-six months.

Tarnished Armour revolves around the world of heavyweight boxing, where there exist so many unforgettable characters that it would be impossible to name and thank all those who were involved in some form or another behind the scenes of the ensuing chapters. However, many were particularly generous with their time and forever patient with my inquiries, telephone calls and personal interviews, and none more so than the book's principal subjects, Monte Barrett and Hasim Rahman, as well as Tim Witherspoon and Larry Holmes.

Outside the ropes, deepest thanks are owed to a number of people for the same variety of reasons: Steve Farhood; Ken Kolasinski, editor of *Boxing Digest*; Nigel Collins and all the team at *The Ring*; Keith Nelson, Paul Hamblin and Rob Carter at Emap; Glyn Leach, editor of *Boxing Monthly*; Al 'Old Timer' Davis, Joe De Guardia, Steve Nelson, Stan Hoffman, Tom Moran, Chuck McGregor, Rock Newman, Greg Juckett at Cedric Kushner Promotions, Donald Tremblay at Main Events, Greg Fritz at Don King Productions, Fred Sternburg at America Presents and Lee Samuels at Top Rank.

Other fight figures to whom I must express sincere gratitude are Vaughn Bean, Lamon Brewster, Shannon Briggs, Tommy Brooks, Mark Butcher, Chris and Tracy Byrd, Curtis Cokes, Tony Connolly, Pat Doran, Buster Douglas, Angelo Dundee, Lou Duva, Jesse Ferguson, Joe Frazier, Marvis Frazier, Michael Grant, Daniel Herbert, Jack Hirsch, Evander Holyfield, Bernard Hopkins, David Izonritei, Bob Jackson, Kirk Johnson, Don King, Cedric Kushner, Butch Lewis, Lennox Lewis, Oliver McCall, Frank Maloney, Oleg Maskaev, Kassan and Lorraine Messiah, Stephen Munisteri, Rock Newman, Jack Obermayer, Kevin Rooney, Lou Savarese, Bruce Silverglade, Renaldo Snipes, Michael Spinks, Kelly Swanson, Emanuel Steward, Obed Sullivan, Pinklon Thomas, Steve Trunov, David Tua, Tony Tucker and Darroll Wilson.

Away from boxing, and on a more personal note, I would like to thank Bill Campbell, Joe McAvoy, Tina Hudson, Caroline Budge, Judy Diamond and everyone at Mainstream for their faith in *Tarnished Armour*, and all their help over the last few months.

From day one, my family have always stood by me. They know my gratitude, but I would like to express it in writing all the same.

My whole American 'boxing experience' would have been virtually impossible were it not for Romy Barron, who housed and fed me for many months. I have since consigned all my mother-in-law jokes to the bin.

I would like to thank my sisters Henrietta (endless cups of tea and sand-wiches) and Victoria, and my brothers Anthony (for suggesting I watch a Larry Holmes fight on ITV with him one afternoon) and Benjamin (many years of shared, obsessive interest).

Many thanks, also, to my brother-in-law Simon Hearn – few others would have been quite so happy about indefinitely surrendering their offices, computers and cartridges of printer ink.

Thanks to Ceci, Daddy, Bobby, Anthony and Camilla Benda, Harry, Xanie, Olivia, Isabella, Antonio, Lorenzo, Bert, Imogen, Richard Shaw and Alex Watson, and also to another brother-in-law, Luke Matthews, who took many of the photographs in this book, as well as those on the front cover; I would also like to thank and remember my late grandparents, Kenneth and Lucy Benda, who tirelessly edited my early, unpublished works, circa 1977.

A big hug and a massive thank-you for my wife Bim; not once did she recoil from these recent pursuits of mine, though it often meant sacrificing evenings watching *Sex in the City* or *Party of Five* so that I could study recordings of grown men beating each other up. Her patience and support remained steadfast throughout the bad times (paying a few hundred dollars to check into a Minnesota hotel, purely to catch the broadcast of the Lennox Lewis v Henry Akinwande fight) and the good times (meeting Lou Savarese face to face)! I love her and thank her enormously.

Finally, and most importantly of all, I would like to thank my mother Rosemary, in whose memory this book is most fondly dedicated.

CHAPTER ONE

Reminiscence

The sunshine filled the moss-green valley town, washed its hills and its bridges, the roofs of its houses and the busy market squares. It was a lovely, warm, bright afternoon, a day for barbecues and drinking cold beers in the garden, mowing lawns and fishing along the steep riverbank.

The fisherman closed the door to his car, patted his stomach, yawned, squinted in the sunlight, and led the three of us across the road. This was where he belonged, where he was brought up as the product of a broken home, where he would return no matter where life's roundabout ejected him along the way; Alabama to work on the railways, Nevada to fight, San Juan to appeal to the consciences of more powerful men than he, and then eventually back to Easton for good, to retire and fish.

The fisherman was also the fighter, the former heavyweight champion of the world. The face and the physique had stayed roughly the same; only the softened attitude signified any great changes in the man who had fought for more than half of his life. There was a hint of resignation, perhaps, a shrug and a glimmer of sadness in his smile as he sat by his bar, inside his restaurant, across the road from his office complex and the courtrooms he rented out as his own property.

He closed his eyes, screwed them tightly shut, droplets of sweat bob-sleighing down his neck and shoulders, the Aertex shirt prickling his skin. He took himself back, back to the days when he ruled the world. Back to the days when he was younger, fitter, stronger. Those impressionable days spent toiling in the gym, jabbing with the dancing king of all heavyweights and enduring the spicy politics which walked hand in hand with the sport which crowned him its leader for just over seven years.

★

With the passing of each fight, they tarnished their armour further still. They weighed in heavy, but the burden of their skills lessened. This was the lost generation of heavyweights, belly-bumping and mauling their way through sideshows which threatened to cast only the dimmest of lights over the one man in the division who could be rightfully accepted as 'The Champ', Larry Holmes.

Holmes built a reputation from the foundations of his work as one of the most celebrated sparring partners of Muhammad Ali. Holmes was undervalued from the start of his professional career, despite his major role in helping Ali prepare for his resounding 'rope-a-dope' victory over the apparently invincible George Foreman in Kinshasa, Zaire, in 1974.

Even as he had gone ahead with a fight against the fearsome Roy Harris, his hands still broken and sore from a previous encounter, his surrender in an amateur bout still signified to the cynics that when the going got tough in the pro ranks, Holmes would quit.

Holmes, 'The Easton Assassin', disappointed the experts in the summer of 1978, when he was matched with the experienced Ken Norton for the vacant World Boxing Council (WBC) heavyweight championship.

Earlier that year, Ali had lost the world title in a baffling upset to seven-fight novice Leon Spinks, but when the WBC ordered Spinks to defend his newly acquired crown against Norton, the new champion elected to cash in on the more lucrative prospect of a return with Ali. Ever since Spinks's decision to take this course of action, the heavyweight championship of the world has struggled along, by and large, in a fragmented fashion.

Ali brought cash and charisma to the table – and, after all, Spinks had beaten him once, so why not again? Conversely, Norton was a dangerous fighter with modest marquee value, despite the fact he had gone 1–2 in three close fights with Ali himself. Spinks and his management's decision to forfeit the WBC crown, but retain the World Boxing Association (WBA) belt and make more money against Ali, is but part of a contingency pattern adopted today by the majority who ply their trade in and around the canvas ring.

The WBC stripped Spinks of the title, and installed Norton as champion. Holmes and Norton clashed, and produced a fight seldom rivalled since, so breathtaking were the swings of momentum involved. First one, and then the other held an advantage, this continuing right up until the very end, when it was ruled that Holmes had edged Norton for the title by a split decision.

Twenty years after the event, sitting in his restaurant in Easton, Larry

Holmes drank a glass of Coke filled with crushed ice. With all of its strength, the sun blazed down upon the valley where Holmes had been raised and where he had remained throughout the intervening years. He had ignored the trends set by his rivals, who started out on the streets, bought condominiums in Florida and LA when they ruled, and then wound up back on the streets when the days of glory had become simple, painful memories.

The championship of the world had been won, but for Holmes, being champ never lived up to all he had imagined it would be.

'Nothing really changed,' said Holmes, belching softly and rubbing his stomach. 'I wanted to talk to my promoter Don King, but Richie Giachetti and all the other trainers kept telling me that I should leave him alone, that it wasn't the time to talk. But I wanted to talk about my next fight, how much money it was gonna make me, who it was gonna be against and where it was gonna be at.

'Giachetti said, "No, he ain't in a good mood, let's talk to Don later." Always, it was "Let's talk to Don later". But I refused to be treated like some chump, sat myself down once in a hotel lobby in San Juan, Puerto Rico, and waited for King to come down from his room. I sat there all day long and Richie said, "He ain't gonna want to talk," but I said he would. He would have to talk to me, because I was the heavyweight champion of the world.

'Eventually he came down, said to me, "Hey, champ, how're you doing? What's up? Talk to you later, okay?" And he kept on going. He did this for three days running, until I said, "Fuck it, I'm the heavyweight champion of the world! Why is it that I'm being kept waiting like some chump?"

'I busted into his room, and he said, "Larry, you can't do something like that." I told Don that wasn't my problem, that I had been waiting to speak to him and I wasn't gonna wait any more. That's how they do it – brainwash you into thinking they can do all the business without you. I told Don then that if I ever had anything to say, I would tell him; I wanted a say in my business. I didn't want Richie Giachetti or nobody else negotiating the money for me to fight. I knew I didn't know exactly how much I deserved – I might have gone too high and I might have gone too low, but I was gonna do it.'

Holmes had given notice that he did not care to be treated as a fool, and King duly went about manipulating his career with more cunning than he required for most other boxers.

★

Three months later, Leon Spinks's life began to fall apart at the seams. Spinks was a party animal, a lady's man, a cavorter and a drinker, with surprisingly little discipline considering he was a former marine. He had lived life to the full after his defeat of Ali, and when he turned up at the New Orleans Superdome to face the man they called 'The Greatest' once again, he was accompanied by an entourage as chaotic and ill-equipped as any in history. There were four people jabbering instructions to him as he plonked himself down on the stool at the end of each round, and George Benton – the only one who might have made a difference – walked away in disgust before the fight was over.

Ali's regaining of the title was unspectacular but memorable nonetheless. It was to be the final victory of a majestic career, and it was also one which threatened to erase Holmes from the public's mind. Ali retired, however, and Holmes continued to enhance his status as the world's best heavyweight with a string of title defences, despite the WBA's decision to declare its belt up for grabs now that the dancing master had disappeared.

None of the subsequent WBA champions could rival Holmes. Many were fighters who would win WBA honours after failing in WBC title matches with him in the first place. Despite their shortcomings and private little Greek tragedies, these men who dwelt in the land of the lost generation each had an absorbing story to tell. Which of their successors would pay them any heed?

CHAPTER TWO

The Mirage of Immortality

*This game is as much a test of mental strength as it is physical. I
will always be prepared mentally and physically, and because of
that, I will never be beaten. I cannot be beaten.*
MONTE BARRETT, MAY 1997

'Big' John Tate won the vacant WBA heavyweight title by decisively beating
South Africa's Gerrie Coetzee in Pretoria on 20 October 1979. The bulky
Tate was an illiterate product of West Memphis, Arkansas, a farmhand who
picked fruit and laboured in mills after leaving school at the age of twelve.
Two years later, he grafted for money by working ten-hour shifts moving
stacks of wood in lumberyards. 'In the winter, my hands would freeze
working in the yard,' he would say. 'You can't work in the winter if you can't
afford gloves.'

Soon Tate moved to Knoxville, Tennessee, where he swept out jail cells
and took up boxing. He had found something he was good at, something
which would reward him with more than he ever could have imagined
when he was collecting piles of wood and cleaning prison floors.

Tate made the revered United States Olympic boxing squad for the
Montreal Games of 1976 (where he was stopped in the semi-finals by
Cuba's legendary Teofilio Stevenson). He was six foot four and weighed
seventeen stone two pounds, and he was coming off two impressive victories by the time he challenged Coetzee.

He had blown away Duane Bobick, the man who once made Larry
Holmes quit, and he had then enjoyed his first taste of South African soil
with a knockout of the highly regarded Kallie Knoetze at the Independence Stadium in Mabatho.

Apartheid was rife during this period, and Tate's willingness to fight not
once but twice in the reported homeland of racism was a cause of some

concern. 'I will show the South African people that there are black people who can be gentlemen,' argued Tate, before defeating Coetzee.

A year later, he had become just another former champion, when he lost in the fifteenth round to Mike Weaver. Weaver had already lost to Holmes in a bid for the WBC version of the championship, and was considered to be a relatively safe proposition for Tate to encounter before his home-town fans in Knoxville.

With moments to go before the final bell, and Tate the proverbial mile ahead on points, he was lashed by a devastating left hook which pitched him head first into oblivion. The two men fell to the canvas – Tate unconscious and Weaver in delirium, kicking his legs wildly in the air and grinning widely at his *Rocky*-esque battle from the brink. Tate had become an ex-champion, humiliatingly detached from his senses by one punch.

'Everywhere I went, it tormented me the way I lost to him,' he admitted several years after the event. 'I guess it will always torment me.'

MAY 1997

Outside, the air was warm and the sky bright. On the second floor of a Front Street corner building, beside the Brooklyn Bridge and a block or so away from an ominous-looking Jehovah's Witness stronghold, stood Gleason's Gym. Inside the gym, just beside the relative prosperity of Brooklyn Heights, a swarm of black and hispanic fighters sweated and toiled, their well-oiled engines recoiling and unloading against grey heavy bags and the oversized gloves of their trainers. It was a beautiful day, a day to remember.

New York City was its usual vibrant self, the weather was glorious, and the gym heaving with activity. Here worked the Dominicans from Washington Heights and the homeboys from Bedford-Stuyvesant; pounding leather, enduring the continual thwack of medicine balls on stomach muscles, turning up the heat against grimly determined sparring partners, biting through the pain, spitting, wiping away the thin ribbons of blood from split lips.

This was not a usual day, however; not for the gym's proprietor Bruce Silverglade, observing proceedings in a paternal nature from his small office, nor for the young local stars, waiting expectantly upon ring aprons, tying the laces to their Timberlands and dabbing at showered faces with their towels.

This was a day for watching and learning, gleaning secrets and inside information, familiarising themselves with the enemy, studying a champion and plotting his downfall.

The Russians were coming, but there was no Reaganist 'damn the commies' fanfare about their imminent arrival. They were not the enemy because of their nationality or politics; they were the enemy because they were the champ's entourage, and while the champ would be accorded a vast amount of respect outside the sparring ring, inside it, given half the chance, their hosts for the day would take him on as their enemy. The hosts would seek to punish, to wound, to hurt, gain mental advantages and file them away in some neat corner of their mind, to be re-examined the day they might duel for real.

A noise emanated from the granite staircase, and the door opened to allow the Russian entourage to enter the gym. Two slim men in tracksuits appeared, with closely cropped blond hair and chiselled features. They smiled, carried gym bags and mobile phones, and led the way towards the changing-rooms. Behind them followed the champ, diminutive but smiling broadly, his face flatter and more interesting, the pigtail creeping down his neck and back. He was the smallest of all of them, but he was the champion of the world – an undefeated champion with bazookas in his fists and the rapidly expanding aura of invincibility.

His father, an Oriental Russian with rough, leathery skin but the same dark hair, joined him. The Russian's manager followed: a big man with a balding head and mean-spirited eyes, and an unnerving way of speaking simultaneously with immense charm and a sense of foreboding. The heavyweight who came in last was a monster, St Petersburg's own Cyclops, well over seven foot tall, with furrowed brow and legs thicker than the torso of a grown man.

The Dominicans and the homeboys watched, intrigued, some staring solemnly, others smiling with undisguised excitement. As the Russians disappeared into the changing-rooms, the hypnotic thrum of the speedballs filled the room once again.

Camera crews from Australia and the HBO studios in Manhattan wandered through the sparring rings, trails of thick black wire following behind them. A skinny Korean girl snapped away with her Pentax, darting in and out of the groups of young fighters and media-relations goons.

The champ emerged moments later, and skipped rope before a large rectangular mirror at the back of the gym. Next to him, the Korean knelt down and took aim, reeled off several films in the space of minutes. In the ring to his right, a bulky seventeen-stoner threw half-hearted shadow punches at another.

One of the shaven-skulled blonds checked a stopwatch intermittently, while the Cyclops limbered up in an empty ring, the floor shuddering beneath him as he threw cumbersome shots at an invisible adversary. The promoter schmoozed with the TV executives.

The champ skipped faster, the rope striking the ground with a continual crack. The sweat trickled down his face and neck; the warring hippos next to him clinched and hugged and wobbled off balance; the Cyclops paced up and down with a blank look on his creased face.

When the time came for volunteers to spar with the champion, there was an abundance of candidates. The unfortunate heavyweight with rolls of fat and five necks was picked out to provide the Cyclops with some target practice.

For nine minutes a Puerto Rican worked earnestly but uneventfully with the champion, trudging forward, parrying when he could, throwing tidy but unspectacular jabs and crosses. The champ moved and poked, hit to the body, moved and poked again.

Meanwhile, the Cyclops took one giant step after another, and the hippo waddled and flinched, cuffed a soft left to the body and wobbled backwards.

The champ had to wake up when his fourth round of sparring began, as a Brooklyn slickster went for him, advancing with a spring in his step and an exaggerated swaying of hips and shoulders. The champ moved and poked, and the fighter from Brooklyn proceeded to sling long lefts and rights to body and face, catching the champ and stinging him.

The Cyclops landed two, three thudding shots, but the hippo took them well, and realising the experience might not be quite the pain-filled horror he had expected, elected to advance with less trepidation now.

Brooklyn's most cheerful whooped excitedly, unloaded, admired his work. The champion leaned against the ropes, swayed, raised his hands. The American tore in, stepped back, shuffled and whooped loudly again as he heard the cheers of his buddies at ringside. At the bell, the champ winked at him.

The heavyweights leaned and embraced, held, grabbed, shoved, cuffed.

The champ clenched his fists, threw to the body and the American moved back. *Bang!* The champ's right hand struck the Brooklynite high on the temple, dizzying him, sending him floundering back into his own corner. The champ winked again, and the sparring partner whooped delightedly. He would have a war wound to show off when he had finished showering. He had boxed with a champ, and it was an experience money couldn't buy.

Twenty minutes later, the Russians departed, vanishing down the staircase in their dark suits and gleaming black shoes which matched the cortège of limousines waiting for them outside. The cars moved off Front Street, turned right and under the Brooklyn Bridge, and eventually slipped into the heated traffic and disappeared from sight.

Inside the gym, the sparring partners chatted amongst each other and changed into their street clothes, and the thrum of the speed ball continued uninterrupted.

A thousand miles away, a challenger with a history of drug abuse prepared to meet the champion of the world.

★

The weather was still holding up, well into the second week after Kim and I had moved to New York, the sunshine luring people onto the riverside boulevards in their rollerblades. Tennis courts were filled, the hotdog vendors were cashing in by charging an extortionate price for cans of Sprite and Coke, and outdoor concerts were staged along the South Street Seaport and around Washington Square Market.

The evenings were humid. The subways and stations which connected commuters from New Jersey to the Big Apple were chock-full of people undoing their ties, massaging their feet, changing from brogues into trainers, and anticipating a cold beer along the Hudson.

During my visit to Gleason's Gym the previous week, I had talked at some length with Bruce Silverglade, mainly about heavyweights, and his words suggested little optimism on the future of the division.

'There are some good fighters out there, but no great ones,' he said resignedly. 'None of them stands out. There's no Mike Tyson out there, no young guy just taking the division apart. The thing is, boxing is in a mess, and the first place to look at to see that it's in a mess is in the heavyweight division. Even if a manager has a guy who can fight, he's not bringing him along properly. He's protecting his fighter, matching him against nobodies.

'The manager is only concerned about protecting unbeaten records. Most of the fighters don't stand up and demand more competitive fights. And the TV stations are to blame, too, because they almost demand fighters with glossy, unbeaten records. You can have a fighter with a 30–0 record, and he may never have fought a contender in the top ten. But it's far better to meet some competition after ten or eleven fights, maybe lose one or two along the way, but *learn*.'

It stood to reason that if there were to be 'another Mike Tyson' on the way up, he was most likely at the embryonic stage of his career. While

Lennox Lewis and Evander Holyfield were looking at defending their world championships against an old Tyson and seasoned but uninspiring men like Michael Moorer and Henry Akinwande, the remaining contenders were either veterans (Tim Witherspoon and Ray Mercer) or new faces who were clearly not in Iron Mike's class.

I had read about Monte Barrett long before I made the trip to New York. He had won two New York Golden Gloves titles (the equivalent of an ABA championship) as an amateur, and was fighting out of the Brooklyn–Queens area, using the appropriately confrontational nickname of '2GUNZ'.

Barrett had engaged in ten professional fights by the time I was put in touch with him by his manager, a Bronx attorney named Joe De Guardia, who had himself won a Golden Gloves title back in 1988 as a middleweight. In those ten fights, Barrett had been opposed by the usual nondescript opposition, though not all would have qualified for the 'tomato can' tip: Liyadi Alhassan, a gangly, awkward Ghanaian who had fought in the Olympics, and Mitch Rose, conqueror of the cult figure 'Butterbean', had both been defeated by decision.

I had a mid-afternoon appointment to meet Barrett at the Starrett City gym, in the far reaches of Pennsylvania Avenue, Brooklyn, and caught the train from the World Trade Centre.

Sunrays glazed the stained subway carriage windows, blinding the passengers and illuminating the floor. The train passed through the tunnels of Manhattan, crossed the Brooklyn Bridge and continued to make its way in the open.

Taking the subway in Manhattan means you don't get to see the cappuccino bars, bondage shops and Mardis Gras outfitters as you roll along underneath Greenwich Village, nor Madison Square Garden and the glittering lights of Times Square as you thunder through the midtown stations at 34th and 42nd Streets. As you wind through northern Brooklyn, though, you can see the landscape: the towering red blocks, the housing projects, the suburban jigsaws.

At Pennsylvania Avenue I left the carriage and the rap music behind me, and walked two flights of steps down onto street level, where blue buses were being crammed to capacity and tramps urinated under bridges. Never too happy taking the bus, whether in London or Brooklyn, I bought a Coke at a Lotto stand, and was given directions to Starrett City. It was going to be a long trek on foot but to my mind it was better than disembarking at the wrong stop and winding up miles away from my destination.

Some blocks weren't too bad: neat, white-painted houses with immaculate patches of garden and rows of tulips. Others weren't quite so delightful, but this was deepest Brooklyn after all, and anyway, my old home in Clapham North was hardly a haven of quaint tranquillity either.

Large flags were hung above front doors, pennants from rearview mirrors in the cars parked along the roadside, proudly announcing the multinational fabric of the neighbourhood: Puerto Ricans, Dominicans, West Indians, Cubans. Cars were sprayed with the colours of Rastafarians, Bajans and Hispanics, reggae and salsa spilled onto the pavement from the open windows of Corvettes and Trans-Ams, blending into a cocktail of electric drum beats and the mountain sounds of the sampona.

Women carried bags of shopping, young men huddled under bonnets and wiped oily fingers on their trouser pockets, teenagers in baseball hats and tracksuits swaggered by, loud, antagonising and restless.

A little under an hour after leaving the train, I reached the gym. It was situated discreetly under a multi-storey carpark, opposite a large sports complex complete with swimming-pools and baseball grounds.

Outside was a battered car with white paint rusting along its edges. I stopped by the door. I faced a photocopied poster on A4 paper, attempting to warn the youths of the area away from the slippery slope of guns, crack, the quick fix and the easy buck. 'Buy one', it said, above a picture of a handgun. 'Get one free', it added, this time above the dark sketch of a child's coffin. It wasn't an unusual piece of advice for a boxing gym to dispense. The gym, after all, was where scores of troubled individuals had turned to over the years as the only productive outlet to vent their fury and frustration at lives of poverty, crime and desperate social circumstances. This was a way out for some, a chance to gain the limelight and riches, a chance to rise above the limits set by their birth, to speak loudly rather than in conspiratorial whispers, to be heard and seen across the world, rather than skulking away in the shadows.

For Barrett, this had not been a short-cut out of the projects, but a chance to realise the lifelong ambition of becoming the heavyweight champion of the world. He wasn't spoilt by the trappings of wealth, but owning his own construction company – and a reportedly successful one at that – meant he was not in the predicament of having to fight his way off the breadline.

Inside the gym, a disgruntled man with an overflowing belly and stubble on his cheeks told me I could wait outside for Barrett's arrival, that I could bide my time talking to the fighter's trainer, Al 'Old Timer' Davis, who was, it transpired, the lucky gentleman who owned the four-wheeled wreck outside on the road.

Sure enough, hunched up before the steering-wheel, sat an elderly man with a bald, marked head and a grey moustache. He pushed dry-roasted peanuts into his mouth, wiped the salt off his lips with a sleeve, eyes staring straight ahead of him as he did so. He confirmed that he was Barrett's trainer, and proceeded to share stories with me about his life in boxing, long before he had ever been introduced to the aspiring 2GUNZ. Stories of forged identity-card rackets (he showed me his from 1947), stories of fighters smoking pot in their changing-rooms only a matter of minutes before challenging the likes of Sugar Ray Leonard in world-title fights. 'And then there's Monte,' he croaked, munching his peanuts. 'I've always wanted a heavyweight champion of the world, and now I have one. Known him since he was seven years old, and he's gonna be the best there is. He can punch, take a punch. Once, I saw him get hit,' he clapped a fist into an open palm, and shook his head from side to side with wide eyes. 'He took it, shook it off, came back . . . bang, bang . . . knocked the other guy out. He's ready for just about anyone out there right now.'

I shifted my squatting position next to his driver's seat, my knees going numb, and my legs tingling from the long walk from the station. Of course, no trainer in his right mind would do any less than profess to know that 'his kid' was a surefire bet for world-title success, but there was good reason to root for the Old Timer.

At eighty-two years of age, and with only a light-middleweight contender keener to roll a spliff rather than take a fight with the great Leonard seriously as Davis's major career highlight to date, the leap into the world heavyweight title frame would be some chasm to negotiate.

'Known him since he was a young kid,' repeated Davis, trying to be aloof, yet sporadically turning to check I was paying attention. 'He's an athlete. Used to catch him sprinting up and down concrete, somersaulting each time he turned, and I made him promise not to do that shit no more, now that he was a contender. That's what I have to worry about. That's all I have to worry about with Monte.'

Minutes later, a green jeep sidled up beside us, and Barrett and an equally heavy-set cousin emerged. Both men wore dungarees and baseball hats, the shirtless fighter's muscles rippling along his arms and shoulders. We bundled back into the gym, signed a visitor's book, and I sat before the sparring ring and waited as the heavyweight changed into his gym gear.

He was recovering from an injury to his hands and therefore unable to spar on the day, but before embarking on a series of callisthenic exercises and shadowboxing, he chose to elaborate on the single-minded reputation that he had carved for himself. 'I won't be a victim,' he said animatedly. 'I'll stand out from the rest of the pack, not just because of my ability to punch, box, move well and improvise, but because I won't let anybody – not even the promoters – talk down to me. Don King, Bob Arum, Cedric Kushner – I'll talk to them exactly how I like, it won't make no difference to me.'

As he spoke, he tilted his head gently from side to side, his eyes round and alert, studying me, making sure I was taking in all that he was saying. He was relaxed, though, in spite of the defensive walls he had built in preparation for the day the promoters would come knocking at his door, and he moved from one subject to another easily.

It was their problem if others took exception to his adamant belief that he would never be thrown upon the heap of broken dreams and promises. He would continue to be deliberate and thoughtful of his own well-being as his career advanced and his name drew more headlines. He was not worrying about the prospect of being made part of a game of checkers. No, the promoters had another thing coming if they felt this young fighter could be enticed by a chest of fool's gold.

'I won't allow them to mess me around, even though they've tried it already,' he said, lifting a set of dumbbells as Old Timer received a kiss on the cheek from the fighter's wife, Taja. 'When Tyson was preparing for Evander last November, they made the call, wanted me to go down to Vegas and work with him. I told them, "Sure, I'll come down." I was gonna go down there to learn, take Al with me, stand up to Tyson, but they said they didn't want my trainer there.'

'Stupid people,' muttered Old Timer. 'That's why Tyson lost to Holyfield – he surrounds himself with stupid people. If you surround yourself with stupid people, you become a stupid fighter.'

The fighter stepped into the practice ring, shuffled and postured, arms shooting out jabs and uppercuts from his shoulders, his chin tucked down.

The telephone rang inside the gym owner's office, and he soon appeared at his doorway, fingers scratching stubbled cheeks, and offered a robust female fighter a date to trade blows that following weekend. The lady grunted her acceptance, price unknown, and continued to throw wide, lunging haymakers at the heavy bag before her.

The walls of the gym were covered with bright posters of Shannon Briggs, a multicoloured character with bleached dreadlocks, dark skin and scarlet boxing shorts. This was once his gym, where he stood proud as the area's top fighter. His stock had dipped, however, after his failure to negotiate the first serious step of his career.

I had met Briggs about two months prior to his first loss, outside the entrance to Madison Square Garden, with the 'Blizzard of '96' still well under way, and a bunch of cops huddled together in their dark overcoats beside us. His fight against Darroll Wilson, he informed me, would be easy and quick. One round, he predicted.

Eight weeks later, Wilson came to fight. He absorbed Briggs's opening barrages, then swamped him in the third and stopped him. Briggs blamed his first defeat on an asthma attack. Wilson was destroyed in the first round of his next fight.

'Briggs used to be the big-shit amateur around here,' said Barrett dismissively, as he continued to hop and skip about the ring, teasing Old Timer and winking at his cousin. 'But I beat his winning record in the amateurs, and now this has become my gym.'

Not enough to make up the rules, though, as the owner emerged once more, reminded the fighter there were ladies present, and told him not to use profane language.

Barrett lifted a hand to his mouth, eyes wide with mock remorse. Here, he was the joker, the laid-back, supremely confident athlete, the man who would not be beaten so long as he was mentally and physically prepared.

'I've got a lot going for me that the others just don't have,' he later elaborated. 'I can box, I can punch, I can move, I can take a shot. I'm also a good-looking guy. I love children. A room just lights up when I walk into it. I dress well, I speak well. I'm the all-round, perfect package. And I'll never be beaten.'

★

Vince Phillips was the underdog, no doubt about that. He was the human sacrifice to be placed upon promoter Bob Arum's altar, a challenger whose right to meet the undefeated Russian phenomenon, Kostya Tszyu, was perplexing. In the challenger's last two meaningful fights, he had been ripped apart in a bid for a welterweight title, and then lost a pedestrian decision to a fragile contender. These were the credentials of an opponent, not a serious challenger for a world championship. This was the appetiser before the feast, before Tszyu sought to rise in weight and challenge the welterweight supremo Oscar De La Hoya.

On fight night, Donald Trump's vulgar Atlantic City recreation of the Taj Mahal had its foyers packed with Americans and Russians. Nationalist jingoism still sold tickets in professional boxing. Years had passed since the dropping of the Iron Curtain, the dismantling of the Star Wars SDI program and the introduction of *perestroika*, but any confrontation between an American and a product of the former Soviet Union was still likely to draw plenty of patriotic attention.

If he hadn't been fighting Tszyu, few people would have cared less about Vince Phillips. He was another ex-junkie from the sport's depressingly fast conveyor belt of wasted talents, but here he was tackling a Russian – so the Star-Spangled Banner was unfurled and 'God Bless America' was belted out before a flag big enough to cover the boardwalk.

The American ladies with their lengthy fingernails and the Russian mobsters in their cheap suits and overcoats took their seats under the winking lights of the ballroom chandeliers.

Tszyu entered the ring behind a buxom card girl waving the flag of his adopted homeland, Australia, the nation he had emigrated to after the amateur world championships in 1991. Phillips trotted in to the strains of 'I Believe I Can Fly' by R Kelly.

Tszyu wanted to be a destroyer. He intended to come out and send a message to the people who mattered: that he was hot on the trail of a showdown with the Golden Boy, De La Hoya. After one round, it was apparent that a quick knockout might not be such an easy goal. After three rounds it was clear Tszyu was in a fight. And after six, it seemed like victory, let alone the knockout, would elude him.

As early as the first, the Russian's big right hand had found its target, and it had landed with shocking impact. But Phillips did not capitulate. His body rocked backwards, his legs bent, but before the Russian could follow through, he swayed forwards, erasing the tingling in his head with a shake, and threw a counter right straight back at the champion.

The contest intensified. The challenger's face was becoming lumpy and bruised, a swathe of purple and yellow crossing his forehead and cheeks, blood dripping from several cuts, but he was winning the war. The more Phillips was able to absorb the champion's punches, the more Tszyu's game-plan fell apart, until he relied solely on a desire to take this increasingly determined veteran out with single shots. Down went Tszyu, but he was up and punching, and Phillips would not budge.

The realisation swept across the ballroom. The junkie was clean, and the junkie was winning the war.

The big ladies with their long fingernails screamed 'USA! USA!' The Russian mobsters, wiping their hands frantically on their cheap suits, roared out a deep-throated chorus which sounded like, 'Zoo, Zoo, Zoo!'

But it was Phillips who was enjoying himself, swallowing the pain which was etched across his face and winning the battle of wills, until he trapped the champion in his corner and unleashed a torrent of shots. Tszyu's arms dropped to his sides. The punches struck home. He was defenceless and his legs sagged. Rights and lefts crashed into his face, spinning his head and blurring his vision.

His body fell slowly, helplessly into the ropes, and the whites of his eyes rolled. There was no such thing as unbeatable.

CHAPTER THREE

Holy Wars

Tony Tucker was undefeated in thirty-five fights when he took on Mike Tyson on 1 August 1987. He was supposed to have been a soft touch for the rampaging Iron Mike, another knockout statistic on Tyson's ledger of destruction, another victim to face career devastation. But Tucker had fought with spirit and tenacity, his long Jeri curls flapping in the Vegas wind as he bounced uppercuts off Tyson's chin, smothered the monster's hungry advances and lasted the distance in a successful bid for respect.

He could have come back for a rematch a better fighter. He could have learned from the first fight and drummed up interest in a return, especially since Tyson was to subsequently embark on a succession of utterly one-sided slaughters, but Tony Tucker – the real Tony Tucker – never ever came back. He became wrecked by drugs and a fiery temper, and when his skills deserted him almost completely, his body systematically broke down. In 1995, his jaw was broken and the orbital bone around his eye smashed. He lost, and he lost again, and each time the spectacle grew more pitiful.

'It's not over yet,' Tucker told me in 1998. 'I still feel like I have more to offer in this game, and with God's help I'll prove people wrong. If I hadn't broken my hand against Tyson I would have beaten him. If I hadn't had the flu against Lennox Lewis, same thing. The Lord will tell me when it's time to hang up the gloves, but for now he hasn't told me anything. My time hasn't passed me by yet.'

★

Las Vegas is an original – a metropolis in the Nevada desert, a shimmering ensemble of lights and showbiz pizzazz. Atlantic City is its wretched bastard child. There are few redeeming features about the East Coast city. Boxing, if you're a fan, is about the only one which comes to mind. The food is awful, the streets are dirty and dangerous, and the atmosphere stiflingly inane. Whether by coincidence or not, though, I always found myself returning from its haven of jackpot machines, leaning against the window by my seat on the Greyhound bus, with the most excruciating of headaches. These mini-migraines were surely a result of the stale air, the hideously patterned carpets designed specifically to keep guests out of their hotel rooms and on the casino floor, the endless pinging of the fruit-machines and the hours of bullshit spoken at boxing press conferences.

The whole prospect of travelling once again to the Boardwalk and its rows of candy-floss stands, repulsive 'all-u-can-eat' canteens effectively charging you five bucks to induce a steady fit of vomiting, and newsagents selling pornography so hardcore it would make an MP blush, was one which filled me with dread.

There is, however, a certain amount of amusement to be found in the prospect of finding yourself seated for the two hour drive next to an obese lady in a lilac jump-suit, fighting your way through an excursion party from Iowa's Over-Eighties Blackjack League, and barrelling your way past the sad individuals playing three slot machines at a time.

Quite literally, I didn't know whether to laugh or cry in Atlantic City. It was monstrous, unspeakably tacky, yet delightfully hedonistic. Greasy burgers, overpriced bottles of beer, the ring-ting-dring of the quarters spilling into metal trays, the hideous sweater shops, the fights. Most importantly, the fights.

My first trip to Atlantic City had been to see Tszyu tumble against Phillips. My next visit came a month later. My return to what is essentially a marshland surrounded by the products of Donald Trump's megalomania, was largely attributable to an all-heavyweight show being promoted by Cedric Kushner.

It was not to be the most spectacular of events – any boxing insider would have been able to guess as much – but my intention was to meet a fighter a level or two above Monte Barrett in terms of experience. In Barrett, I had found a sprightly young prospect with a single-minded belief in his destiny. Now it was time to learn more about the motivation of a fighter several rungs further up the ladder, one who was knocking on the door of title contention.

Kushner had been signing up an enormous amount of heavyweight talent, mostly from what would have been the lower echelons, but there were one or two top league names on his books. By giving these fighters regular work on his *Heavyweight Explosion* shows and exposure on the Cedric Kushner Sports Network (CKSN) cable station, the promoter was keeping his clients' names and reputations alive.

The shows, which were dragged through remote locations such as Des Moines in Idaho and Baton Rouge in Louisiana, and occasionally into more celebrated surroundings like Atlantic City and New York, were scorned by many. Main events often pitted a rated fighter against journeymen or no-hopers with losing records, but Kushner was cleverly covering a sector of the market seldom navigated by his more established rivals.

Bob Arum and Top Rank had had about as much success in the heavyweight division as Napoleon had invading Russia. Main Events looked after two or three top heavies only, and it was Don King's style to wait for champions to be groomed before he would even contemplate swooping in to snatch them away from their mentors.

Kushner, meanwhile, had cleared house. The majority of his main events left something to be desired from the standpoint of entertainment, but once in a while the wealthier forces of HBO, the nation's main cable channel, would crop up and buy a show with two quality pairings.

King controlled Evander Holyfield, and had sublet old champs Oliver McCall, Tony Tucker and Greg Page to a business partner named Jimmy Adams in Nashville, Tennessee. Main Events and the Duva family were putting most of their eggs into one basket case (Andrzej Golota) and any others left over into the threat posed by the hard-hitting Samoan David Tua.

Kushner guided the careers of promising talents like Shannon Briggs, Lou Savarese, Larry Donald and emerging contenders Hasim Rahman, Obed Sullivan and Ike Ibeabuchi.

This was not Kushner's opening foray into the division. After immigrating to the US in 1971, he had started out working as a ferris wheel operator, then a ticket tout, and eventually a promoter of rock concerts. Steppenwolf, Van Halen and Fleetwood Mac were some of the bigger names he worked with, but after a short stint in jail for touting, Kushner moved on to the business of prize-fighting. By 1983 he had his first world champion, South African heavyweight Gerrie Coetzee, who had surprisingly knocked out the drug-addicted Michael Dokes for the WBA crown. Kushner's association with Coetzee proved short-lived, though. Don King eased his way into Coetzee's confidence, and soon after the win over Dokes, Kushner was left out in the cold.

Fourteen years later, and King had still managed to retain a grip on sport's most formidable of prizes, now handling the career of a fighter who had once stood as the antithesis of the kind of heavyweight who would associate himself with a convicted murderer: Evander Holyfield.

The early June show in question was to feature a tepid double-header, with Larry Donald taking on the squarely built Anthony Willis in the headliner, and a rematch between fallen prospect Terrance Lewis and his conqueror Levi Billups as chief support. Obed Sullivan was to appear on the undercard in an undemanding bout against the always worrying opponent TBA (To Be Announced).

Kim and I caught a late-afternoon Greyhound from New York's Port Authority station to Atlantic City. This was to be the decidedly unluxurious form of transport we would use to cover the breadth of the United States a week later, and back again. Not only would these metallic-grey-and-blue beasts be our means of transport during our month-long round trip, they would also prove to be hotel rooms for half the duration of our journey, strapped for enough cash to stay in Travelodges every night of our 'holiday', as we were. The drivers were usually an entertaining bunch, but the temperatures rose and plummeted alarmingly from sickly, suffocating heatwaves to blasts of Arctic freeze-breezes. The seats were surely designed to cause passengers the utmost discomfort, and the average Atlantic City commuter tended to be a maudlin, sixty-something poised to blow his or her monthly pension in five ill-spent hours trooping from one violently lit casino hall to the next.

Kim's back began playing up an hour into the trip. Such medical dilemmas did not bode well for the four-week trip which awaited us. By the time we arrived at the Hilton garage, her back – and her head – were killing her. She knocked back two Anadin and a bottle of mineral water and I cheered her up with the encouraging information that all would be well once we had settled down into our seats at the modestly named Trump Plaza.

What crap. Three hours spent watching grown men pummel the living daylights out of each other, enduring the bellowing roars of their family members from ringside, gazing up at the dazzling chandelier lights and bending an ear towards the monotonous *ching* of the coins dropping from slot machines all combined to form a recipe highly unlikely to alleviate the stress to her ears and pounding forehead.

It was with some surprise, but also with much relief, that I found Obed Sullivan unwittingly saving the day. Disappearing into the bathroom for a minute, I left Kim standing outside beside the pretzel and hotdog stands, and on my return found her engrossed in conversation with the boxer, who was leaning against the wall, asking her name and how she was doing. His flattering attention, it seemed, was doing wonders for her headache.

Five minutes later, and we were still milling along at a snail's pace in the queue to get into the ballroom for the show. We bought hotdogs and Pepsis, and, as we did so, the heavyweights arrived in their navy tracksuits and gym bags: Donald, looking like a bulkier version of Carl Lewis; Anthony 'T-Bone' Green – a massive Denis Rodman lookalike, with lemon-dyed hair, dark shades and a sneer on his lips; and finally the scarred Hasim Rahman, not on the bill tonight thanks to the plaster-cast covering his right hand and arm, an injury sustained in his previous fight and part and parcel of the sacrifices a heavyweight puncher so often had to make.

The show began with little fanfare. There was the customary standing for the 'Star-Spangled Banner', a tedious opening contest, wolf-whistles for the round-card girls in their blue-and-silver peacock outfits.

If Kim's head was getting better, the people seated directly in front and behind us seemed determined to block any further recovery. The woman who kept chattering over our shoulders was more bearable than the loathsome individual before us. She was with her young daughter, and clearly only one was a rabid fight enthusiast. She leaned over and offered us her collection of photos to admire: pictures of her in small, floral-patterned dresses, gripping champions like Virgil Hill, Roy Jones, Riddick Bowe and Bernard Hopkins. She told us the names of all the fighters she had met and posed for photographs with. It was not overly interesting after the first five minutes, but music to our ears compared to the loud-mouthed git in front.

There on row six, the John Gotti Jr lookalike sat, his thick arms wrapped around the back of the chair in front of him when they weren't helping his hands stuff his face full of mustard-covered hotdogs, spraying us all with globs of onion as he screamed for one fighter to 'Kick that mothafucka's ass!'. Relish spewed everywhere as he catcalled and announced to all who were interested (no one) that the fight was 'Boring! Fight, you fat fucks!'

His slobbering jowls were evidence enough to prove a certain amount of hypocrisy on his part, but I could have endured all this disrespectful jeering so long as he didn't elect to start a conversation with me directly. Some chance. Overhearing my English accent, the jerk with the manners of a starving jackal, chose to inform me with all the details of his uninformed and particularly unwelcome opinions. Lennox Lewis was 'a pussy', apparently, who wouldn't stand a 'fuckin' chance' against either Mike Tyson or Evander Holyfield. And The Prince was 'a fag'.

I was glad to see the emergence of T-Bone Green from the dressing-room, not because I was overly excited about seeing him beat up on one Rodney Blount, but because it distracted the attentions of America's biggest bore.

Green cut quite an imposing figure, with his huge shoulders, exotic hair-do and groovy shades, and his story was pretty interesting too. The fighter had spent half of his life in prison for a variety of offences, and was now looking to make a name for himself as a serious title contender.

I hadn't bargained on seeing such a chaotic exhibition of 'skills'. In the opening round, he stormed at Blount with wild urgency, bombarding the smaller man with wide-armed shots and a mass of grunts and groans. He looked mean for the first two minutes, and then the reason for his sense of urgency suddenly became obvious. Technically, he could not box.

He took the second and third rounds through aggression alone, and the fact that his size was intimidating enough to prevent the camouflage-trousered Blount from launching any substantial counter-attack. Come the later rounds, however, it was Green on the defence.

And what a defence: his hands held up high, but at quite some distance in front of his face, his palms and the insides of his arms facing his now emboldened foe, and a wide-eyed look of uncertainty across his face.

T-Bone survived, and won a unanimous decision. By the time the next fight was halfway through, he was mingling with the crowd, all smiles, posing for pictures in a pair of baggy, unzipped suit trousers, dark shirt, and a black-and-white-spotted leather tie.

Everything became less comical a short while later, after the fight had ended between Kim's new admirer, Obed Sullivan, and Isaac Brown. Sullivan had won easily, despatching his opponent in the first round. He was holding his arms aloft as I stood up, eager to catch a further glimpse of the man some insiders had been touting as a possible opponent for big George Foreman.

As I stood, Sullivan swayed. I thought it was me for a moment, losing my balance after rising so quickly to my feet, but Sullivan's face proceeded to dull, his eyes close and his body topple as his legs buckled below him. He fell, hit the floor, and I could see that awful twitching in the leg muscles, which so often indicated that something was seriously wrong.

For five or six seconds, a sense of dread filled the arena as aides and officials rushed to place the stricken fighter's head upon a soft base. The drama was over quickly, as Sullivan snapped back into consciousness and slowly regained his feet to comforting pats on the shoulder and sympathetic glances.

His sudden collapse was made all the more mysterious by the ease of his victory, and Brown's failure to land a single outstanding punch. Some worried that Sullivan might have been affected by some form of neurological disorder, but he simply responded that a small cut inflicted during the contest had made him panic about the thought of losing the chance to cash in on a fight with Foreman.

It sounded like a gravely implausible reason to faint so dramatically. Ironically, it was announced soon after that Foreman had no intention of fighting him anyway, instead preferring to take on the more unproven but bigger-hitting Rahman, who had observed Sullivan's stumble from ring-side.

Before the show was over, I arranged to meet up with Rahman prior to his duel with the much older Foreman. He scribbled his numbers in Baltimore and Houston on a piece of paper, handed them to me and told me to call him in August once his training camp arrangements had been made.

★

In the heavyweight division, the colour was purple, evangelical purple: the colour of the trunks and the gloves specially designed for the WBA champion of the world, Evander Holyfield.

When a fighter is considered finished, his words either fall on deaf ears or are construed as being part of his sad demise from glamorous champion to fallen warrior, destroyed by the years of abuse he has subjected his body to.

When Holyfield said his defeat to Riddick Bowe in their third fight was down to a virus, heads had been shaken sadly, and appeals for the little heavyweight to retire had resumed. Hands were washed when a deal was made to match Holyfield with Mike Tyson in 1996, but when the medical liability had administered to the former kid dynamo the hiding of his life, bewilderment was explained away by pseudo-intellectual rationale.

Perhaps the joke was on everyone: fighters, fans, writers, promoters. Who ever truly knew who stood as the best heavyweight in the world? There was no formal infrastructure running the sport – no grand slams matching the best against the best, no ranking system which was not subject to the manipulative and self-serving intentions of bureaucrats and crooks all the way from New Jersey down to Caracas and Mexico City.

Perhaps Tyson was not even the second best heavyweight on the planet, let alone the best, by the time Holyfield set his fists upon him. Perhaps Holyfield v Tyson was a duke-out for third place all along, with Riddick Bowe and Lennox Lewis occupying the top spots.

Those on Tyson's side were not about to concede to the superiority of Holyfield or anyone else on the basis of one bad night. Tyson, they insisted, remained the 'baddest man' in existence, save for two evenings when he had underestimated the fighters before him.

It was an insignificant hiccup in Tyson's comeback, according to his followers. There were 'many more important things ahead in the life of Mike Tyson', said the fighter's co-managers, John Horne and Rory Holloway. Tyson, said his defenders, would do now as he should have done the first time, and knock out Holyfield in double-quick time.

History would have suggested otherwise. The winner of a fight was usually a more emphatic victor the second time around. It took a fighter of real character to return from defeat and beat his conqueror in a rematch. Tyson had yet to prove he could return from such adversity. Holyfield had done so, memorably, the night he stayed in Riddick Bowe's face and gutted out a majority-decision win in 1993.

Holyfield had survived Tyson's punches, and now knew for sure he could endure the worst the younger man had to offer. He had been replenished by his first victory to such an extent he even seemed to be speaking in a clear, concise fashion, as opposed to the mumbled drawl of the days when Bowe stood out as his biggest rival. He had been obsessed for a long time with proving the bully in Tyson, and now he was born again, both as a fighter and a person. In the immediate aftermath of Holyfield v Tyson I, there had been a brief respite from the hostile comments of Horne, Holloway and even Tyson. But as time went by, the one-sided war of words resumed.

There were suggestions that the first defeat had been set up by an early-rounds head-butt on the part of Holyfield, and Tyson's new trainer Richie Giachetti rubbished the 'overplayed' role of Holyfield's trainer Don Turner in the defeat of Tyson. After his man had beaten Tyson, Turner had become the man of the moment, winning Trainer of the Year awards from various boxing organisations and publications, and he proceeded to wax lyrical about the game-plan devised for the monster's destruction. The blueprint had been for Holyfield to fire from a distance, to move to the left, shove Tyson and follow through with the right hand. Move again, keep the young terror off balance and unable to unload.

The two fighters and their teams spoke and acted in ways that could not have been more dissimilar. Tyson and his people spoke street jive and swore habitually. Holyfield spoke cleanly, throwing in biblical references at every opportunity, and never using an F-word stronger than 'fight'.

Tyson entered the ring for the rematch to a rap song full of foreboding. Holyfield made his entrance to gospel music, and sang loudly all the way from his changing-room to the ring. This was not, however, a simple battle between Good and Evil. Holyfield conducted himself in a far more civilised manner than Tyson, and lists of muggings and gang-bangs did not fill his CV, but Tyson was not devoid of humanity, and Holyfield was not a man ever in a position to cast the first stone. On the night of the rematch, though, Tyson was going to put himself to the sword once more and invite further descriptions of base vulgarity.

The rematch was bigger than the original showdown in terms of pay-per-view and public interest. It was no longer perceived to be a mismatch. It was the chance to watch Tyson take another hiding or see the monster wreak havoc and revenge, and to take care of business.

The MGM Grand Hotel was a sell-out within days of tickets being put up for sale, the majority of decent seats in the house taken up by the WBA and the IBF, their wives and girlfriends, Hollywood celebrities and the latest stars of rock'n'roll. You could pay fifty dollars to watch the bludgeoning from the comfort of your own home, or you could watch the event in one of the millions of sports bars around the country charging a twenty-dollar admission for the privilege.

Kim and I were by now into the second week of our travels, and found ourselves in Phoenix on the day of the fight, holed up in a Travelodge next to a main road and some of the city's less welcoming suburbs.

A short taxi ride took us into an area littered with science museums and a collection of shops and restaurants named the Arizona Center, and as early as 7.30 p.m. I had decided it was time to sit ourselves firmly down at our 'ringside' table. The bar was pretty empty at this stage, with the majority of locals keen to watch the rematch, but not so enthralled with the prospect of viewing Don King's other fighters box listlessly through one mismatch after another.

We ate tacos, drank Bud lights (it was going to be a long evening, after all), and played pool on one of the numerous little blue tables surrounding us. The walls were festooned with college football pennants and trophies, and huge screens had been hired for the night to display the Showtime pay-per-view telecast of the big boxing event.

As the locals arrived and the bar heated up, it was difficult to distinguish between those who would cheer for 'the good guy', Holyfield, and the ones rooting for the brooding Tyson. They all looked the same. The Holyfield fans drank as much beer and smoked as many cigarettes as the Tyson fans.

The Holyfield supporters did not wear evangelical robes, and the Tyson fans were not to be seen donning black capes and hats.

The men played pool together as Julio Cesar Chavez waddled his way through a typically undemanding tune-up fight, and the women chatted with each other as King's female fighter Christy Martin smudged her lipstick and mugged an opponent for silly money.

It soon emerged that there was one change in Tyson's strategy from the first fight with Holyfield: the strategy of madness. Holyfield dominated the opening two rounds, but Tyson came out strong in the third, even appearing to push the champion into a zone of great discomfort.

Then Tyson was hit by a butt, and his temper exploded. He bulled his way in close, grabbed, leaned in and bore his gold-capped teeth down hard on Holyfield's right ear. He snarled and chewed and tore at the side of the ear, spat it out upon the canvas and the victim leapt into the air, his knees bent, howling in pain. Holyfield spinned towards his corner, glove cupped against the wound, and then turned back to show referee Mills Lane, only to be shoved in the back by Tyson – who now thumped his chest and taunted his former conqueror.

There was a long pause, while Lane attempted to take in all that had occurred, before deciding to dock Tyson two points.

As they inspected his wound in the corner, Holyfield's trainers Don Turner and Tommy Brooks wanted their charge to sit on his stool and take a disqualification, but the champion ordered them to put his gumshield back in.

The action resumed. Tyson thumped his chest again, went for Holyfield and, as the two men locked in together, the challenger once again bit into Holyfield's flesh, this time targeting the other ear.

Disqualified, Tyson took his anger to another level, performing a one-man riot in the ring, charging towards the blood-soaked Holyfield and lashing out at all who stood in his way, whether Holyfield's trainers, Vegas police officers, even his own corner men.

A week later, Tyson was suspended from boxing in the state of Nevada for a period of twelve months by the Nevada State Athletic Commission (NSAC). With the recent passing of the Professional Boxing Safety Act, devised by Senator John McCain and passed by Congress, all other states felt compelled to fall in line and accept the ban as unilateral.

There were to be offers for Tyson to fight in China and the Middle East, but King and the boxer wisely decided that it would not have been to their advantage to respond to these overtures. To have done so would have meant jeopardising their chances of being reinstated the following year.

★

Such was the aura surrounding Holyfield by now that the greater his success, the wider people's ears opened to his spiritual message. Apart from his fervent belief in a greater power, his forgiving tones in the wake of the Tyson rematch only solidified his humble, Christian image.

You do not, of course, have to be a professional boxer to receive inner strength from God, though many of them profess to do so, but it is an occupation you might not normally have associated with the vast number of scriptures which urge peace and goodwill to all men. On the other hand, some argue, the Bible is renowned for being one of the most violent books in history, so perhaps the contradiction between adhering to such words while punching people in the face for a living matters less than we think.

Holyfield always entered the ring to the strains of 'Glory to Glory', and talked about winning all three major heavyweight titles before retiring – one each for the Father, the Son and the Holy Ghost. All around him, a host of rival heavyweights and champions from other divisions were echoing his words. Others claimed they were simply jumping on The Real Deal band-wagon.

'Everything is done in God's time,' said heavyweight Michael Grant one afternoon as we sat drinking coffee in Philadelphia. 'Why should I worry about a time frame in boxing when I know that it is God who ultimately decides when it will be my time to rule?'

There seemed little evidence to suggest these fighters had anything but the most steadfast belief in the words they spoke, but for many of their rivals there was a feeling that some pugilistic version of a Jimmy Swaggert con-job was taking place. 'What makes him think God takes sides?' argued IBF champion Michael Moorer while discussing Holyfield's 'relationship' with God. 'I believe in God too, so what makes him believe God will choose him over me?'

Holyfield may have had the reputation as the sport's 'Christian Warrior', but a history of adultery and illegitimate children, and an episode in his life when he claimed to have been 'cured' of a heart defect by faith-healer Bennie Hinn, was more than enough to draw the cynic out of even the most open-minded of people.

When I was in Philadelphia talking with Grant, I also paid a visit to the Joe Frazier Gym on North Broad Street. Grant had spoken to me about the snakes who crawled along the grass and bit people – both in the Bible and in the world he currently traded in. At the gym, I sought the opinions of a preacher named Marvis Frazier.

★

Philadelphia's rich association with boxing is personified by its fighters with reputations as gutsy, never-say-die predators. A Philly fighter is nearly always a blue-collar fighter, a left-hooking, durable, unrelenting machine, subjected to a diet of gym warfare as ideal preparation for the rigours of professional fighting.

Different gyms have different rules and methods: in Sheffield, Brendan Ingle forbids his young protégés from targeting the head; in Detroit, Emanuel Steward keeps the temperature in the 'Kronk Recreation Center' at a simmering heat. Philadelphia indirectly encourages wars. The Philly fighter's reputation precedes him: his heart, his will to win, his refusal to submit. This ethic contributed to the ruin of men who were too brave, yet too vulnerable, for their own good, like Meldrick Taylor and Tyrell Biggs. And it helped make heroes of men like Bennie Briscoe, the middleweight champ that never was; Bernard Hopkins, 'The Executioner'; and most of all, Smokin' Joe Frazier.

As is the case with so many American cities, a block or two's walk can lead you from a high-finance district to an area of social deprivation. So it is with Philadelphia, where the town hall's Parisian architecture and the office blocks and luscious boutiques stand only a matter of a few blocks or so away from the less salubrious regions of Broad Street.

The walk from the centre of town to the Joe Frazier Gym is more intimidating than the one from Pennsylvania Avenue station in Brooklyn to Starrett City. After seven blocks, the shops and the cafés are replaced by garages and off-licences that have bars to protect the shopkeepers from the customers.

I passed the famous arena known as Jimmy Topi's Blue Horizon – an old theatre, restored and used regularly on Tuesday evenings for the soon to be disbanded USA channel's *Tuesday Night Fights* show. This was considered by some to be the 'purest' venue for watching the fights, a venue where only blue-collar fighters were welcomed, and where fancy-dans with sequinned robes and sharp footwork were heckled. Conversely, its detractors would claim that the routinely packed houses attracted a mob, baying for blood and blind to any of the technical nuances which separated a boxing match from a pub brawl.

Just the night before, the Horizon had been filled to the rafters for an unusually exciting heavyweight pairing, featuring Darroll Wilson – the man who had burst Shannon Briggs's bubble, and a big puncher from Soweto named Courage Tshabalala. Fans leant over the balconies and roared their approval as the South African hammered Wilson to the canvas with a jab in the opening round, and sent him sprawling in the third, with his legs caught underneath himself like a new-born foal. Somewhere between the count of nine and ten, Wilson had got back to his feet. He had survived the round.

As Tshabalala's enraged trainer Lou Duva, the veteran patriarch of Main Events, launched into another of his trademark tirades, the round card girls removed their tailcoats and sauntered around the ring in wonderbras, g-strings and high heels.

The crowd whistled and bellowed, as Wilson came out for the fourth a rejuvenated fighter, while Tshabalala wilted, his last reserves of energy spent, finally crumbling to the ground in submission. Both heavyweights were returning from bad knockout defeats, and in this classic crossroads match-up, Tshabalala sunk further into journeyman status, and Wilson gave his career a boost towards a return to becoming a legitimate contender.

The heavyweights donned their robes, stepped out of the ring, and headed for the changing-rooms. The round-card girls handed out free admission passes to the post-fight party at their strip joint, and the TV executives rubbed their hands with glee after one of the most thrilling heavyweight encounters of the year.

A further seven blocks up from the Horizon, and the streets are sparse. A man sleeping rough here, another guzzling beer from a brown paper bag there. I remembered once visiting Bernard Hopkins at the James Shuler Memorial gym in South Philly, recollected him pointing out of the first-floor window at men sleeping under dirty woollen hats and men selling crack on each street corner. I remembered him telling me there were places not even he, the middleweight champion of the world, would care to tread.

I made it to the gym uninterrupted. I hadn't been whacked on the head with a brick and robbed, as former contender Bert Cooper had been the previous month, and I hadn't been accosted by some crackhead speaking in high-pitched riddles as a friend had been during one of his visits to the City of Brotherly Love.

The gym was dimly lit, but giant murals depicted colourful scenes of Frazier battling against the man he now referred to as 'The Butterfly', Muhammad Ali. Most of these illustrated re-enactments were taken from

'The Fight', the first of Ali and Frazier's three gruelling encounters, and the only one which Frazier won. To the left of the ring, another mural had Joe standing proudly among his four fighting sons and nephews, one of whom was Marvis.

Marvis greeted me in the gym, bespectacled and gentle-looking, wearing a dark blazer and trousers, and a grey waistcoat. I followed him into his office, with its laden bookshelves and mirrored ceiling, and framed posters of 'The Fight' staring at visitors from every angle.

Beyond his office was his father's own study. The door was closed, but I could hear the gruff tones of an angry man on the telephone, and as if sensing my curiosity, Marvis said, 'Don't go in there. Dad's not in a great mood today.'

Unlike his contemporaries from the 1980s, like Tim Witherspoon, Tony Tubbs, Leon Spinks and James 'Bonecrusher' Smith, Marvis had not won a world title, had not enlisted himself into the ranks of the Alphabet championship-holders. An IBF title challenge against Larry Holmes in 1983 had been disastrous, and a subsequent first-round annihilation at the fists of the young Mike Tyson had effectively ended a career which could never hope to emulate the success of his bigger punching, physically more formidable father. What Marvis had now, however, was something Witherspoon, Tubbs, Spinks and Smith could only dream of obtaining: stability, peace of mind, respect rewarded for services rendered outside of the ring.

It was over ten years since Marvis's last fight. There had been no embarrassing defeats; in twenty-four fights he had lost only to Holmes and Tyson. These losses had been absolute, but at least they had been suffered against two of the best champions of the modern era.

Now, Marvis was an ordained minister, and one whose tranquil lifestyle led him to be called 'The Deacon' by his more 'adventurous' father. Joe Frazier, like Holyfield, was a churchgoer who openly admitted a tendency to engage in 'dalliances' with the fairer sex.

Religion, I argued, could lead to some dangerous situations in the sport. So often it seemed a shot fighter, a fighter who was clearly at the end of his career, sought to bolster his deteriorating skills by turning to the Good Book. The results were seldom beneficial, and I ventured to Marvis that perhaps Tony Tucker should come to him and ask whether he was receiving the right message from God.

'Sometimes God talks to people and they don't listen,' was Marvis's response, as he leaned forward in the leather chair from behind his desk.

'God told me when it was time to move on and end my professional career, and that's what I did. I don't know, but maybe Tucker's been hearing the wrong message. When God speaks to you, it can be through any number of ways. It can be directly, through your friends and family, or through events which happen around you. God could be speaking to Tucker through his friends and family telling him to stop, but he just doesn't know it yet.

'With me, I even felt a physical sensation sometimes when God spoke to me. I fought James Broad as a pro, and he had beaten me in the amateurs. In the dressing-room before the fight, I was warming up and my daddy began to pray out loud. Then he asked me if I had anything to say, and I just said, "Lord, you know me. You know you are strong in my heart." And I knew for that night He would be with me; the feeling you get when the Lord is with you is more than emotional.'

As Marvis spoke, the room next door became quieter. The doors to the gym downstairs opened, and the first few visitors of the day arrived, preparing themselves for hours of shadow-boxing exercises and sparring.

'It's a wonderful feeling, knowing that God is with you,' continued Marvis. 'The difference between a coward and a bully is the ability to overcome nervousness, and with God in your corner you have the ability to become a hero. Now that's not to say that God chooses against another man. God is in everyone's corner, it's just that not everyone is in His corner.

'Look at Evander's win against Mike. As the Bible says, "I will use the weak and the foolish to confound the wise," and that is what God did that night. He took Evander, a man everybody thought was too weak, and he took the foolishness of boxing to confound the so-called wise people who felt that he had no chance of winning. God showed how much he loved Evander that night, and Evander showed how much he loved God by telling the world that he could not have done it without the help of our Lord and Saviour.'

If Marvis's beliefs had helped him make such a uniquely impressive transition from life inside the ring to one so secure outside, then there was surely something to be said for any man wishing to draw strength from religion.

Yet the whole holier-than-thou mystique surrounding Holyfield at this time was a little hard to swallow, and I found myself more sympathetic to the words of Bernard Hopkins, a recent convert to Islam, who told me on the same day he had pointed out the debris and sorrowful sights of South

Philly, 'Religion is not something which should define us. What it does is give your mind another path to explore and learn, and it can clear away a few of the worries you take with you into the ring. As a fighter, a belief in something will always help you, but as an individual human being it really doesn't matter what you believe in. We're all going to the same place, it's just that some of us are getting there in a different car.'

CHAPTER FOUR

Houston Rock

Oh God no, not another bus ride. As I waited in the solemn queue for the Houston bus by Gate 47 at New York's Port Authority station, it crossed my mind more than once to turn back, head for the subway, get home, and book a flight out to Texas on American Airlines.

By continuing to succumb to my fear of flying, I left myself open to more abuse from friends sure to continue labelling me 'a big girl's blouse'. I didn't care; no one had as yet constructed a bridge to connect New York to the British Isles from across the Atlantic, so flying was my only route back home, but if I was only going to Houston, I preferred to travel by land.

Big girl's blouse, indeed! Taking the bus was probably as hazardous to one's health as flying over the sea in an old Tiger Moth, but given the choice I would always plump for a false sense of security in those trusted old Greyhounds than the cold statistics which kept telling me I had more chance of winning the lottery than crashing into the waves while inside a jumbo jet.

I leafed through a copy of *George* as the bus headed for its first stop, Washington DC. I temporarily forgot about fighters as I admired the sultry cover photo of Liz Hurley in a black leather outfit, revolver in hand. Before we reached the nation's capital, I had eaten all my rations. Only another forty-one hours to go, I comforted myself. Ten hours' listening to the old man next to me snore incessantly all the way to Virginia. Forty-one hours' surviving on a diet of Doritos and cups of watery Coke from vending machines at the bus stations along the way.

By the time we arrived in Houston early on Thursday afternoon, I was hoping to call Hasim 'The Rock' Rahman, arrange to visit him at the Main Street Gym, conduct the interview we had loosely arranged, and then get the hell back to New York as fast as I could. There was a 10 p.m. coach departing on the evening of my arrival, and even though my neck was stiff and my mouth filled with the sickly taste of crisps and soda and stale air-conditioning, I intended to be on it.

I walked from the Greyhound station to the city centre, and called Rahman at his hotel on a payphone. His sleepy voice answered.

'Hasim, it's Dominic. What time are you in the gym this afternoon?' I asked.

'The gym? I've already been to the gym!' he replied. 'I'm resting now. Why don't you come see me tomorrow morning, I'll be there from eight o'clock.'

My heart sank for a brief moment. The cost of my bus fare had been $150, and a night's accommodation in Houston, at least according to my *Fodor's* guide, was going to set me back another fifty. The best thing to do was to forget about boxing for a while, and enjoy the experience of staying in Houston for a day.

I traipsed around the town for half an hour, and eventually came to an ugly-looking building which I had been led to believe was a hotel. It looked more like a condemned ruin from the outside, but as first appearances are so often misleading, and a flag was waving outside its front entrance with the rather grand title of 'Houston Metropolitan' written across it, I ventured inside.

I hadn't been misled by its appearance. The place looked like it belonged in downtown Sarajevo. Only one of the five lifts was working, piles of rubble stood where one expected coffee-tables and sofas, and water dripped from naked light bulbs behind the receptionist's desk. The whole scene reminded me of the chaos followed by the dismal loneliness which ensued after those evil plants had taken over the world in John Wyndham's *The Day of the Triffids*. The receptionist looked at me in a strange way, the kind of way you'd examine something unusual you'd never seen before – in this case, most probably the arrival of someone without either a bottle of cheap rum or switchblade in hand.

Pretending to be completely unfazed by the abysmal condition of this hell-hole, I calmly and without irony asked the man if he had a room. He responded by handing me a cardboard box containing about seventy keys, each with a number scratched onto its handle, and told me to choose any room I wanted.

I wanted none of them. I took the lift to the seventh floor, and entered rooms ankle deep in dust and litter, rugs spotted with cigarette burns, windows shattered, glass sprinkled on the sheets. Not a television, working shower or light bulb in sight. In the distance I could hear some muffled sounds, someone coughing, another throwing up. Some lucky bastard even had a TV that was working, but I had already seen enough to know I would rather have had my toenails extracted with a pair of pliers than to stay more than another five minutes at the Metropolitan.

I called back the lift, but it had obviously decided to pack up like its four companions. Walking down seven flights of stairs didn't fill me with too much delight, in fact I even felt a small rise of fear in the pit of my stomach as I realised I would have to do so in the pitch dark. Down each stairwell I went – not so slowly I would be caught up by the imaginary beast lurking behind my shoulders, but not so fast I would run smack into some slumbering prostitute strung out on heroin.

I reached the foyer with great relief, politely told the receptionist I would look elsewhere and returned to him the set of keys and the mass of cobwebs which came with it.

I decided to spend a few more dollars than necessary, and quickly caught a taxi to a quaint bed-and-breakfast establishment just outside the city centre, in Houston Heights. This was more like it: a pretty, five-bedroom guest-house, with four-poster beds and newly fitted bathrooms with monogrammed towels. Sixty-five dollars, and that included free use of the landlady's extensive video library and a cooked breakfast in the morning.

The next day began well. I woke up early, stood under a steaming shower for twenty minutes, and then sat myself down in the breakfast room/conservatory for a meal which consisted of two poached eggs, home-fried potatoes, bacon, muffins, melon, strawberries, pancakes, toast, blueberry jam, and coffee. The diet could wait.

The morning newspaper, however, momentarily ruined my day. I picked it up, turned immediately to the sport section, and there before me were the names Hasim Rahman and George Foreman in bold print. Excellent, I thought, a decent read about the build-up to their scheduled November fight, and then I would be off to meet the challenger himself back in the city.

'Foreman pulls out of fight with Rahman', said the subheading. I sighed, asked for a refill of coffee, and read the small article again. Foreman had indeed reneged on a deal to take on the Baltimore puncher, and was instead looking for a 'more suitable' opponent. At first this seemed about as bad news as I could take, having travelled all this way to write a pre-fight story.

Quickly, though, I figured that Rahman would have been aware of Foreman's withdrawal when I spoke to him the day before, and that had he been too dismayed to meet me he would have said so then. So, the interview was still all set. And the story? Actually, the story was always going to be more about Hasim Rahman himself than the fight with Foreman.

The Main Street Gym was a large, corrugated-iron hall only two blocks away from the bus station. I arrived early, well before Rahman, and sat myself down against a wall and next to Rahman's trainer, Tommy Brooks.

There were two rings in the centre of the hall, and men and women skipped rope along the perimeter, in time to the beat of the rap music blaring out of a stereo system. By one of the rings, heavyweight boxers Garing Lane (nicknamed 'The Freight Train' for his enormous dimensions rather than his speed), and Ricky 'Action' Jackson limbered up for a morning's sparring with Rahman.

Brooks was a patient, well-regarded trainer, with plenty of experience for a man only in his forties. He had learnt how to box at former light-heavyweight great Archie Moore's Boys' Club in San Diego, and after winning US Airforce titles as an amateur welterweight but nothing as a pro had decided to train fighters rather than swap punches of his own. Years later, and he had worked with some colourful characters, from the ill-fated John Tate, through super-featherweight champ Rocky Lockridge, lightweight eccentric Livingstone 'Ras-I Alujah' Bramble (who used to take a snake charmer and a voodoo magician into the ring with him), multi-weight champion Pernell 'Sweet Pea' Whitaker (one of the best defensive fighters ever) and bantamweight assassin 'Poison' Junior Jones. Nowadays he was working with heavyweights, assisting Don Turner in the corners of Evander Holyfield and Michael Grant, and running the training programmes of Rahman and Rahman's friend, Larry Donald.

If that seemed a fairly incestuous set-up, it was the norm rather than the exception in boxing. Brooks's wife, Donna, was the daughter of Lou Duva and the sister of Dino, the co-controllers of the Main Events promotional outfit. At the time of our meeting, neither Holyfield, Grant, Donald nor Rahman was under the umbrella of Main Events, yet several were on their way towards duelling with Main Events fighters: Holyfield against Michael Moorer, a bout which had been signed and sealed a while before my arrival in Houston; Donald against the veteran Tim Witherspoon, and Rahman against the Duvas' Samoan terminator, David Tua.

Houston was a favourite place of work among the heavyweights. Holyfield would always move out here after commencing his training programme at home in Atlanta, pointing towards the population's ability to acknowledge his presence with smiles and winks, yet refrain from interrupting his busy schedule with requests for photos and autographs.

Grant's emergence as Holyfield's protégé was developed here, and when Rahman and Donald both initially voiced a desire to spar with the heavyweight who had risen more times than Lazarus, it was in Houston that they ended up. Others worked here too: Obed Sullivan, the former marine who had fainted in Atlantic City, and Lou Savarese, the media-friendly New Yorker who had taken Foreman to a close decision only five months earlier.

I told Brooks I had come to see Rahman, and asked him how Holyfield's preparations were going for the rematch with Moorer – a man Holyfield had lost to in 1994.

'He's doing real good,' said Brooks. 'Holy's gonna stop him inside five rounds this time. He's got a clean bill of health this time around, and that's what will make the difference. Moorer's still a good fighter, even if he did lose to George, but Holy's better now than at any stage of his career.'

I asked Brooks when he had heard about Foreman's change of heart about the Rahman fight.

'Yesterday morning,' he replied. 'It really didn't surprise Rock or me, though. He must have seen something in the Jeffrey Wooden fight that he thought he could have taken advantage of, and then I expect he saw some more tapes of different fights, and realised that Rock can really fight.'

I liked Brooks. Not everyone in the sport had to strut around in a pimp's evening wardrobe, nor did they all have to struggle under the weight of such over-inflated egos. Brooks turned up for work in his jeans and his tracksuits and baseball hats and made no bones about the fact that the sport was a business, that they were all in it for the money. He didn't curse and growl, or physically assault writers who had criticised him, or boast tales of knife fights in San Diego and of putting gun barrels to adversaries' heads. He came to train fighters, that was what he did for a living, and he felt content enough in the knowledge that he did so well, without feeling the need to spout pseudo-intellectual rubbish at every available microphone.

'Rock's good, but he's still green,' he said. 'He needs to keep listening and learning, and we'll get there. When I first took over as his trainer, he could hardly hold his hands right, but he learns well. He would have beaten George, but that's not happening now, and we've had to accept that. Now we're hoping to fight Obed Sullivan.'

Well, it wasn't a world-title fight, but Rahman v Sullivan was a good match-up of top contenders, and even if I shuddered at the memory of Sullivan's fall into unconsciousness after the win over Isaac Brown, it was clearly a good quality fight which was likely to end up on HBO. After years of top contenders avoiding each other like the plague, HBO's renewed vigour in trying to match the best with the best by paying top dollar had suddenly rekindled interest in the sport, particularly the heavyweight division.

Three months beforehand, David Tua had taken on another undefeated fighter, the Nigerian Ike 'The President' Ibeabuchi. The two clashed in Sacramento, and after twelve hectic rounds in which CompuBox records for the most number of punches traded in a fight were broken, The President had received all three of the votes which mattered, the ones made by the ringside judges.

Sullivan and Rahman, meanwhile, had yet to make their HBO débuts, instead featuring regularly on the lesser USA network against adequate but unexceptional opposition; Sullivan boxing his way to tidy, undramatic victories over the squat Levi Billups and Native American Sam Hampton, Rahman blowing away similar types with his wrecking-ball right hand.

Rahman arrived in sleeveless grey T-shirt and cut-off cotton tracksuit trousers, arms bulging, gym bag slung across his shoulders. He was six foot four, approximately seventeen stone, skin and eyes darker than Monte Barrett's. He was a big heavyweight; not a giant like Michael Grant or Lennox Lewis or Riddick Bowe, but if he failed to stand as ominous as those three, it was only by two or three inches and several pounds. His face gleamed, the thick scar tissue splayed high across his right cheek, the result of a truck crash as a teenager, when the vehicle had rolled over him, burst into flames, and killed one of his best friends.

He shook hands with me, suggested we spoke after his workout, and then sat down to have his hands wrapped methodically by Brooks as Action Jackson stepped first into the ring, his headgear covering most of his face.

Rahman was the star today. There was no sign of Holyfield or Grant. Jackson was from the second division, a reasonable fighter who did not excel in any particular department. Garing Lane was one step away from what the Americans called 'Palookaville'. He was grossly overweight, with thick tyres creeping over his waist and a flabby but kind face. Lane seldom won, but his ability to go the distance and avoid being knocked out or stopped meant his services were often in demand from promoters keen either for their rising stars to get in some rounds, or else become one of the select few to be able to pound through his resistance. It paid the bills, but one feared he would be forced to pay a dearer price when old age beckoned. He had just taken Sullivan the full twelve rounds in a dull fight. Sullivan had jabbed and speared, but Lane had hardly blinked, and just trundled after the marine in the orange shorts, prodding out the occasional cuffing left.

I wanted to talk to Lane about his views on the Rahman v Sullivan contest, but he preferred to begin discussing how he was about to embark on a comeback (even though to my knowledge he had never been away), and how, when he was in shape, he could take anyone out there.

'Gonna get my weight down, get a few wins under my belt, and then I'll be ready to surprise some of these guys,' he said unconvincingly. 'Sullivan? He's okay, nothing special. I give him a two out of ten. Rahman? He can fight, and he can really punch. I give him an eight. Rahman's gonna knock Obed out.'

Rahman sparred for six rounds with Jackson, and after drying the sweat from his back, face and shoulders with a towel, invited me over to an open doorway to conduct the interview. A cool breeze hit our faces as we sat down upon a ring apron.

We talked about his fight with Trevor Berbick, whom he had knocked down early but failed to put away, and with Jeffrey Wooden, in what had been his most recent fight.

'Man, you keep bringing up my worst fights!' he protested with a wry smile and a shake of the head. 'Let me tell you now, there will never be a repeat of the Jeffrey Wooden fight. I'm glad it gave George Foreman the belief he could beat me, even if he did pull out and become "Chicken George", but I'm letting everyone know – I'm knocking them all out now. All of them!'

Actually, I hadn't really picked out the Berbick and Wooden fights because they were his worst showings, but because they were his most high-profile outings to date. Berbick had reigned as WBC champ until getting blown apart by Tyson's tornado in '86, yet nobody had stopped him since. Rahman had come close, with a sledgehammer of a right hand in their opening round, but Berbick had survived not only The Rock's power, but the embarrassment of tearing his shorts to such a degree that they had revealed a fetching pair of spangled underwear.

The Wooden fight had been intriguing and it had been brutal; the sad-faced Wooden could not punch, but defensive guile and the cunning which a fighter garnered with experience had helped him detect a possible weakness in Rahman's ability to ship punishment to the body. Body-punching was a dying art in boxing, and few had tested Rahman's resolve in this department – and for too many rounds he had appeared wanting, almost doubling over in pain and seemingly tiring beyond hope as the middle rounds arrived. Come the ninth, however, and after some eccentric refereeing which had allowed Wooden to continue after being driven to the canvas by some fearsome blows, Rahman emerged victorious.

'I feel like I'm ready to fight for the title now,' said Rahman. 'You've got Evander fighting Michael Moorer, and Lennox Lewis against Andrew Golota. I think Holyfield will beat them all and then retire, and then you'll have me in there fighting for one of the vacant titles. The politics doesn't bother me. Holyfield's with King and I'm not, but once you get to number one in the rankings, it doesn't matter who you're with.'

That was easy enough to say, but what Rahman seemed to overlook at the time was the fact that he had to get to number one in the first place. For now he sat at number seven, with Sullivan at number three. The winner of their fight would be in a strong position to succeed the existing IBF mandatory contender, Vaughn Bean, who unfathomably remained at the top of the pecking order, despite already failing at his first crack at the title against Moorer six months earlier.

I asked Rahman if he saw a potential rival out on the horizon, a man whose name might be linked to his as the heavyweight rivalry of the next decade, just as Ali and Frazier were in the 1970s, Tyson and Spinks in the 1980s, and Holyfield and Bowe in the 1990s. I asked him if such rivalries were important to him.

'There are some good guys out there,' he said. 'Chris Byrd, Michael Grant, David Tua. They're all good fighters, and I can't take nothing away from any of them, but I believe in my ability to be the best heavyweight in the world. I've got the best jab in the world, a jab that will shut opponents down and let me get them in a position to knock them out. No one else can do that. Lennox Lewis paws with his jab, Foreman telegraphs his so you can see them coming. But I can't concern myself with what anyone else is doing, and who is or isn't gonna be the ultimate opponent for me. It's me I have to worry about, no one else.'

In the space of four years Rahman had transformed himself into a viable heavyweight threat, having turned pro at the late age of twenty-five after a brief amateur stint under the tutelage of Tyson's old trainer Kevin Rooney. He had tried his hand at boxing after a series of successful body-slamming brawls (light-hearted street fights where opponents solely aimed for the stomach and chest) with his neighbourhood rivals. He had not been born in the crack-dealing neighbourhood of Brownsville as had Tyson and Bowe, and nor was he a sharecropper's son, like Joe Frazier. Rahman's parents lived comfortably in Maryland, and his brother was studying to be a surgeon back home in Baltimore.

In the bigger heavyweight picture, people were growing frustrated with the failure to match Holyfield and Lewis for the undisputed championship of the world. Rahman may have seen their imminent retirement and disappearance from the scene, but the rest of the world wasn't so sure. At worst the two would get beaten but continue to fight on, but the best possible scenario involved them clashing for the right to be called the real champ, the one and only champ that mattered, in order to bring some form of closure to the fracturing of the titles which the paying public had put up with since Riddick Bowe last held the undisputed crown in '92.

Perhaps Rahman's belief that neither champ would have much of an impact on his future was down to their inability to generate the sums of money associated with men who took on Mike Tyson. And so it was that as our meeting together wound to a halt, it was Tyson's name which signalled the last word.

'Tyson'll be back,' said Rahman, without a shred of doubt in his voice. 'And when he comes back, it'll be me he'll have to come through to prove he's the best.'

★

Soon after my return from Houston, I wanted to see how things were developing with Monte Barrett. Still unwilling to forego his independence and sign with a major promoter, he and his manager Joe De Guardia agreed to appear on a Cedric Kushner 'Heavyweight Explosion' show at Foxwoods casino, a Native American-run casino complex in the heart of the Connecticut forests near Uncasville. They were testing the waters with several promoters, and Kushner looked like their best option on the basis that he could supply them with several dates for their calendar and a wide range of opponents to choose from.

Main Events, who had sponsored Barrett as a young pro, were not interested in him, and Don King was reportedly still smarting at being rejected by Monte – the fighter had been shown a briefcase containing $80,000 and simply responded by shrugging and saying, 'I have money.'

Monte was scheduled to appear on a tepid undercard, but there was a little confusion as to the identity of his opponent. The posters advertising the main event – Larry Donald against the washed-up Tyrell Biggs – stated that Barrett, 'the New York sensation', was to take on Sam Hampton, who himself was fresh from a decent effort against Obed Sullivan. Some of Kushner's representatives, however, stressed that was not the case, and that good old TBA would be Barrett's foe until further notice.

TBA proved to be as elusive as Sam Hampton. Barrett arrived at the arena, a converted theatre stage within the casino, cheerful and early. He wandered around with his ever-present cousin, a tan Banana Republic cap on his head, jersey, white T-shirt, baggy jeans and Timberlands, still – as he put it – 'dressing well, looking the part, lighting up rooms'.

The first sign of a problem occurred ten minutes later, as the early arrivals started to filter into the arena and order beakers of Budweiser from the waitresses dressed in toothpaste green and shocking pink. Barrett wasn't walking with his self-assured swagger any more, rather he prowled from one corridor to another, swearing under his breath, visibly harassed, searching for someone to speak to.

I glanced at the bout sheet in my hand. Had he trained for Hampton and now found himself in with a 'tomato can'? Was he being thrown to the wolves by Kushner, matched against an opponent even more capable than the durable Hampton? The answer was that he had prepared in vain. There was no fight featuring Monte '2GUNZ' Barrett, no mention even of Hampton. Barrett was off the show, and he had travelled in his truck all the way from Brooklyn to find out.

Agitated beyond belief now, eyes smouldering, lips pouting, acknowledging me curtly and without the friendliness of our time together in Starrett City, Barrett mentioned something about 'that's the last fucking time I fight for that motherfucker Kushner', and then cornered his manager Joe De Guardia in a hallway.

The two sat down and talked animatedly for fifteen minutes. I watched inconspicuously from the doorway to the arena, disappointed by this mess; I had not come to see a once fine fighter like Tyrell Biggs only increase the sadness of his demise with another sorrowful capitulation to a young contender. I had come to see Monte fulfil the potential which he insisted he possessed.

The very animated Monte was being calmed down by De Guardia, who was doing wonders explaining the situation to him. Monte settled somewhat, but he was still seething when he explained to me his removal from the card.

'My opponent tested positive for hepatitis,' he said. 'Sam Hampton? No, I wasn't fighting no fucking Sam Hampton . . . I don't know who the fuck the guy was, but like I said, I ain't fighting for these motherfuckers again. They let me come all the way here before I'm told I'm not fighting. Someone fucked up, but I'm not letting anyone fuck with my career. I trained real hard. I was ready, prepared . . . I'm sorry man, but . . .' His words trailed away as his temper cooled, and he looked at me again. 'Okay, man,' he sighed, patting me half-heartedly on the back. 'You take it easy, now. Give me a call when you get back to New York.'

With that, he wandered back towards the throng of friends and friends of friends who had come to watch him fight; guys in black string-vests and their girlfriends, his squad of lumbering cousins and brothers.

I felt tired and weighed down and I imagined that I felt his disappointment. I would call him the following week and find out what the next move in his career was to be, but meanwhile the show was about to begin. I hoped for the opportunity to see a flicker of emerging talent, before the certain defeat of a man who had once been bursting with promise – Tyrell Biggs.

As Biggs entered the ring, cheers rippled across the arena from all directions, but this was not the Olympic Games, nor the evening of a world-championship fight. This was September 1997, almost ten years since Biggs had been ruined by Mike Tyson in a premature title bid. It had been years since the friendly, slick-boxing stylist with the exceptional left jab had even been considered a contender, but his name still meant something. It could still be traded in for a small pay-day when times grew hard.

It soon became apparent that there would be no minor miracles in a confrontation between Biggs and another former Olympian, Larry Donald. The soft-hitting Donald sensed immediately that he was for once up against a foe who might fall rather easily.

Ten years earlier, Biggs fought like Donald, only a fair bit better. On this night, he came out with his long jab and tried to step and move, but his legs quaked from the opening bell, and come the second he was down and out from a swift left–right combination.

Biggs winced and raised his head drowsily, blood dribbling from his nose. The fight was over. Surely it was all over for his career, I thought to myself sadly. It was terrible to watch him dismantled so effortlessly. It was pitiful observing him grimace and gasp for breath, as officials sat him down gently upon his ring stool and checked him over as a corner woman stemmed the flow of blood from his nose by packing it with cotton wool.

'I tried to ignore some medical problems,' he told me afterwards. 'I shouldn't have taken this fight. I just haven't been feeling myself lately, and I don't feel good.'

Later still, doctors detected an irregular heartbeat, and he spent three nights in hospital hooked up to an intravenous drip until the condition was rectified. If God's message had been vague with Tony Tucker, this surely sent a clear signal to Biggs, or so I hoped.

'I'm just looking for small club fights now,' said Biggs, in his husky Barry White tones when we spoke on the telephone after his release from hospital. 'Maybe if the time is right, and another big fight comes along, I'll take it. If it doesn't happen, it doesn't happen. I don't want to be like George Foreman and Larry Holmes, fighting into my fifties. I want to settle down, find a decent job and raise a little family. I want to try and live a normal life. That's what I want the most.'

It didn't seem too much to ask for.

CHAPTER FIVE

Breakfast at Terrible Tim's

I miss the roar of the crowd, the buzz you get as you leave the
changing-room. If I can get back any of that, no matter how small,
I'll be happy.
PINKLON THOMAS, JULY 1992

I tried warning them. When I fought Tim Witherspoon, I said to
him, 'Timmy, we're friends, no matter who whips who. Don't let
the assholes around you talk shit. You're supposed to be getting
$130,000 but by the time they give it to you, you'll be lucky to
see $30,000 of it.' I told him, 'They're gonna cut your purse here
and there,' but he just didn't listen to me. All Timmy said was,
'Fuck you, motherfucker, I'm gonna knock your fuckin' ass out!'
But I told him to remember what I had said, and two months later
he was broke.
LARRY HOLMES, JUNE 1998

Towards the end of 1997, there were still three world heavyweight champions in existence – four if you gave credence to George Foreman's standing as the 'linear' title-holder. But Foreman and IBF champ Michael Moorer were really the bit-part players in a play largely believed to be held together by the WBA king Evander Holyfield, and his British WBC counterpart Lennox Lewis.

Holyfield was widely regarded as the number one heavyweight in the world, and not just at home in the US. The rest of the world's press also recognised him as such, but there was an obvious need – or so many felt – for him to turn back the six-foot-five Englishman with the torpedo right hand and canoe-sized feet.

I had admired Lewis for a long time, especially the laid-back way he had oozed into the ring against British champion Gary Mason in 1991, arriving for battle to the background of a smooth reggae beat, totally unflustered by the prospect of dealing with the limited but big-hitting Londoner. He had put on a remarkable defensive display that evening, the best such demonstration, I felt, since Tim Witherspoon soaked up Frank Bruno's shots on the arms and shoulders back in '86. By the seventh round, he was pinning Mason with jabs, and tearing at his eye with venomous right hands, all the while shifting stance and keeping his defences watertight.

Since being walloped by Oliver McCall at Earl's Court, however, Lewis had changed a great deal as a fighter. He now fought with a cloak of uncertainty, a tentative tactician against the obscenely ill-prepared Lionel Butler, for example, and clumsy and unco-ordinated against Henry Akinwande before winning by disqualification in the fifth round of their July fight in Lake Tahoe.

Holyfield had built up greater momentum as the two fighters' lawyers and managers sought to clear the path for a unification match. The WBA champ was riding the crest of a wave after two inside-the-distance defeats of Tyson, wins which encompassed excitement, controversy and more thrills than Lewis had been party to in quite some time. Now Holyfield was preparing to unify the WBA and IBF crowns by taking on old foe Moorer, and were he to emerge successful from this venture, he would have even more bargaining power should the Lewis fight be his next target. Two belts against Lewis's one. Holyfield's new-found popularity within the fight fraternity against the lukewarm reaction handed to Lewis.

Lewis, conversely, was on a roll of three thoroughly unconvincing wins; a too-close decision over Ray Mercer, the fifth-round mental collapse of McCall and the dire wrestling contest with Akinwande. While Holyfield was looking terrific against Mike Tyson, Lewis was struggling to overwhelm recovering alcoholics, junkies and awestruck survivors. Now, more than ever, Lewis needed to face a credible opponent, a man considered to be talented, dangerous and marketable.

With Tyson suspended from the game, Bowe developing into a serious liability in every respect, the young guns like Rahman yet to break into the public's consciousness and Foreman sticking to an agenda of his own, only one man fitted perfectly into this description; Andrzej Golota. In spite of his ludicrous tactics against Bowe during two fights in 1996, Golota was the boxer the fans wanted to see in action again. Lewis, the man who had walked into the ring to face Mason and Razor Ruddock with ice running through his veins, would surely have his back against the wall in this one.

As the countdown to the fight began, the talk centred predominantly around the Polish heavyweight's propensity to strike his opponents' family jewels. He had also made liberal use of head-butting skills and had even sunk his teeth into the shoulder of the unfortunate Samson Po'uha in 1995.

Golota's chaotic temperament was not confined to the boxing ring. Some strange things had happened to him in the past, not least the night he found himself celebrating an amateur victory in a Warsaw bar. The foolhardy soul who had dared to engage in a war of words with the hulking boxer was unceremoniously guided into the toilets, where he was thumped and made to strip, his clothes stolen and dumped in a dustbin several streets away. A prison sentence for assault had been delivered in Golota's absence, but by this time the fighter had moved his family to Chicago, where he trained at the Windy City Gym and fought professionally for the Duva family.

Golota's tactics against Bowe (he had twice thrown away victory over the former world champion after punching below the belt) were a clear indication that his mind worked in mysterious ways, and not only when he was in action against the best heavyweights in the world. Ken Kolasinski, editor of *Boxing Digest*, was more than a little taken aback while watching the Pole during one particular workout, about a week before the fight.

'He was hitting the pads with his trainer Roger Bloodworth and hitting them really well,' said Kolasinski. 'And then Bloodworth began to tell him to lighten up. Golota's eyes were manic, like he was on some other planet. He just kept on punching, harder and faster, until eventually Bloodworth dropped his hands and panicked as Golota rushed him, still firing punches.'

Lewis brushed aside the perceived notion that Golota would bombard him with low blows and other foul shots, saying it mattered more what he had in store for Golota than what his opponent had in mind for him. Even so, at the conference announcing the fight, Lewis's manager Frank Maloney played up the low-blow angle, producing a human-sized punch-bag wearing boxing shorts. Golota played along with the gimmick, pounding his fist into the stomach area of the dummy, and sending it and Maloney flying backwards.

I was staying in Greenpoint, Brooklyn, during the week of the fight. It was an appropriate place to be, especially as I had decided to watch the fight at a friend's place rather than jostle for a decent view at the massive Convention Center in Atlantic City. Greenpoint is one of the largest Polish neighbourhoods in America. Street signs are written both in English and Polish, video shops stock the latest blockbusters from Katowice, butchers ply their trade behind windows crammed with dried meats and dubious-looking sausages, the grocery stores are piled high with jars of pickled red cabbage and shredded onions in vinegar. The off-licences boast the widest variety of flavoured vodkas I've ever seen – everything from cherry, orange and lime to Bison grass and chocolate. The majority of the restaurants are Polish, as are the dental surgeries, newsagents, bars and Catholic churches. I noticed the women had pale, suspicious faces, their hair bunched back into buns, dark lipstick applied firmly but not too heavily. There were a lot of men with blond hair, moustaches, broad shoulders and chins dotted with stubble.

Outside stationers and tailors' shops, badly photocopied black-and-white posters of the fight showed Golota standing alongside the Englishman, above a swarm of words written with an extraordinary amount of Js, Zs, Xs and Ks. You didn't have to understand Polish to get the gist. Every bar in town was going to be showing the fight, and every Pole in the vicinity was certain to pay a minor cover charge in order to guzzle copious amounts of honey-flavoured Kropnik and cheer on their glowering hero come 4 October.

The night of the fight, it was clear even on the HBO pay-per-view broadcast that Lou Duva and Bloodworth were growing increasingly fidgety at the tardiness of their fighter, who was to arrive over thirty minutes later than planned in his dressing-room. He turned up just an hour before the showdown with Lewis, distracted and tight, his body cold having walked from a surgery where he had taken an injection for a knee injury, and his manner awkward. Duva and the other trainers were not made aware of the medication that had been administered to their charge until after the fight.

When he made his way into the ring, Golota was as stony-faced as ever. Around him, from the balconies high above the main arena, rows of red-and-white flags were draped across walls and around the shoulders of Polish youths who had been knocking back the drink. They welcomed him, their hero, the Polish icon, a God of War.

Lewis emerged to his customary reggae tunes, his shoulders, neck, head and arms twisting and turning to the rhythm as though he were made of rubber. Then the tune transformed itself into a techno version of Sergio Leone's spaghetti-western themes. The gunslinger was in town. Lewis was a flexible giant. Golota stood still, solid and pale, bumps of acne riddling his back and neck. He stared around him as though hypnotised.

Last-minute instructions from the referee. The order to return to their respective corners. Round one. Golota stalked Lewis, and Lewis used his mobility to work the angles. He wasn't running, merely waiting for an opening. Golota backed the champion into a corner, as he had done so productively against Bowe on so many occasions. But Bowe had waited to be hit. Lewis grabbed Golota, spun him around, and now Golota was the hunted. Golota was in the corner, getting hit; getting hit by fast, accurate punches.

The action moved to ring centre, and Lewis's right hand slammed against Golota's temple. Down went the Pole, but the most profound sight of all was not seeing the monster on the deck, but the startled, crazed look in his eyes. The eyes betrayed him, betrayed the shock and bemusement with his condition. He blinked, shook his head, but the eyes were still wide, his body unused to taking the sort of punishment being fired so deftly in his direction. He was up, but he was finished. Lewis exploded, unleashing a stream of shots: uppercuts to the chin, hooks to the side of the face. Golota crumpled. He slid to the floor. It was all over.

★

I met Tim Witherspoon for the first time on a sweltering September morning in the Pocono Mountains of East Pennsylvania. Tim Witherspoon, the fighter who could fill his belly with junk-food and a few beers, smoke some pot, and still be able to suck it all up and perform with skill.

The former two-time champion's comeback had steadily gained momentum since 1994, and he had looked good in defeating the mobile, smart-boxing Alfred Cole, a former cruiserweight champion, and in stopping the Cuban giant Jorge Luis Gonzales.

Seven months after the Gonzales win, however, Witherspoon had lost a split decision to the granite-tough Ray Mercer on the undercard of the Bowe v Golota rematch in Atlantic City. It was a loss which, although hurtful to Witherspoon's pride, did not instigate a sudden fall from the ratings. Mercer was a proven warrior with an impenetrable chin, and the decision could have gone either way.

Witherspoon's unofficial manager and long-time friend Tom Moran collected me from Trenton train station, about two hours away from the training camp, and during our journey he spoke candidly about the twenty years the pair of them had spent together. Moran was a proud Irishman with dank, ginger hair pulled back into a shabby ponytail. I had seen a picture of him once in a magazine, wearing a T-shirt with a cartoon depicting a white dove removing the Union Jack gag from an Irishman's face. I sensed politics might crop up eventually, but suspected that his humour and general good nature meant I was not about to be roasted about British activity in Belfast.

'I'd better warn you about Tim,' he said with a chuckle, the wind whipping his hair into a mess. 'He's the kind of guy who likes to joke around and have fun. He knows you're coming, and that you're English, and he might try and stir some trouble up between us. Nothing serious, it's just his way of having a laugh. I visit Belfast quite often, and I'm keen for Tim to come out with me. I've already been introducing him to decent beer, had a few pints of Harp with him the other night in Philly! He knows all about the Troubles, and after what happened in the ring after he beat Frank Bruno he isn't ever that sympathetic towards British people!'

There had been many highs and lows in Witherspoon's career; from two world-title-winning efforts and the night he crushed Bruno at Wembley, to the torrid years battling Don King in court in a successful effort to release himself from the shackles of his promoter's slave empire.

Moran had met Witherspoon in their hometown of Philadelphia, bumping into each other at parties and discussing each other's plans, hopes and dreams over bottles of beer and the occasional joint.

Moran's talents lay in video-editing and filmography and he had recorded reels of tape chronicling the formative years in Witherspoon's career, all the way up to this latest, and so far – successful – comeback. 'Tim's interested in managing local musical talent in Philly,' said Moran. 'With his and my skills combined, there's a real good chance we can make a go of things once Tim's finished with boxing. Right now, I truly believe that the last chapter in Tim's boxing career has yet to be written, but when it's all over, I don't want him falling into the same trap as the others.'

Boxing remained in the blood of all those who chose to participate in its sometimes wonderful, often brutal world. Fighters retired and became trainers, sometimes managers, a few even went on to promote. Nearly all of them came back to fighting. There was a cycle which kept repeating itself; one which began with a comeback embarked on with a real sense of purpose, a belief and confidence that titles could be won and seven-figure purses secured. Another setback would lead the fighter into a period of denial, a time of excuses and self-pity and a mistaken sense that he would eventually turn back the tide and prevail as a champion. Thereafter comes the lonely resignation, the acceptance that the wonder years have gone, the admission that money is all that keeps him going. He realises that the millions of dollars have been spent on a series of ill-advised investments and a courtyard full of sports cars. Now, he just wants one last chance at saving and putting aside for his pension, but it is never enough. When you are used to millions, a thousand dollars provides little more than a quick fix of comfort.

Finally, and most distressing of all, there are those who fall deeper into the well of despair and failure, the ones who turn to drugs, alcohol, violence and eventually wind up committed or behind bars or dead.

Witherspoon had a shot. One shot at helping bring about a fairy-tale ending to a career which included more than its fair share of wicked warlocks. He intended to fight for the title, spurred on by his recent signing with Main Events and the promise of an HBO date before the end of the year.

Then he would move on, help Moran package a film of their lives together on the road: partying in Philly, flying to London, fighting in Vegas, screaming at Don King while staying at his ranch in Cleveland, searching for cannibals during a trip to Jakarta with Muhammad Ali, negotiating to fight by the Great Wall of China. And then they would set about getting Philly's best rappers and R&B artists on the radio, on VH-1 and MTV.

In the heart of the Poconos on that steaming end of summer morning, Witherspoon was getting ready for a match-up on the USA channel. Politically, things were looking promising. He had just split from yet another promoter, the hawkish Denis Rappaport, and having signed with the Duvas, was on the right track to get a shot at Lewis, Main Events holding the promotional rights to the WBC champion in America.

'Is he gonna give us a shot?' asked the ample-bellied Whit Lowry, Witherspoon's assistant trainer, slumping into the back seat of Moran's car after we picked him up at the airport. 'I hope so, cos Tim has the right hand to knock him out.' He poked a finger at a picture of Lewis on the cover of *Boxing News*, and showed it to me.

'You really think so?' I asked.

'Yeah, Tim's the best heavyweight I've ever worked with, and I've worked with a lot,' muttered Lowry. 'Mitch Green, Oliver McCall, Bert Cooper – Tim's better than all of them. He knocked out Mitch in sparring; hit him once, and Mitch fell down like a sack of shit. Beats up Bert so bad, we can't even use him for sparring no more.'

Up into the hillside and mountains, into the trees veiled in hues of red, copper, orange and emerald, we drove into a complex of rented cabins. It was here that Witherspoon was living, as he got back into training, waiting for the USA opponent to be announced, then the HBO date for December, and then hopefully his longed-for crack at regaining a world title – an opportunity which had thus far eluded him.

Moran tapped on the door as I helped Whit with his bags, and when it opened there were laughs and loud greetings, embraces and jokes. Tim Witherspoon stood taller than I had imagined he would, well over the six foot three he was listed as in the various record books, or so it seemed. Witherspoon's physical dimensions had always been called into question. He was too fat, too slovenly, fought out of a crouch which only accentuated his girth. Here, on this afternoon, he stood tall, even if his stomach crept over his jeans waistband and his cheeks looked fleshy and well nourished.

He greeted me with a strong handshake and one of his big smiles. 'Here's the Englishman,' he said lightheartedly, tugging slightly at the animal tooth earring which dangled from his left ear. 'You gonna get me a fight with Lennox?'

'I'm not that influential, Tim,' I replied. 'How's the training going?'

'Not yet, uh-uh,' he said with a quick shake of the head. 'First, we eat. Come on, we're gonna have some breakfast!'

This sounded like an altogether brilliant idea to me, having caught the train from New York's Penn station to Trenton at some ungodly hour in order to meet Tom. As I had left the apartment earlier in the morning, a quick swig of orange juice was all I could muster without waking the household, and I suddenly realised my stomach was growling angrily at me.

We trooped into the cabin, which was laid out on three separate floors. The basement was where Witherspoon slept and washed, the ground floor had a kitchen, a dining-area and a living-room with two sofas and a TV, and upstairs were the trainers' rooms.

More whoops of laughter and back-slapping followed as we closed the door behind us. The others were already inside the cabin: Witherspoon's brother Stevie; Robinson, a nephew of Witherspoon's long-time trainer Slim; and James Thornwell, aka 'Country', a bald-headed man who acted as camp co-ordinator, cook, spit-bucket man and all-round helper.

Stevie was hyper, talkative and jocular, even if I only understood half of what he said. Robinson was sullen and humourless but Country was a character, a friendly guy with a contagious sense of humour and cackling laughter and, as I would soon learn, an oracle for the former heavyweight champ's most interesting stories.

'You want some breakfast, man?' he asked.

It seemed impolite to say no. I remembered Kim warning me I was putting on too much weight, and, glancing over at the generously proportioned Witherspoon, I wondered all of a sudden if perhaps breakfast with the boxer was not such a great idea after all.

'Hey,' said Witherspoon, reading my mind. 'It's all good food. Look, Country looks after me; he takes all the yolks out of the eggs, trims the fat off the bacon. This is gonna be a good, wholesome, fat-free breakfast.'

Indeed, Witherspoon did not lie. Country did take the yolks out of the eggs. All two dozen of them. And yes, he did trim the fat off the bacon, but Christ, how may packets had he bought? There were only seven of us eating, and he had enough sizzling in the pans before him to invite Tony Tubbs, Greg Page and George Foreman over for an impromptu reunion if he'd wanted to.

'Help yourself, man,' said Tim, as Country delivered the platters of scrambled eggs, bacon and toast. 'Look here, you've also got grits, baked ham, home-fried potatoes. And just so you know I'm eating healthily, you can have some of this afterwards . . .' He gestured towards the enormous metal bowl he had beside him, the contents of which he was now scooping into his mouth. It looked like a sensational fruit salad of raspberries, plums, apricots and juice from a mixture of forest berries. I would have been mightily impressed had that been the boxer's sole intake at breakfast time. It wasn't. No, breakfast with Tim Witherspoon was to be a banquet, and at least two courses were necessary before his hunger pangs disappeared.

As we ate, Stevie and Robinson played the video of the Mercer fight. They studied the flickering images of their man dipping and moving in, sneaking through Mercer's defences and sending a looping right bouncing off Mercer's head.

Mercer steps forward, and is caught again by the overhand right, thrown by Witherspoon as though he had been studying Curtly Ambrose coming hurtling in from the Pavilion end at Lord's. *Boom!* Mercer's body shudders, his legs tremble like a lamb's, and he frantically stumbles forward to grab Witherspoon. Witherspoon lets him hold. The moment is gone.

'I had him there,' muttered Tim, tipping the excess berry juice into his mouth. 'I just didn't see how bad he was hurt at the time. He was out, and I didn't see it.'

Stevie took the VCR controls, rewound the tape, replayed the lost opportunity over and over. I thought this might be considered a little tortuous for his big brother, but it didn't seem that way. The punch landed again, Mercer froze, grabbed. The moment lost again. And again.

'I still won the fight, though,' Witherspoon said to me matter-of-factly. 'The judges robbed me.'

'There was a round before that one,' chipped in Moran, 'when both Tim and Mercer slugged it out on even terms, and yet one of the judges scored it a 10-8 round for Mercer. That told me something. We knew it was close, and I knew it was gonna go down to the wire. Tim faded, we all know that. As usual, he didn't train the way he should have done. But I felt he won, and I know there wasn't a 10-8 round during that whole fight.'

'You want a drink of something, man?' asked Tim. 'Juice, tea? We got tea, man. All you English drink tea – at four o'clock, right? Sure, I know what you English guys get up to. Tea for two at four, right? Heh-heh, I had a good time in England.'

Tea did sound good, but not the sachets of blackberry-and-honey herbal delights Witherspoon had bought at the local shops. I didn't ask if he had a box of PG Tips in the house, but declined his offering.

'You play cricket?' he asked, standing up, stretching and yawning.

'Not as much as I'd like to,' I replied. 'I bet you played a bit once upon a time.'

Witherspoon had obviously watched a match or two during his summer visit to Basildon before the Bruno fight, as he understood what I was referring to. 'Sure, sure, I know . . .' he said with a chuckle, and threw an exaggerated right hand from way behind him, over his ear, and down towards the ground, without bending his elbow. 'Listen, you wanna rest for a bit? I'm gonna have a sleep for a couple of hours. You want a bed to lie down on, there's one upstairs. Or you can watch videos if you want, only stop watching me against Mercer!'

Witherspoon hit the sack. It was nearly ten in the morning, Stevie and Robinson departed for the gym, Moran had set off for the store, and I sat down to watch tapes with Lowry and Country. We watched the Mercer fight once more, and then the destructive rematch between Riddick Bowe and Andrzej Golota.

'Do you really believe Tim can get it all back?' I asked them both.

'Sure!' yelped Country, leaping to his feet. 'Look, Tim's never lost it. It's like Tom says, he just never got used to training right. If Tim had the same work ethic as a guy like Evander Holyfield, he would be unbeatable, I'm tellin' you. See, Tim's had four losses in his career, and we only accept one of them – when he was beaten by Pinklon Thomas. He was robbed against Larry Holmes, there was a whole lot of shit going on before the Bone-crusher Smith fight, and then the Bigfoot Martin fight . . .'

His voice trailed off for a moment, and I remembered the stunning news several years before, that Witherspoon had travelled to Michigan to drop a decision to Bigfoot Martin, a sluggish, durable journeyman who had lost to nearly every big-name fighter in the division. There had appeared to be no turning back for Witherspoon after that.

He had returned to action a month later, fat and with his hair dyed orange, and outpointed a fighter named James Pritchard, who usually found himself knocked out when taking on class opposition. That had been Tim's last fight since this latest, surprisingly progressive return to the ring.

'That was a bad fight,' said Country. 'Tim didn't train for that one. We went to Michigan, the home of Michael Moorer, who was world champ at the time. We arrived in the afternoon, calling out Moorer, and the people there didn't like us for it. Come the fight, nothing happened. Tim didn't do shit, but Martin didn't do shit either! They gave it to Martin to teach Tim a lesson.'

For two hours, Country and I talked, as Lowry snoozed on the sofa after his hearty breakfast. We talked about Witherspoon's fights with Holmes and Thomas, his war with Don King, his trips to England. We talked about the highpoint of this comeback, the wins over Cole and Gonzales, and the fact that at that time the heavyweight championship was solidly in King's grasp.

When Moran returned from the store, he joined Country and Lowry on the outdoor sports yard for a game of basketball, set at a frenetic pace. I watched the three of them dribble, bump heavily into each other, seize the ball away, shoot it through the iron hoop, repeating the exercise for forty minutes or so. When the game was finished, they panted heavily, soaked to the skin in sweat, chests heaving. I told them I was ready to take them on at that stage.

We woke Witherspoon up and watched as he proceeded to strap a harness around his tracksuit, snatch up an axe from the hallway, and march outside. Behind the cabin, by the edge of the woods, were litters of tree stumps like a battalion of giant mushrooms. The harness was in place to protect a back which had played up frequently during his career. Chopping wood at all may have been unwise if the problem was indeed a serious one, but the fighter felt he had a good enough reason to soldier on and dismember the trunks before him. 'Always get knockouts when I do this,' he said, and smiled broadly as he hacked into the stumps, chips of bark flying hazardously close to his unprotected eyes.

Our next stop was a local health spa, where the training camp had been set up in a makeshift gym next to a swimming-pool. On arrival, Stevie and Robinson were hovering like bees around two young amateurs, who pounded on each other with gruesome disregard for defence. For intense, three-minute periods, the boys pummelled each other with vigour as their 'teachers' instructed them to increase their work-rate, show more aggression, punch harder, strike faster. At the end of the third session, the exchanges were completed, and the boys wearily removed their head-gear to reveal faces reddened and stung by the whip of leather.

Witherspoon's sister-in-law, Shakira, stood before the speedball in singlet and tracksuit trousers. She was petite and attractive, and she hit the ball hard and fast, her eyes never straying from her target.

Next to her, moving almost effeminately on some rubber matting, was a chunky heavyweight. This was Gerald 'The Jedi' Nobles, a newcomer from Witherspoon's hometown of Philadelphia, who moved and swayed his arms and legs delicately to the sounds of Puff Daddy.

Behind him, taping his hands slowly with a forlorn look on his face, was Mark Young, a veteran fighter – a former one-round knockout victim of the young Mike Tyson, and now battle-weary beyond belief.

'Tim likes Mark,' whispered Moran. 'He really can't do much any more, but Tim took pity on him, makes sure he gets paid by Main Events as a sparring partner, and takes it easy on him when they're in the ring together.'

He turned to the fighter and called out a friendly hello, and Young replied sweetly and softly, asking Moran how he was doing, before returning to the task of binding his own hands. When you're no longer at the top, you don't have high-paid trainers doing these tasks for you. You're a sole trader.

Today, Witherspoon would not be sparring with Young. It was Nobles who had been providing him with his real work, and so it was on this day that the two engaged in six rounds of variable intensity. As was the case when he fought for real, Witherspoon was a trundler, a fighter who used his experience and seasoning to spend rounds working out his opponent's strengths and weaknesses before moving in for the kill.

His sparring with Nobles was restrained and bordered on the dull, until the midway point, when the youngster grew increasingly confident and pitched into his employer with heavy crosses and hooks to the former champ's soft body. Witherspoon leaned against the ropes, ducked his head low, fiddled, moved out of range, trundled and threw lazy cricketer right hands. Nobles stayed on him, whacking more power shots to the liver and ribs.

After the end of the sixth round, Witherspoon stepped out of the ring, sporting a patch of purple around his left eye courtesy of one of Nobles' bombs. He moved on to the speedball, avoided the heavy bag, called out to a smiling Nobles, 'You're in shape, man!' and decided it was time to leave.

It was time to eat again. Witherspoon was hungry, and on the drive towards the town centre, kept saying how much he felt like Chinese food.

'Lewis is the guy I want the most,' he said, swivelling around in the front passenger seat of Country's car. 'He's a good guy, and I like Frank Maloney and Emanuel Steward, too, but this is a business and they have something I want. He's got a good right hand and I've got a good right hand. But he don't have no defence, and I've got the greatest defence in the world. Evander Holyfield, same thing. If you ain't got no defence, you can't beat me – and those two guys don't!'

'You won your day in court with King,' I said, knowing that the fighter had long ago spent the million dollars he had been rewarded in damages. 'How do you feel about him now?'

'Well, it seems like they're all out to get Don at the moment,' he replied. 'I really don't have nothing bad to say about Don no more. We went to court, I proved my point. They all want to stick the knife into Don King, but Don King don't do nothin' all the other promoters don't do too. They all lie, rob, cheat you. They ain't no different, it's just that everyone knows who Don King is. Bob Arum, the Duvas, Kushner, they're all the same. This is a business, and they're all businessmen. That's the way it is.'

On entering the Chinese restaurant, Tim caused dozens of heads to rise from bowls of ginger prawns and wonton soup, and gazes to be focused inquisitively on this giant who towered above the old ladies in the buffet queue, the waiters who scurried around tables, and the waitresses delivering pitchers of Coke and Dr Pepper.

We filled our plates at the buffet, Witherspoon piling his high with curried mussels, and sat ourselves down at a table. We drained our glasses of soda, asked for refills, stabbed at mussels and prawns, and dabbed at the yellow sauces staining our lips.

'So, you been to Ireland?' Witherspoon asked me, winking at Tom. 'It's okay, you can tell us the truth, I'll be your back-up, man! You think the soldiers should be in Ireland? Did you like Margaret Thatcher? You like your prime minister? Why do you guys not like each other?'

'Tim, it's not the English people we don't like, it's their government. The people are great people, and most of them don't agree with their government's policies towards Northern Ireland,' Tom announced, before I could answer any of Witherspoon's questions.

I almost blurted out an argument to Tom's claims, but thought the better of it. I didn't object to the idea of debating Bloody Sunday, the decommissioning of arms, SAS hit-squads, kneecappings, hunger strikes, Ian Paisley, Bobby Sands, Orange parades or anything else associated with the Troubles with anyone be they Republicans, Loyalists, Englishmen or even ill-informed American romantics, but I somehow saw such a discussion taking way too long. I turned the conversation back to boxing with as much subtlety as I could manage, keeping the subject of England firmly in the frame by asking Witherspoon how much his title defence at Wembley in '86 had meant to him.

For an hour, all of them – Tim, Country, Tom and Whit, all joked and laughed aloud, remembering their times in Essex, chasing barmaids and waitresses, arriving in London, making friends everywhere they turned. To them all, England reminded them of good times.

The fight had been hard. It had taken a lot out of Witherspoon, but he kept referring to that now famous all-night bus ride around the capital after the fight, singing to rap songs, drinking, watching the empty bottles roll across the aisle, sitting back and grinning drunkenly through the pain of Bruno's blows.

When you talked to Witherspoon about the greatest moments of his career, this was what was mentioned first: the WBA championship defence against Frank Bruno, the successful defence of his world title, abroad, against the shattering power of Britain's HP hero.

For that whole day, Tim Witherspoon never instigated any talk about his world-title wins over Greg Page and Tony Tubbs. These were triumphs enjoyed with the slightest of pleasure, victories secured after spending debilitating weeks in a training camp with the very men he had to fight. Weeks spent smoking dope and lounging around with Page and Tubbs, only to discover that it was each other they had to punish in order to reach the top. But the Bruno fight, that was a different story. It was the night Tim Witherspoon at last felt like a world champion. And it was the only night he ever did so.

Two weeks after our Chinese meal, Tim Witherspoon advanced on opponent Levi Billups, and scorched him with that Curtly Ambrose right hand. Billups, normally a survivor, was knocked cold in the first round by that one serious punch.

That evening it was not the win over Billups that filled my mind, but the words of Ray Mercer, whom I had first met in a converted garage in East Orange, New Jersey. As his hands were being wrapped by his trainer in preparation for some light sparring, I looked up from the blotches and scars on Mercer's arms and neck, and into his creased, weary eyes. He twitched his neck, recently broken, and hardly on the mend at a rate which would encourage getting into the ring in the foreseeable future.

'That fight with Tim Witherspoon,' he snorted. 'It didn't mean shit. They were just trying to match up two experienced guys, two old men, so that they could at least take one of us out of the picture. That's all that fight ever was. It was never gonna mean anything more than that, we were just being led along.'

CHAPTER SIX

The Commodity

The Broadway Grill restaurant on the first floor of the Crowne Plaza hotel was filling up by the time I arrived for the press conference. Photographers were setting up at the front, asking unsuspecting souls in the front if they were 'shooting', and if the answer was no, kicking them back a few rows. TV and newspaper people chatted together in small groups, drinking orange juice and snacking on the titbits being offered around.

This wasn't a title fight being announced, but it wasn't chopped liver either. Obed Sullivan v Hasim Rahman had been set for 1 November as the chief support to Lou Savarese against Nigeria's David Izonritei. An all-heavyweight undercard was also set to include Monte Barrett tackling Val Smith, a cousin of Michael Moorer. They would be two decent heavyweight matches, and HBO was going to carry the transmission on its acclaimed *Boxing after Dark* series, a platform for new faces on the big scene like Sullivan and Rahman, and for decent champions with modest crossover appeal like Bernard Hopkins and Vince Phillips.

Sullivan conducted himself like a star in the making. He arrived at the conference in a fern-green suit and smart brown shoes, listened attentively and conversed easily with men like Steve Farhood, the former editor of *The Ring* magazine and the acidic Wallace Matthews of the *New York Post*. Savarese was good at mixing with the media, too, laughing and mingling with the suits and the press in his long suede coat and cap. Rahman and Izonritei, meanwhile, took a back seat from the small-talk. Izonritei sat quietly but happily in the background, while Rahman arrived late and joined his managers Steve Nelson and Bob Mittleman, as well as trainer Tommy Brooks, at their table.

I wandered over to Rahman's table, shook hands with Brooks and caught Rahman's eye. He was busy examining a new set of trunks: solid black with the silver image of that old Marvel comics hero, 'The Thing', emblazoned upon them. Next to the man of bricks was the legend, 'The Rock'.

'It's gonna be a knockout,' said Rahman. 'I know Obed pretty well. He's been all smiles with me back in Houston, but behind my back I hear he's been talking. He's gonna get knocked out, that's all that needs to be said.'

When the press conference formally kicked off, each combatant was asked to say a few words. Rahman, Izonritei and Savarese stayed seated and talked about how much they were looking forward to the following Saturday night.

Then it was Sullivan's turn. He stepped over to the centre of the dais and addressed the crowd like a presidential nominee. 'This is my first time here in New York, and it's true what they say – it's a great city,' he began, opening and closing the palms of his hands, scanning those before him in an effort to make eye contact with everyone. 'The people here have been great, and they've made me feel really welcome. This is going to be a great show and a great night for boxing.'

'I just hope you'll be ready,' said Rahman.

'Oh, I'll be ready, Hasim, believe me – I'll be ready,' replied Sullivan with a snigger.

The show was to be held at the Apollo Theater in Harlem, a venue which had enjoyed a long and rich history in the world of entertainment. It had staged concerts by Ella Fitzgerald, Gregory Hines, Aretha Franklin and James Brown among others, but apart from an exhibition of pugilism by the first ever black heavyweight champ, Jack Johnson, and a tap-dancing show with Sugar Ray Robinson, there had been no boxing events. In recent times it had become a beleaguered sanctuary for amateur talent, men and women being granted as much time to sing and dance, indulge in stand-up comedy or play the trombone, until the audience either cheered their mass approval or jeered derisively. Cheers could mean an invitation to return, jeers resulted in being dragged off stage by a man wielding a crook.

The weigh-in was held at the Planet Hollywood restaurant near the Rockefeller Centre in midtown Manhattan. Heavyweight weigh-ins were always purely for spectacle rather than the result of any official necessity, heavyweight fighters not needing to come in under any particular weight limit. Although colourful, most such ceremonies can be tedious affairs, with much waiting around and little to see apart from fighters standing upon scales, flexing their muscles and then staring at their opponents for the benefit of the photographers.

It was no different here: a supermodel in a metallic spacesuit introduced the four fighters, oohed and aahed at their impressive physiques and asked permission to touch their biceps. Savarese and Izonritei raised their eye-brows in exasperation as the cameramen pleaded with them to look meaner during their stare-down. Instead, they couldn't help but laugh, and at the end of the afternoon shook hands before departing.

There were no such pleasantries between Rahman and Sullivan, who by now were finding each other's presence the source of some needle. As they came into pose together, Rahman whispered something inaudible to the former marine, and Obed stepped ever closer, so their faces almost touched. For thirty seconds they froze, eyeball to eyeball, as the photographers went wild, reeling off films and eventually breaking away to reload their cameras. One of their number cursed as he dropped the new film, and by the time he was ready to take more shots the two protagonists had broken away. 'Hey, Obed, can you just stand next to Hasim again for a second, please?!' he beseeched.

'No, man, I don't wanna do that,' said Sullivan. 'It's getting too close now. If he comes anywhere near me again, I might have to lay one on him, you know what I mean?'

On the night of the fight I caught the subway to Harlem. Getting off at 96th Street station, the Apollo was only a couple of blocks' walk away, and a short distance only from the popular soul food restaurant, Sylvia's. It was a fun venue for a fight card, but the staff were sour-faced and graceless, distinctly nervous at this new enterprise their bosses had decided to foist upon them, and were treating the arriving press with about as much regard as New York cab-drivers did their passengers.

The fighters were to duel not on an elevated ring, as was the norm, but on a flat, matted surface on the main stage of the theatre, with the press watching from the stages left and right and photographers occupying the balconies.

I sat behind Michael Katz of the *New York Daily News* as he belly-ached about some terminal problem and close to Muhammad Ali's biographer, Thomas Hauser. All the other American reporters, the ones whose stories I had read for so many years, were there: Matthews, Farhood and the inimitable Jack Obermayer, Chris Thorne of the *Newark Star-Ledger* and Tim Smith from the *New York Times*.

The fighters would be descending from their changing-rooms and entering the stage from right behind us, where the HBO crews now busied themselves preparing for the live broadcast to follow the preliminary bouts.

Directly across from us all, over the ring, the HBO commentary team were having their hair combed and faces powdered: colour commentator

Larry Merchant, his colleague Jim Lampley, and Sugar Ray Leonard guest-ing as the third man. They stood beside each other, in the smart casual wear used for the *Boxing after Dark* shows (black tie for the more illustrious *World Championship Boxing* telecasts), and conversed over their little red, green and blue microphones.

Beyond the ring, from where the fans sat, and to my left, the usual mix of celebrities and wannabes filtered onto the stage. Some were true fight fans like film director Spike Lee and tennis great John McEnroe who arrived before the first bout, while oily gentlemen with white scarves and slicked-back hairdos waltzed in just before the main event with bored-looking girlfriends in tow.

After the first fight of the evening, Rahman and then Sullivan took it in turn to test the feel of the canvas. At approximately nine-thirty, Val Smith slipped between the ropes and was followed in by Monte Barrett, who was wearing a shimmering scarlet outfit and a scowl on his face.

'This should be a decent test for Monte,' said Joe De Guardia, crouching momentarily beside my seat. 'This guy's no bum, but Monte knows that.'

After receiving the referee's instructions, Smith went back to his corner and shook his feet anxiously from side to side. Monte opened his mouth, and Old Timer inserted a rinsed gumshield across his teeth.

Smith didn't look like a bum, and he had come to win. Barrett wanted to be all things to all people, alternating his style from flash to determined banger. He snapped a jab, then pushed it lazily, rushed at Smith, but found himself in too close to unload when he had trapped his opponent against the ropes. 'Left hook to the body, move to the left and throw the hook to the body,' called out his corner.

But Smith was wily and aware of the trap they were attempting to set. He covered up well, moved to the side, shot out a jab of his own and then a right. Both landed, drawing a smear of blood around Monte's nose. Monte smirked, shook his head, posed and moved on.

Smith jabbed, landed another right, pedalled backwards. The pattern continued for three more rounds, with the underdog holding a small but psychologically effective lead in the scheduled six-round contest.

Monte wasn't being whipped but Smith was staying with him, and doing so with a little more precision and more of a game-plan. There were only two more rounds for Monte to make the difference on scorecards which had to be close, and it wasn't the most comfortable of times for his corner as the one-minute rest ticked by.

It looked like Monte was out of breath and, as he came out for the fifth, there didn't appear to be any hint of a change in his tactics. Smith was resilient, nowhere near succumbing to Monte's unbeaten aura, nor playing along with Monte's assurances not so long ago that he could never be beaten, that he would always show up mentally and physically conditioned and ready.

Monte's left hook was improving, but it was the uppercut which won the day, launched as it was from knee level and bouncing destructively off Smith's nose in the latter stages of the fifth. Smith's head flew backwards, a spray of blood from his nose splashing his white trunks. He grimaced, his eyes burnt and he half turned away. Monte rushed into him, threw another uppercut, another hook to the body.

Smith was enraged. Hadn't his opponent recognised his surrender? He pushed Monte away from him, away from the crimson-covered shorts and the broken nose drizzling blood all over his face. The referee stopped the fight, and Monte celebrated with a somersault in the middle of the ring.

Savarese v Izonritei was the main event, but only because Lou had a swarm of local support, mostly of the female variety. Izonritei, an African amateur star now based in Florida, was an inconspicuous presence in the American fight game, with the notable exception being a brave stand against David Tua before falling in the twelfth and final round.

Obed Sullivan and his corner (trainer Chuck McGregor and assistant Jimmy Glenn) made their way into the ring dressed in gold and orange. Rahman and Brooks, as well as Don Turner who was helping out for the night, turned up in sheer black. The sounds of Queen's 'We Will Rock You' reverberated around the stage.

Sullivan paced, Rahman bounced and glanced around him. He was always looking out at the crowds at his fights, as though trying to search out a particular individual, but more likely seeking the approval of those in attendance.

The fighters disrobed and the live broadcast commenced. The referee gave his final instructions. I looked at their faces. Rahman had a hint of a smile. Sullivan, his face glistening with vaseline, looked a lot older than his years, his brow furrowed and lined.

Rahman stalked, Sullivan retreated slightly, boxing behind neat jabs and straight rights, covering up as the aggressive, bullish Rahman moved in. They tied each other up, banged heads once or twice, wove light punches through their guards. Sullivan wrong-footed Rahman, covered up, jabbed, hit him again. Rahman blinked, then blinked again. A small nick had been opened above his left eye. Sullivan speared with more jabs and rights. Rahman swivelled, lowered his body and moved in with a moderate body attack.

By the middle rounds, Sullivan was less decisive. His tactics were becoming negative – occasionally snapping out the jab, usually holding. Rahman was forcing the pace, but he was struggling badly to take advantage of any opportunities for landing the shocker right hand.

I had been waiting for the Rahman explosion for six or seven rounds by the time it looked clear the fight would go the distance. Maybe Sullivan's fainting spell against Isaac Brown really had been due to a panic attack, even if it had seemed like such an unlikely story at the time.

Rahman won the fight by a majority decision, but I wasn't the only person at ringside left with a feeling that both men had done more harm than good to their careers by failing to take advantage of their exposure on primetime TV.

Izonritei, the quiet police inspector from Lagos, had other ideas. He struck the amiable Savarese with a thunderous right hand in the fifth round, sending the favourite down in a heap. Savarese looked to be in such bad condition that many questioned the wisdom of the contest being allowed to continue.

But continue it did, as Savarese somehow made it to his feet, only to be stampeded by Izonritei's subsequent onslaughts. The press screamed for the referee to wake up, the girls in the stands covered their eyes and shrieked hysterically. Savarese tipped through the ropes in slow motion, his legs jack-knifing over his body, his eyes blurred and unfocused.

Savarese had been defeated. The photographers rushed to snap the African victor being embraced by round-card girls wrapped in live pythons. Fighters left the buildings with dreams intact, others with their illusions of grandeur shattered.

Bob Lee, the beleaguered president of the IBF, shuffled slowly through the crowds, accompanied by two younger men. As he made his way out of the building, the hostile whispers clawed at him, and even though the taint of corruption was to scald him badly, to me he just looked like a sad old man with watery eyes and an uneven gait. There were no horns protruding from his head, nor garish trinkets dripping from his fingers. He was more frightening than that, because he looked like a normal man, a man whose normality – according to subsequent FBI investigations –had been seduced and corrupted by the lure of profiteering in a business which so easily allowed itself to be exploited.

★

It wasn't long after the heavyweight show at the Apollo that old George Foreman once more pulled his weary limbs from the rocking-chair, dusted himself down and entered the ring for another defence of his 'linear' world title. Since belting out Moorer for the championship in 1994, he had been taken the distance by Germany's Axel Schulz, and a pair of Americans, Crawford Grimsley and Lou Savarese. Foreman's power was waning, or so it seemed, and his reflexes had greatly dimmed. Perhaps it was down to these reasons that when he picked up HBO's list of acceptable 'challengers' he ignored the likes of Rahman, Izonritei, Ibeabuchi and Tua, and instead went for a man considered to be as psychologically fragile as one might find in the sport. Foreman chose Shannon Briggs.

Shannon Briggs was the product of a brilliant marketing operation, run by Marc Roberts. Roberts, a New Jersey-based promoter and sports agent who became involved in boxing in the late 1970s, also represented and secured lucrative endorsements and glossy contracts for stars of American football, basketball and ice-hockey. His company was called World Wide Entertainment & Sports, and Shannon Briggs was its most recognisable client.

Briggs was a colourful character, not least because of the crown of golden dreadlocks on his head – a hairstyle inspired from his days spent with the Village trendies at Washington Square Market in New York, where he hustled chess matches and hung out with the hippies and rollerbladers. As an amateur fighter he had impressed Roberts and former *New York Post* writer Michael Marley, and was signed up to a generous contract before he had even turned pro. In an international meeting between Cuba and the USA, though, Briggs was knocked out in a single round by Felix Savon, having claimed he was destined for an easy victory. A year later, at the US Olympic trials, he had to pull out with an injury in the early rounds and was not permitted to rejoin at a later stage of the competition. Even so, when he turned pro after failing to make the Olympic squad, there was still talk of him becoming the next star in the division. He had the looks, the flair and the natural ability. But could he stand, fight and take it when an opponent absorbed his thunder and fought back with some of his own?

The partnership between Roberts and Marley soon disintegrated, and it was Roberts who kept hold of Briggs. Fighter and manager had a close relationship, and the business side to their dealings was like few others in the sport.

You could buy shares in Roberts's company, WWES, on the stockmarket, and so indirectly a small stake in Briggs's career. The fighter had a pretty interesting portfolio already started up for him by Roberts. This was boxing in the 1990s: all business. There were some who bemoaned this fact, recalling the pre-war days when the best supposedly fought the best; to some extent this was true, but boxing had always been filled to the brim with businessmen, duckers and divers, schemers and manipulators. At least today, the fighters themselves had become more directly involved in reaping the rewards of their careers. Boxing was a business in the 1920s, but Harry Wills was powerless to break through the colour barrier and challenge world champion Jack Dempsey. Boxing was a business in the 1930s and 1940s, but no one ever helped set up a portfolio for Joe Louis, who instead wound up as a greeter at some tacky Vegas casino. And boxing was a business in the 1950s, too, but it was one which only men with names like Blinky and Frankie ever succeeded in.

Briggs's opposition, however, left much to be desired. For his first four years as a pro, his reputation was built around potential, rather than cold, hard statistics. The longer he refused to step up his level of competition, the more doubts became suspicions, and the stronger these suspicions grew. What was Roberts hiding from the rest of the world? Sure, Briggs had looked awesome annihilating the Calvin Joneses and Jimmy Ellises of the world in less than three minutes, but which of his peers wouldn't also have done so?

On a cold January evening at Madison Square Garden, during the famous 'Blizzard of '96', Briggs was among the crowds who had gathered to watch Roy Jones blitz the sturdy Dominican Merqui Sosa. Even in the grey shroud of shadow which engulfed the back of arena seats, Briggs could easily be spotted, his crop of corn-coloured hair bouncing up and down each time he moved or turned. He was to fight Darroll Wilson next, a definite step up in competition, and despite the noise which signified the imminent arrival of Jones, I thought that that moment was as good as any to ask 'the next big thing' how he saw his first decent test going.

'One round,' he replied immediately. 'Darroll Wilson isn't in the same league as me.'

Two months later, Briggs tried to make his prediction come true. He fired on all cylinders against Wilson, trying desperately to take him out in the opening round, but Wilson weathered the storm.

The underdog, a former shopping-mall security guard, refused to be disheartened by Briggs' power-punches, and the balance began to shift late in the second round as he fired back with a barrage of his own. Wilson's punches swamped Briggs in the third round as the New Yorker retreated to the ropes. The favourite wilted to the canvas like a dying lily and rolled onto his back, gumshield hanging from his lips.

The defeat had shattered the illusion that Briggs was a budding superstar. His chin, heart and desire were all deemed to be too weak to succeed at the highest level, and it was hard to find anyone apart from Roberts who felt he had even the remotest chance of bouncing back from such a setback.

'That fight was so hyped,' laughed Wilson the day we met in a converted gym outside Atlantic City. 'They had hyped Shannon up so much, telling everyone that he was going to be the next great heavyweight champion of the world. I had seen Shannon's technique, everyone had seen it. He always came out in the first three rounds to try and get you out of there. He didn't like going the distance, because he got tired so quickly. He always throws a lot of bombs, but as rounds go by he gets real tired.'

For the Wilson fight, Briggs had Tyson's former trainer Teddy Atlas in his corner. Atlas walked away after the fight. He was not one to suffer fools gladly, and there were many such individuals, according to Atlas, who were ever present in the world of Shannon Briggs.

'Shannon was surrounded by these three friends – one to make his bed, one to wash his underwear, another to make his breakfast,' Atlas told the press. 'It got ridiculous. After the fight he complained about having an asthma attack, but he had never mentioned this problem to me before. What bothered me most, though, was that after the loss, his chief concern was the situation with his share portfolio. How much had the loss affected its worth? This was not what a fighter should have been concerning himself with.' Atlas left, and a little-known Cuban, Carlos Albuerne, was drafted in by Roberts to continue Briggs' development.

Shortly after their encounter in March '96, Darroll Wilson and Shannon Briggs saw their careers head in opposite directions. Wilson was continually matched tough, and lost in a single round to David Tua in his next outing. Briggs returned with some uncomplicated wins. Briggs was marketable, despite his serious deficiencies. He could sell tickets. Wilson could not even fill a school gymnasium, which was where one of his post-Tua fights took place. Briggs received a call from George Foreman.

'That Foreman fight should be mine,' complained Wilson on hearing the news that Briggs was about to become $5 million richer. 'George obviously saw me as being too dangerous. He's seen something in Shannon to make him think he can beat him. He knows that Shannon's got some power, but he also knows that you can never tell if Shannon's about to have another asthma attack. The truth is that Shannon just don't like tough boxing matches. When they're tough, he gets asthma.'

'Shannon can't beat George, and George knows that,' agreed Michael

Grant. 'Look, Shannon won't win against a top heavyweight, and his manager knows that. They're selling Shannon to the public, but it's a con. Shannon can't fight, so they have to cash in on a big fight like this one with George, and see how it goes from there. Roberts once called up Lou Di Bella at HBO, and asked him how he felt Shannon would do against me. Di Bella told him that Shannon couldn't go more than three rounds with me, and Roberts never got in touch with my people after that. What does that tell you? It tells me he has no confidence in Shannon's ability to fight. They're more interested in their share certificates.'

Briggs fuelled more jealousy and ill-feeling among the heavyweights than even the IBF's pin-up boy, Vaughn Bean. Briggs, it was felt, was a nice enough guy, but his image of 'coming up from the streets' irked many of his rivals. Stories of sleeping rough, poverty and battles to keep food on the table were all dished out to the press, but other fighters did not buy these tales. To them, he had always been a glamour boy surrounded by privilege.

'Shannon Briggs says he's from the streets, but he's not – and he knows it,' snapped fellow New Yorker Monte Barrett. 'Shannon Briggs is a big wuss!'

Briggs could not help but feel hurt by these barbed remarks. Much worse, though, was that shortly after the loss to Wilson, his best friend was murdered and his mother passed away. How privileged an experience was that? If he could beat George Foreman, and look good doing so, he would make the critics eat their words and force his rivals to get in line for their own shot at the big time.

★

The air was full of salt and smoke, and wisps of pink candyfloss floated before those of us strolling along the wretched boardwalk. Cycle-cabs creaked along the promenade, the old women bought more lycra sweat-shirts and the gulls gnawed at the pizza crusts lying beside the overflowing rubbish bins. Good old Atlantic City. I wondered what it would have been like to live here all the time, and shivered at the thought.

Al Bello, a photographer with the Allsport agency, had once told me that he had visited the homes of Evander Holyfield and Bruce Seldon within a short space of time when he was working on a photo-shoot for *The Ring*. Visiting Holyfield at his marble mansion in the hills of Atlanta had been akin to waiting for an audience with a maharajah. Seldon lived in an Atlantic City 'shack', with drug-dealers loitering on his street corner. Holy-field had greeted Bello in a conservative suit and led him into his smart, mahogany office. Seldon had stripped to tracksuit pants and played basket-ball on a nearby court with a gang of street kids.

Life had got even better for Holyfield since then, and a lot worse for Seldon. Holyfield had increased his riches several times over with another victory over Mike Tyson, and then, a fortnight before Briggs challenged Foreman, with a masterfully executed eighth-round win over old foe Michael Moorer. Holyfield was now the WBA and IBF world champion.

Seldon hadn't fought since losing to Tyson. One bright afternoon he had been driving along Atlantic Avenue when a girl caught his eye. He drew up beside her, began to converse, and in no time at all she was in the front passenger seat and heading back to his place. On the way there, the two smoked dope. In his own home, Seldon proceeded to show off to her his illegal firearms collection before the two had sex. When the girl said good-bye later that evening, she headed for the nearest police station. She was fifteen years old. Seldon was convicted of statutory rape and sent to prison.

Donald Trump had secured the Foreman v Briggs match-up at the Taj Mahal hotel. On the morning of the final press conference, a sea of familiar faces filled the ballroom – the press, TV executives, contenders like David Tua and old warhorses like Tim Witherspoon.

I headed for the press room first, just next to the souvenir shop selling newspapers at three times their normal price, commemorative bars of Trump chocolate and 'I've been to the Taj' T-shirts. I sat myself down at one of the tables and over the course of an hour spoke to Tua who was recover-ing from surgery on a chipped elbow, Lou Duva and then Angelo Dundee.

Tua wasn't the most enigmatic of contenders, but his ruthless left hook more than made amends for that. He was a sawn-off shotgun of a heavy-weight, and as he sat there before me, whispering about his love for rugby, Samoan mythology and poetry, I was reminded of those times at school I had spent listening to the soft, lisping tones of a young Mike Tyson on TV.

'It's time for the new wave of heavyweights to take over,' said Duva later, his jowls creasing as he spoke. 'Where d'you say you're from again?'

'England,' I replied.

'Well, just make sure you speak slowly, and I'll have no problem under-standing you,' he quipped. 'David here, he's gonna be the heavyweight champion of the world the moment he gets a shot at the title. It's inevitable. Holyfield and Lewis are getting too old. It's time for them to make way for the next generation. We'd fight Shannon Briggs, we'd love that fight.'

'What about Hasim Rahman?' I asked.

'Sure, we'd love that fight, too. My son-in-law, Tommy Brooks, he's

Rahman's trainer. Let's make the fight. It would be a family affair!'

'But surely you would have some reservations about fighting Holyfield,' I pressed. 'You were like father and son for so many years when he fought for Main Events; surely it would hurt to work in a corner against him.'

'Look, I love Evander, but this is a business,' responded Duva matter-of-factly. 'I would love that fight for David.'

Dundee joined us at the table, his face aglow, his skin tanned by the Miami sunshine. Foreman's co-promoter, Jeff Wald, wandered over and showed off the latest in a batch of T-shirts which had arrived that morning. The image on the front of the garment was of a scowling Foreman raising a mammoth fist. 'You Tell Him To Retire' was the legend printed above it.

'Who would have thought it?' said Dundee to himself, as we all looked on. 'Who would have thought in Zaire that twenty-three years later I would be working with Big George Foreman. Isn't it great how this sport works? It's just magical, absolutely magical.'

Back in the conference room, Briggs and Foreman had already accentuated the generation gap with their wardrobes for the day. Foreman staggered around in his fawn trousers and cream woollen waistcoat, looking for all the world like he was in need of a pair of slippers and a cup of cocoa. Briggs was the funky hustler from the Village, in his untied Tommy Hilfiger boots and designer sweatshirt and ankle shorts, his hair bunched up like a bale of straw.

As they waited to take their places behind the podium and its microphones and tumblers of water, Foreman limped in an exaggerated fashion over to a group of reporters, men who had followed him for much of his career, from Kingston to Kinshasa all those years ago.

'At this stage of my career, I'm looking for an excuse to get out of the game,' said Foreman. 'But someone's got to whip me. That's all they have to do – whip me. And I don't mean by doing all of that running and holding stuff. Fight me and beat me like a man. I need somebody to show me that it's time to get out.'

Briggs hovered before a table spilling over with posters of himself beating up on some hapless opponent. Roberts and some WWES flunkies carefully laid the posters out flat, and Briggs signed them. Roberts dictated and Briggs scribbled.

' "To my good friend Mr Trump",' began Roberts, and the cynic inside me wondered why a man who was about to put his life on the line should have to address anyone as 'mister' – with the exception of the one whose very fists threatened him. I couldn't see Trump referring to the fighter as 'Mr Briggs'.

When they moved on to the podium, Briggs swaggered and Foreman tottered upon his gammy leg. 'This is a dream come true,' said Briggs. 'I'm in good shape. I'm not stressed. I'm myself. I'm going to be myself on Saturday night.'

'I am the true heavyweight champion of the world,' said Foreman. 'I want to have a big fight with one of those other so-called champions, but where are they? I don't hear them calling for me. As far as this fight with Shannon is concerned, I'm ready to shake, rattle and roll!'

Away from the TV cameras, however, Foreman was in a more philosophical mood. 'I came back to rescue my youth centre in Houston,' he said. 'I really don't like being away from there, but my progress in this comeback accumulated to the point where I am at now. I'm a professional boxer at the moment, but generally I'm an evangelist. I would prefer to be working back home as a preacher, but I came back to boxing to make some money because the centre was running out of it. So far this has all been pretty lucrative. I'm having a ball – boxing is the best place to be. A lot of fighters would love to be in this position, a lot of sports personalities in general.'

While Foreman was being questioned about the amount of time he felt was left in his boxing career, Briggs was explaining to all who would listen the circumstances of his loss to Wilson. 'I'm still getting over it,' he admitted. 'It will take a long time, because of the things which took place afterwards; with Teddy Atlas saying the things that he did, and with my mom dying. I could not breathe during the fight. I was working, though – I hit him with a jab, and he flew across the ring, but I just could not catch my breath. I came back to the corner. I was getting oxygen in, but I was not letting any out. He wasn't a good puncher at all, it's just that I couldn't do anything with all this oxygen filling me up, making me feel bloated. As for Teddy and the things he said – that hurt a lot. Teddy is paranoid. Look at his history. Talk to some of the other fighters he's worked with.'

Foreman v Briggs went twelve rounds and was to go down as being one of the most controversially judged fights in recent history – labelled by some as a bigger robbery than any heist orchestrated by Butch Cassidy or Jesse James.

Briggs began in sprightly fashion, using his movement and jab well although seemingly unwilling, for fear of an onset of asthma, to take the fight to Foreman other than in brief spurts. Foreman's jabs thumped Briggs with regularity, the straw hair sent tossing in all directions, the youngster's mouth agape. Occasionally Foreman came through with ponderous combinations, and more than once Briggs's eyes seemed to give warning of yet another surrender.

But something else was happening. The audience were cheering and applauding all of Foreman's shots, even the ones which missed their mark. The crowd, sentimentally rooting for the old man, were exaggerating whatever slim command he had of the contest. Briggs was still jabbing and moving well. The crowd expected the younger man to attack with more ferocity and purpose. Anything coming from the fists of the forty-nine-year-old champ was beyond what was expected.

It was the kind of fight you could watch from start to finish without it requiring any great degree of analysis, and come away believing there was only one winner – George Foreman. But pick apart each round, without the sound of the crowds or the commentary team encouraging you one way or the other, and the result is not so obvious. The judges gave the fight to Shannon Briggs by a unanimous decision, and the crowds and the press wailed with horror.

Whether one believed that Briggs was the rightful winner that night or not, something even more mysterious was to emerge. It was soon discovered that two of the three judges working that night – Lawrence Layton and Calvin Claxton – had little experience working on major fights. The last time Claxton had done so had been the night Ray Mercer was awarded a tight decision over Tim Witherspoon. Mercer, as it happened, was also managed by Marc Roberts and WWES. Two Marc Roberts fighters getting the nod in watertight contests, in the space of eleven months, both contests taking place in Atlantic City. The gossip mill cranked into action. Had anyone checked with Claxton and Layton to discover if the pair owned shares in WWES? Was the New Jersey commissioner, the snappily dressed Larry Hazard, involved in a conspiracy to unseat Foreman?

Hazard, much to his chagrin, was hauled before a New Jersey court. Layton and Claxton were investigated for any alleged improprieties, but no scandal broke. Shannon Briggs had not been impressive, but he had won the decision fair and square.

'Listen to yourself say the words "Shannon Briggs – Heavyweight Champion of the World",' Jack Obermayer said to me a while later. 'It just doesn't sound right, does it?'

★

One minute Tim Witherspoon was a happy man; the next, things did not look so bright. His big opportunity, the high-profile fight on HBO had seemingly been set and the opponent, John 'The Quiet Man' Ruiz, suited the veteran Philadelphian down to the ground. At his age, Witherspoon needed fights which could be ended early with big overhand rights, or at the very least ones which did not involve struggling to catch up with 'runners'. Ruiz was not a runner, and he had been taken out early by David Tua.

Then, a few weeks before the scheduled December match-up at Fox-woods, Ruiz signed up with Don King, pulled out of the fight, and agreed to take on Tony Tucker the following January instead. HBO and Witherspoon's team were mightily upset. The cable station assured Ruiz and his management that they had burnt their bridges.

Tom Moran called me a day after Ruiz's withdrawal. 'We were preparing for a one-round knockout,' he said. 'Ruiz would have been the perfect opponent for us, and from there I'm sure Tim would have been able to put himself in line for a title shot. Now we've got to fight Larry Donald instead, and it's no secret that Donald's style will be very hard for Tim to handle. I mean, if he stands and fights, I have no doubts Tim will be able to deal with him physically. It's just that with Tim's back condition I'm worried about how much chasing he'll have to do.'

Indeed, Donald was an entirely different proposition to Ruiz; neither was about to set the world on fire, but whereas the pugnacious Ruiz was predictable and vulnerable to a good shot, Donald was athletic and slick – a spoiler who had lost only to Riddick Bowe in a fight which had gone the full 12-round distance.

The outcome of the match was not in much doubt after the first couple of rounds. Donald bicycled, and Witherspoon trundled despondently forward, slinging lazy overhand rights but failing to follow up with any-thing else. Donald pipped away with the jab, and easily evaded the few shots launched in his direction.

By the middle rounds, Witherspoon's back needed constant attention from a masseur. Donald was winning the fight, but he was doing so with so little imagination or lustre that his own management continually rushed to ringside and bellowed for him to step up the pace.

Witherspoon was dejected by now; he was fighting like a man who felt he was owed something – in this particular case, a world-title fight – and the hell he was expected to overcome someone as awkward as Donald in order to get that shot. Tim Witherspoon felt he had paid his dues already.

In most respects, he had. It would have been a glorious finale to a career ravaged by Don King, but boxing's sentimentalities only went so far and Donald won an easy decision.

Witherspoon had wanted but a taste of what it had once been like, that far away night in London, that solitary moment of joy. His desire had been denied. Nostalgia was all that remained.

CHAPTER SEVEN

Faltering

My client's actions were wholly out of the ordinary, and were due –
as I shall prove – as a direct consequence of the brain damage he
sustained as a professional boxer from 1989 to 1996.
JOHNNIE COCHRANE ON RIDDICK BOWE, FEBRUARY 2000

I just want to put this all behind me. I accept I have a problem, but
I never wanted to do anything to hurt my family, the ones I love.
RIDDICK BOWE, FEBRUARY 2000

I had never subscribed to the opinion that the state of the heavyweight division was as dire as the naysayers insisted. Whether already spoilt by the rich pickings of the 1970s, when Ali, Foreman and Frazier sent each other reeling across continents, or yearning for the days of a relentless terminator like Mike Tyson, there were a great many who felt that the heavyweights were plummeting back into the dire straits of the 'Lost Generation' of the 1980s.

What I did agree with was the sorry state of affairs which saw the most notable contenders avoid each other if at all possible. Ike Ibeabuchi had upset David Tua the previous summer, but before the African was able to capitalise on this stunning win, certain legal 'problems' stalled his career. Ditched by his long-term girlfriend in their hometown of Austin, Texas, an enraged Ibeabuchi had kidnapped the girl's teenaged son, carted the boy off in a stolen vehicle at breakneck speed, and crashed head-first into a motorway overpass. Arresting police officers and ambulance crews were to find the boy in a state of shock, with collarbone and ribs fractured – injuries not all deemed to have been caused by the impact itself, but rather courtesy of the fighter's flailing fists. Oh, happy days.

With the temporary loss of The President from the picture, Rahman, Grant, Tua, Chris Byrd and Canada's Kirk Johnson seemed poised to emerge as viable contenders. Rahman had met Obed Sullivan but had failed to impress. Grant was to hammer Lou Savarese's conqueror David Izonritei but reject the challenges of his chief rivals. Tua was being brought back from surgery via the soft route. Johnson was struggling to make any headway with Bob Arum and Top Rank, and everyone was avoiding Byrd.

I went to Atlantic City on several occasions in January, the first of which was to attend a show of wanton mismatches thanks to America Presents, a relatively new outfit which had promised to bring a certain integrity in matchmaking back to the sport. I hadn't arrived in expectation of a night of upsets, but instead to see Monte Barrett in action, as he was up against an opponent named Guy Sonnenberg.

Early in the day I took Kim, her brother and a friend to the weighing-in for the following night's HBO show, which was to include Grant against Izonritei. Grant was sitting by the door as we entered, and I still only reached his shoulders. He was oblivious to those around him, his eyes closed and head bobbing in time to the music from a Walkman.

The chasm had widened in his relationship with the wizened Bill Cayton, and seldom had it been so obvious. Cayton was busying himself moving about the room, making small-talk with a fixed grin on his face, but there was no communication between fighter and manager. His attempts at transforming the giant Grant into a Tyson clone had been disastrous and, in the long term, damaging to their relationship. Grant had already spoken to me of a temper seriously tested by Cayton and his team shouting out the old Tyson numbers routine from ringside at his fights: 'One . . . four-four . . . seven-seven-two,' each number signifying a certain shot heading for a specific destination.

As it happened, this was to be the last of Grant's fights for which he would be contractually obliged to Cayton as his manager. The official severance was announced shortly afterwards, with Grant stating that they had grown apart.

That evening, the greatest excitement of all for most in attendance was the appearance of Mr T to introduce the show's main event – a hopeless and thankfully brief encounter between Lawrence Clay-Bey and the startled Mario Cawley. It was worse than poor: men with unbeaten records were pitted against ones with more losses than victories. Up-and-comers with potential were paired up with ex-cons who hadn't fought since the retirement of Muhammad Ali. And, worst of all, the only prospect to be extended beyond the second round was Barrett.

Sonnenberg was muscular and aggressive yet he completely lacked any semblance of boxing ability. With his bleached, cropped hair and sunbed tan, he looked better suited to a role on *Baywatch*, but he gave it his best effort against the more skilful Barrett and made the younger man look bad.

Barrett's attempts to succeed in capturing the fans' imagination only stretched as far as his wardrobe on this evening. He sauntered into the ring in white shorts covered with a star-spangled kilt, but his approach in the ring remained as frustrating as it had been at the Apollo two months previously. His arsenal was impressive, his movement graceful and poised, but he was lunging in with his shots, thereby detracting from their ultimate effect, and Sonnenberg lingered for too long – as Val Smith had done before him.

By the fourth, the meagre crowd was either booing or heading for the beer stands. Sonnenberg, his tanned face now a mask of blood, was mercifully halted before the end of the round. Despite Monte's trademark back flip in the centre of the ring, he knew it wasn't a satisfactory end to the evening.

Monte wasn't in the finest of moods, leaving the arena cut above the eye and distinctly bothered. The smooth edges of a career which he had been adamant would run without hindrance, were beginning to fray. He had spoken to me often of his patience and willingness to wait his turn, but fighting the likes of Sonnenberg for too long was going to be detrimental to his plans. This was a sentiment echoed by his trainers.

Old Timer looked up from yet another batch of peanuts, as he sat among the crowd alongside Barrett's co-trainer Artie Cintron. He gazed at me through large spectacles, his legs crossed awkwardly before him, and smiled as I approached. 'He needs to get those kinds of guys out of there faster,' he sniffed. 'He didn't do the things we had worked on, and that's why the guy lasted as long as he did.'

'He was fighting a garbage fighter tonight,' Cintron chirped in. 'If you carry on fighting garbage fighters for too long, you become a garbage fighter yourself before you know it.'

Boxing trainers were full of these little anecdotes, many of which could be used to relate to so many of life's lessons. They were everywhere – in the minds of the old sages like Cus D'Amato, proven fistic geniuses like Emanuel Steward, upon the blackboards and the lockers in the gyms of Brooklyn and Detroit.

Barrett's manager, Joe De Guardia was around, too, although he looked pleased enough just to see his charge add another win to his expanding ledger. It was the beginning of a new phase in Barrett's career; having fought as a sole trader for almost two years now, he was being steered towards a promotional agreement with America Presents. Such a move came with an equal share of reward and risk. Work would be guaranteed as would greater financial backing, moral support, wider TV exposure and the promise of a route which would lead to a title shot. Conversely, in signing with the Denver-based promoters, Monte would become a small fish in an ever-expanding ocean. America Presents had signed up more heavyweights than any other promoter apart from Cedric Kushner – Olympic dis-appointment Clay-Bey, the six-foot-eight Mount Whitaker, Nigerian Duncan Dokiwari and Paea Wolfgramm, whose physique reminded me of Obelix the Gaul.

'We're close to making a deal,' said De Guardia, while the technicians dismantled the ring at the end of the evening. 'As long as the money's right, we'll sign the contracts.'

'Aren't you concerned about Monte getting lost in the mix?' I asked him.

'No. If I see that starting to happen, it'll be my job to keep reminding them of Monte,' he replied. 'But I don't think that'll happen; Whitaker's a novelty act, and so's Wolfgramm. Clay-Bey looks good, but his age will work against him, and it's too early to tell with Dokiwari.'

Moments later we were all surrounding a circular glass bar which resembled a spaceship. Beside us the chatter of the fruit-machines was in full flow as the ballroom cleared into the hotel foyer. Trainers and managers sat hunched around the bar drinking bottles of Heineken and Miller Lite, smoking cigarettes and talking boxing. Some of the fighters had showered and changed, and were now hitting the blackjack tables. Monte strode past in his red tracksuit and black beanie hat, his boots unlaced, his cousins and pals from Queens rumbling along behind him.

'He's off to the hospital for some stitches,' said De Guardia.

Several beers later, I wandered around the casino, resisting the question-able temptation of emptying my pockets into Donald Trump's. In the distance I could see Kim's brother and his friend stagger slightly as they returned from the change counter with cups of quarters. I couldn't see Kim anywhere.

Two of the undercard fighters walked past me in smart new suits and faces happy from their successful evenings in the ring. One of them was a fresh-faced eighteen-year-old coming off a win over a man old enough to have been his father. The other was the weary Bryant 'Special K' Smith, who had scored a rare win on the show, and in only thirteen seconds too.

Beyond them, I saw the lads guzzle bottles of beer, plunge coins into slots, sway, laugh loudly, and wipe chins with their sleeves.

It was getting late. I had had a few beers and sleep seemed like a good idea. I saw a woman rummaging through her purse beside the 25-cent section, and recognised her as Monte's wife, Taja. Assured that I was several drinks away from disgracing myself with some unintelligible slurring, I greeted her with a friendly hello, and was relieved to see she didn't stare at me as though I were some drunken lunatic.

'Hi, Dominic, how are you?' she asked softly.

'Fine,' I replied. 'How's Monte?'

'Not great. He's been taken to the hospital for some stitches and he's not in a great mood right now.'

I wanted to wish her well, a pleasant evening at the least. But my intentions were short-lived as, to my horror, I noticed a drunken form lurch towards me, beer dribbling down his shirt, mouth open wide to release a staccato of 'wuh-heys!'.

I managed to wish Taja a good evening, while deftly moving into the next aisle, before my unnamed companion tripped up and careered towards her. He fell on his chest, arms outstretched, a tumbler full of coins sent flying all over the place, the unmistakable aroma of lager wafting around his prone form.

★

Two weeks later, America Presents staged another show on the Boardwalk, and this time the quality of fights was substantially better. It was a heavyweight co-feature, which meant I had to make that dastardly bus trip once more.

Since struggling past Obed Sullivan, Hasim Rahman had scored a quick knockout at the Pepsi arena in Albany, and had now secured another outing on HBO. This time the opponent was the veteran Jesse 'Boogieman' Ferguson. The suspicion was that the spectacular finish Rahman had failed to achieve against Sullivan in New York could now be fulfilled against the brave but ageing Ferguson.

Sitting at ringside that night proved to be more than a little chaotic. Finding myself in the front row with Nigel Collins, editor of *The Ring*, and Michael Katz of the *Daily News* was a surprise in itself. Looking on as the notoriously quick-tempered Katz engaged in a row with one of Larry Hazard's lime-suited sidekicks was as entertaining as any of the evening's bouts. 'If anyone's going to get upset tonight, it'll be Rahman,' said Collins, clearly not taking too much notice of Katz's face turning a dark, pulsating mauve with rage and indignation as Hazard's man called him a 'fat mother-fucker' and turned intentionally to block his view of the fights with his own massive bulk.

Rahman was not to be upset, but again the full potential of his skills was not revealed to a high-profile audience. He jabbed well, but not enough, and like Barrett against Sonnenberg, struggled to find the range before pulling the trigger on his best weapon of all – a destructive and heavy-handed right cross. Had Ferguson been assisted by the fountain of youth, things may have turned out differently, but as it was, experience and guile were not enough to upset the younger, stronger man.

A booming left hook floored the self-styled Boogieman in the tenth round, but he recovered at the sound of the bell and Rahman refrained from seeking to end it inside the distance in the last two. Instead, the Baltimore fighter clutched and retreated, jabbed and evaded, looking out at the crowds expectantly, never seeming to find what his eyes were looking for. As the seconds ticked by in the twelfth and final round, he unashamedly pedalled backwards, flicking out a hard jab at the grim-faced, advancing Ferguson.

The crowd booed long and loud, understandably unimpressed with the youngster's performance against a man who had failed to stand up to one solid punch against Frank Bruno several years before.

On the way out, I bumped into Rahman's co-manager Bob Mittleman, who told me he wouldn't put his fighter in with a Michael Grant or a David Tua unless they were paid a million dollars.

Rahman mumbled something about staying up all the previous night drinking coffee with relatives and friends, and swore there would never be a repeat of that kind of performance again. Other sources told me it hadn't just been the coffee keeping him up, but that he had been playing poker late into the night, with his companions' cigarette smoke invading his mouth and nostrils.

I caught up with Ferguson too, shuffling along a corridor and towards the elevator which would take him to his hotel room. 'I don't think anything of Rahman at all,' he said through what crooked teeth remained in his mouth. 'I'm over forty years old and he couldn't do anything with me, so why should I be impressed? He couldn't beat most of the guys I've fought – Seldon, Mercer, Bruno, none of 'em!'

Another of Jesse's former opponents was only a matter of feet away as we spoke. He was a huge, looming figure, his face rumpled and fleshy now, but still recognisable. It was Riddick Bowe, the former heavyweight champ, and one whose demise had been as depressingly fast as any in history.

He walked past us, greeted us with massive palms and mumbled 'how ya doin's', and enveloped one of Ali's old foes, Chuck Wepner, in a bear hug. Next to him stood his mother, Dorothy, a painfully slight woman in a rose dress, and the stories came flooding back to me of Bowe's noble exploits as a young son in the dreaded Brownsville projects. Back then he had completed school each day, and immediately headed to his mother's place of work in order to escort her safely through the rancid apartment blocks, up stairways transformed into crack-dealers' dens and disconnected elevators littered with used syringes.

Boxing, so it had seemed, gave him a focus for the future. But it had also broken him, cruelly and without repentance. And as he stood there, overweight and battling to speak coherently, his frail mother watching him with wide, friendly eyes, the world around him was tearing at the seams. Since formally announcing his retirement in April 1997 after the two masochistic skirmishes with Andrzej Golota, Bowe had tried to set about accomplishing other goals. HBO had been keen to use him as an ambassador for some of their social outreach programmes, but little materialised. The most publicised attempt to divert his mind and body away from the gym had been an abortive bid to enlist in the marines. After eleven days of basic training at Parris Island, South Carolina, Bowe dropped out. On a televised interview the following November, the former world champion spoke about a drill instructor who had badgered him consistently, telling him to run faster, try harder, and '. . . telling me to do sit-ups properly, even though I had been doing sit-ups for twenty years. He gave me such a hard time, and that day changed everything – I just decided to come home. I should have been meek and humble and just dealt with it.'

He had wanted to enlist again, but the marines did not allow as many comebacks as prize-fighting. Intermittently, Bowe would mention the idea of a return to the ring, especially during the build-up to Evander Holy-field's rematch with Michael Moorer three months prior to Rahman's fight with Ferguson in Atlantic City.

Behind the scenes, however, the gravity of Bowe's lack of focus was getting out of hand; in October he had faced the humiliation of appearing at a court enquiry with regard to a complaint lodged by his wife, Judy. She complained he had assaulted her in their Maryland home, and that he had committed similar offences many times beforehand. With the complaint pending, Bowe remained estranged from his wife and five children.

In January I had arranged through Bowe's manager, Rock Newman, to interview Bowe during one of his trips to New York, where most of his family still resided. 'Riddick has always been someone who really looked at this sport as a means to an end,' said Newman as we planned the following week's interview. 'He wanted to use his talents to secure his family. Once he accomplished that goal, he started talking about the day he wouldn't have to fight any more. His motivation slipped after the third fight with Holyfield. His focus wasn't there, and the fluctuations in his weight really took a toll at the end of his fighting days. We've come to the conclusion now that Riddick needs a greater balance in life. He's been doing things that have not been particularly well thought out.

'His ability to reason has become somewhat impaired, and he is making some very personal and emotional decisions which have ended up being against his and his family's best interests. He's making an effort now to turn this situation around.

'I don't know how much of all the problems he's going through now are owing to the way his career ended, or the fights he had. I don't know if it all took some form of physical toll. But he's having tests now to determine both from a physical and a mental point of view what is behind some of his impulsive and unreasoned behaviour.'

The morning of my interview, however, Newman's secretary called me early and informed me that my meeting with the self-styled 'Big Daddy' had been shelved. She couldn't divulge too much information, but the next day's newspapers were full of it.

On visiting his relatives in Brooklyn, an altercation had taken place between Bowe and one of his nephews. Blows had been exchanged and arrests had been made. A man once destined for heavyweight greatness was now treading the path of the shambolic. It was embarrassing, and it was to grow worse.

As things transpired, on 2 June 1998, Bowe's attempts to 'turn things around' were obliterated. After arming himself with a knife, pepper spray, a set of handcuffs and some binding tape, he drove all the way from Maryland to North Carolina. On arriving at the house his estranged family were staying in, he marched Judy and the children into his car and drove for two hundred miles of the way back to his home in Fort Washington. When the car stopped at a McDonald's *en route*, his wife was able to give the game away to an employee, who duly notified the police.

The authorities caught up with Bowe. He was charged with kidnapping and assault. He faced a maximum of ten years' imprisonment and a minimum of two. Someone, somewhere, must have shed a tear.

CHAPTER EIGHT

Dark Dealings

As he was serving his one-year ban from the sport, Mike Tyson started the process in March '98 of breaking all ties with Don King. For years, the fighter could not have helped but pay heed to the warnings from outside sources that his bank account was dwindling with alarming speed.

His career – his very existence – was in jeopardy during those tumultuous times which led to his imprisonment for rape. He had been largely responsible for the majority of his predicaments, but the lessons supposedly learned during four years inside seemed not to include the belief that people were, to a large degree, reflections of those whose company they kept. The feeling had been strong that on his release from the Indiana State Penitentiary, Tyson would leave King stranded. Instead he had reaffirmed his belief that 'Don King is the best promoter in the world', and he elected to stay with the man who many felt had robbed him of millions.

Now, almost three years after being released from prison for the rape of Desiree Washington, Tyson was finally cutting the cord with King, in the ominous shape of a lawsuit. Amongst other charges and accusations, it was claimed that the promoter had cheated Tyson out of more than $100 million during his career, an extraordinary amount, even if it had been siphoned off over the course of twelve years.

'King's total control of Tyson's profession, business and finances, and the trust placed in him by Tyson, enabled King to defraud Tyson year after year,' stated the lawsuit. 'King knew that Tyson had a fundamental inability to read and understand contracts and fully appreciate the effect of business transactions on his life. It was King's and King's company's (Don King Productions) duty as fiduciaries to advise and counsel Tyson in the development of his career, to bring him business opportunities, and to do so with their eye solely on the interests of Tyson. Unfortunately, King and DKP continued to defraud him and grossly abused the trust that he placed in them.'

The suit also claimed that King hid his illegal dealings by surrounding the fighter with 'puppets, whom the boxer trusted to be his own independent advisors'. John Horne and Rory Holloway were being publicly exposed, and the whole process was proving to be more than a little humiliating for King too. Tyson denied literally kicking the promoter out of his car in Los Angeles days before the lawsuit was filed, but his fury had certainly been ignited by the knowledge that the promoter 'owned' the legal rights to the former champion's 'image'.

King also induced Tyson's fury before the charges were filed, when he sought to be paid directly for the boxer's scheduled appearance on a wrestling show promoted by the founder of the World Wrestling Federation, Vince McMahon. Tyson, after all, had come to an arrangement with McMahon without the assistance of King.

The lawsuit also pinpointed isolated occurrences of mismanagement:

1. Tyson once asked his 'independent bookkeeper' to transfer files to a new account. The bookkeeper allegedly responded that he couldn't, because the files were kept in cabinets owned by Don King.

2. King skimmed huge amounts from the top of Tyson's purses, and *then* extracted additional amounts for his wife Henrietta, his stepsons Carl and Eric, and his son-in-law Greg Lee, in the guise of consultation fees. Substantial fees were also paid to King's daughter Debbie, as payment for her role as president of Tyson's fan club. (Tyson was not aware that such a club existed – indeed, most rabid Tyson fans were in the dark about this one too.)

3. King illegally used Tyson's money to purchase fancy cars, renovate DKP's headquarters in New York, buy a luxury home in Las Vegas and pay for all of King's legal fees in his on-going court battles with Lloyd's of London.

4. King bought Horne's and Holloway's services by giving them each an initial payment of $4.3 million, a 20 per cent cut each from Tyson's future purses, and additional stock in the MGM Grand hotel.

5. King struck a deal with rival promoter Murad Muhammad, then working for heavyweight Razor Ruddock, in 1991, when Ruddock fought Tyson twice. Unbeknown to Tyson, King was alleged to have paid Muhammad $2 million from Tyson's purse,

in return for options clauses on Ruddock should the big-punching Canadian have won.

Indirectly, these developments were going to cause yet another disappointment in Lennox Lewis's stumbling career. Lewis and his manager Frank Maloney had just forged an unlikely alliance with King after King had fallen out with his previous British partner (and Maloney's rival) Frank Warren. The plan, or so it had seemed, was for the Lewis camp to cut a deal with King which would have led to at least one of the two big match-ups Lewis craved – against either Evander Holyfield or Tyson. While Holyfield remained part of the equation, Tyson had now rid himself of King, and was having his affairs looked after by a pair of former rock music entrepreneurs, Irving Azoff and Jeff Wald.

Soon after brokering a deal between Tyson and promoters America Presents, Azoff and Wald stepped back into the shadows, and renowned fight agent Shelly Finkel (one of the sport's few characters with an unsullied reputation) took over the marketing of this latest Tyson incarnation.

Tyson appeared to be seeking to make sure that if he were to have his licence reinstated by the NSAC that July, he would make as many changes as were necessary to give him the best chance of success. There were, of course, many who immediately sought to attach their names to the Tyson publicity machine, most notably the former basketball star Magic Johnson, who was 'whispering' pretty loudly that he was the new mouthpiece for Team Tyson.

The astute King was measured in his response to the media's request for a reaction to these developments. A lot of people, however, were more interested in the responses of Horne and Holloway. Holloway's was fairly mute, but Horne predictably lashed out in the manner of a child who could no longer play with his favourite toy, so instead sought to break it rather than share it with others.

Not long after Tyson gave King his marching orders, I was back in Easton with Larry Holmes. 'I've always said he's smarter than all of us,' Holmes said of King. 'He's smarter than Bob Arum, smarter than the Duvas, smarter than HBO and Showtime. He's a good-assed businessman, and yet they always underestimate him. Don King is good for boxers if the boxers are good for themselves. If he tells you he's gonna pay you $5 million, and comes back the next day saying he's gonna give you $4 million, then don't let him. You have a contract which says $5 million. He can't get away with just giving you the $4 million unless you let him. All these other guys, they let him.'

Everyone knew what King was about. Mike Tyson probably should have known from the start. Perhaps he did but chose to hurl himself further into a well of trouble surrounded by a wall of self-pity, in the misguided hope that he would continue to be portrayed as the victim in this, sport's wackiest soap opera.

Horne and Holloway were a different matter, though. Holloway had been Tyson's buddy growing up in Brownsville. Horne had been a comedian but was now just a clown. Holloway may have sincerely cared for Tyson, but he had been corrupted by King when the riches had been waved before his eyes – riches which bought both him and Horne the Armani suits, Versace shirts and ugly waterfalls of jewellery which poured down their chests. These were the fruits of their pillaging of an ignoramus named Mike Tyson.

From many quarters, Tyson received sympathy to counteract the 'told you so' attitude of his detractors, and few defences were mounted as succinctly as that presented by Darrell Dawsey of *The Source: Sports* magazine: 'We embrace him as "our" fighter,' said Dawsey. 'Meanwhile, Holyfield . . . remains cherished but slightly aloof from black youth, separated by a barrier of Christian piety that we respect but don't always "feel". Holy's the cat we wave hi to as he cuts his grass or heads off to church. We know *of* him more than we know him. But not Tyson. That brother, we know . . .'

These were comments which fairly represented a large portion of public opinion, though the portrayal of Tyson as a better role model for any youths (whether black or not) to relate to was strange to say the least; Tyson was not the epitome of evil and Holyfield – a serial adulterer – was not a bastion of pious goodness. But Holyfield had not raped and he had not torn the flesh from another man's face with his bare teeth.

Tyson's own reflections on his behaviour that night were conveyed to Alex Wallau on ABC television shortly prior to his separation from King. A degree of remorse had crossed Tyson's conscience during the intervening months, but his 'me against the world' attitude was still prominent throughout. 'I feel really sick when I see the fight,' he told Wallau. 'I was in trouble [from a cut eye]. He was butting me in the third round, and I was blacking out. I must be the most extreme fighter that ever lived, and that's just the way I am.'

Wallau asked Tyson if he had ever made any attempts to apologise personally to Holyfield, and the disgraced former champ replied that he had. 'I've called him twice since the fight, and he didn't return my calls,' said Tyson. 'He didn't return the calls, so I guess he believed I wasn't sincere. So now, I probably wouldn't take his calls either.'

It was Tyson's wife, Dr Monica Turner, who was being credited by many as the instigator behind his decision to leave King. Turner had made repeated demands to look at Tyson's portfolios; when they were eventually forthcoming, she noticed at first minor and then more suspicious discrepancies. Tyson openly admitted that, even now, his wife was putting most of the work into their relationship, but it would also have been true to say that she had been gearing a sizeable share of her time seeing to it that his professional life was being better looked after as well.

For Tyson, the enforced hiatus from boxing had brought him elements of peace and happiness, aside from a motorcycle accident in Connecticut, which resulted in a punctured lung.

He loved the sport of boxing, but he loathed the business and the media engagements which came with it. He was deeply suspicious of the press, most of whom he regarded as 'parasites', and he had learned at last that there were money-men who robbed and cheated. He liked to fight, but the dealings and the 'trickerations' were the dominant aspects of the game. The trouncing of a Frank Bruno or a Bruce Seldon was almost incidental.

Tyson was having fun during his lay-off. He played the part of an 'enforcer' during a WWF heavyweight title fight between 'Stone Cold' Steve Austin and Shawn Michaels in Boston, and relished the opportunity to fulfil what had been a childhood ambition. First he was brawling with Austin in his role as a supposed spy for Michaels's 'Generation X' posse. Then, when the big night arrived, he decked Michaels and declared Austin the new champion. 'It was all a con job, just like life,' he declared philosophically afterwards, with a conspiratorial grin sneaking across his face.

The most fun Tyson had, however, was pursuing his passion for music. He formed his own label, Tyson Records, with the assistance of Irving Azoff, and he signed up several R&B and rap stars. This was his peace. He gave interviews to music magazines, and attended the World Music Awards at the invitation of Prince Rainier of Monaco, after being given permission to leave the country temporarily by his probation officer. He rocked his head and sang along with Erykah Badu, rose to his feet for Puff Daddy and danced and posed for pictures with the girls from All Saints.

This was a freedom of spirit Tyson had not known under the gaze of King or Horne. He stood firm on his decision to put distance between himself and King, despite pleas made on King's behalf by a number of respected public figures. The Reverend Jesse Jackson called for Tyson to 'return to the fold', as boxing was now 'in the hands of its children' – a reference to King's standing as a black man who was the sport's most influential figure, a position for so long occupied by whites. This was a bold statement to make, but one was left to wonder precisely which of King's former fighters had supplied Jackson with such glowing character references.

'King and I can get on just fine when we see each other,' Larry Holmes said to me, as I pressed him on King's ability to make the race card work for him with every ethnic grouping under the sun. 'But the important thing to understand with King is that for him it's never been a case of black and white. It's all about who can do the most for him.

'It's true that he's the only minority in boxing worth talking about. I don't care what anyone says about your Butch Lewises or your Murad Muhammads; Don King is the only minority with power in this game. That much is true.

'But he will tell you you're trained by a white man and managed by a white man, and that these white men are all stealing from you – if it helps him. But if it helps him more, he will make deals behind closed doors with those same white trainers and white managers, to the detriment of the black fighter. The bottom line is that he does what's best for him. It's never a matter of colour.'

And, in doing so, King simply played the game brilliantly while the rest of the boxing fraternity tried to get its head around the rules. The truth? There were no rules to speak of. Boxing, as those who lived in its strange yet addictive world would confess, was a small family which while often looking upon itself distastefully, nearly always closed ranks when one of its number was threatened. There were monsters, spineless double-crossers and wide boys aplenty, but they were an integral part of pugilism's calypso kaleidoscope, and they would be missed if government legislation buried them alive in red tape.

King, his rival promoters and the TV corporations controlled the big money. Every so often a champion came along, like Evander Holyfield, who accumulated riches, saved the riches and parted from pieces of silver as ruefully as Shakespeare's Shylock. But Holyfield was an exception.

CHAPTER NINE

The Last One Standing

For Lennox Lewis, the waiting game continued, even if there was only one fight out there which truly mattered on the world heavyweight stage. With Tyson having the time of his life joshing with actor Mickey Rourke at music awards in Monte Carlo, and Riddick Bowe being sucked into one drama after another, Evander Holyfield and unification were Lewis's twin targets now.

Holyfield sat in the driving seat, and Lewis knew it. Holyfield could not make the kind of money which seemed to follow Tyson everywhere, but the recognition and acclaim – after destroying Tyson twice (once physically, the other mentally) – were all his.

A deal between the Lewis and Holyfield camps could not be made – unsurprising really, when you considered the various factions involved and all their financial demands and bloated egos. Instead, Lewis chose to schedule a March 1998 defence against Shannon Briggs, the unlikely 'linear' champion who was still smarting from the criticism he had received as the recipient of a controversial decision over George Foreman.

Despite his outward appearance of icy calm, I could not believe that deep down a sense of real frustration and helplessness failed to burn inside Lewis. From the outset of his career, the six-foot-five-inch chess enthusiast with the numbing right hand had spoken frequently of his ability to fulfil his 'destiny'. He had not been so naïve as to presume he could remain un-touched by the film of dirt which covered all aspects of the sport, but it was clear from the start he did not intend to be tainted by boxing's reverse Midas touch.

With these thoughts in mind, I caught the subway to 42nd Street and Times Square station in January, and headed for the Hard Rock café to await the formal announcement of the Briggs fight. I wound my way through the yellow cabs and the hotdog stands, momentarily distracted by a hoard of teenagers camped outside the MTV studios, screaming excitedly at yet another boy band being interviewed beyond the massive windows one floor above the sidewalk. Girls with ponytails and quilted jackets jostled for position and waved placards around wildly in a successful effort to grab their heroes' attention. To capture such a market was to secure a golden future, even if the fawning admiration only continued for as long as the band was able to make an impression on the charts.

Lewis's marketability, in contrast, had proven to be an extraordinarily unpredictable factor. When he took over the domestic scene from Frank Bruno and Gary Mason, there had been a feeling that this sleek, panther-like tactician would appeal more to the hearts and minds of black youths than his predecessors had done. He appeared to be more 'street cool', a snappier dresser with a love for reggae and garage music, and his entourage contained more young black faces and less of British boxing's old school. But Lewis's appeal never seemed to take off; and even if Bruno's pantomime dame act had worn thin, his jovial, self-effacing nature was always better received than Lewis's perceived air of aloofness.

In America, the situation was worse. Even beyond the obnoxiously partisan who closed ranks and sniped at Lewis for the most trivial of reasons, there was a serious consequence of his failure to ignite emotions across the pond. To many in America, Lewis was a hesitant fighter, a strategist devoid of the passion and spirit in Holyfield. He was not explosive and rough like Tyson, nor as overly witty and instinctive as Bowe. To America, Lewis was passive and dull. He struggled with mediocre opposition and he had been vanquished once already by the easily forgettable Oliver McCall.

Holyfield quoted from the Bible and talked about his self-ordained role as God's warrior; Tyson spoke of smashing bones and 'having fun' demolishing opponents; Bowe did impersonations of Ronald Reagan and persistently called Lewis a 'faggot'. Lewis just smiled sardonically, spoke of himself in the third person and allowed the managers, media, promoters and rivals to fluster around his oasis of calm.

'They all know the deal with me,' he said to me inside the Hard Rock, as he gazed around him from behind designer shades. 'Patience is my key, and the desire to go out there and do what comes naturally. As long as I stay focused and train hard I will always win. In a room filled with men, I will always be the last one standing.'

The conference room was busy, full as it was with reporters and cameramen, and even a few bizarre models dressed in togas and Cleopatra wigs as this event was to be sponsored by the Caesar's hotel in Atlantic City.

Lewis's penultimate sentence triggered a memory from my meeting with Monte Barrett. 'As long as I train hard, I will always win,' Lewis had said. Barrett's sentiment had been almost entirely the same: 'As long as I am mentally and physically prepared, I will never be beaten.' At first I suspected that such statements were surely the fighters unconsciously setting themselves up for a fall. It did not take long for me to decide, however, that far from being impossible targets to attain, these missions to retire without further loss were more like mantras for the steely ambitious to repeat to themselves. They were not fooling themselves into a pompous sense of immortality, but more accurately cementing their grim determination to succeed. So it had been that Holyfield, training for his first, supposedly hopeless task of defeating Tyson, had told himself over and over that he could, rather than taking a more measured and logical look at his chances of causing an upset.

Meanwhile, with Lewis floating upon a calm sea of matter-of-fact confidence, Briggs had been stung into a counter-attack against the press, who relentlessly questioned the validity of his win over Foreman. He waded into his critics, warning them that any further shows of disrespect would mean no more interviews and no more pictures. His frankness in admitting he had been surprised by the result of the Foreman fight had been mistaken as him conceding that he had lost. That was not the case, he now insisted. He had simply been taken aback that the judges had ruled in his favour against a man of Foreman's stature, in what had been a close fight.

'This is all bigger than Shannon Briggs or Lennox Lewis,' said Briggs, hunched over his microphone in a rugged outfit of dark brown suede. 'This is my destiny. The belt is mine. No question about it. Even if I didn't want it, it would end up being mine, and there's nothing anyone can do about it.'

He sounded like he meant business, and standing beside the dispassionate Lewis, who himself wore a designer check suit and prim lilac shirt, the American looked to be the more obvious pugilist of the two.

'I have to take him seriously,' Lewis said to me after the microphones had been switched off and Cleopatra and Caesar had headed to the tables for a burger beneath rock music memorabilia. 'This is a real fight. Shannon and I have no hate for each other, but when millions of dollars are involved, I think friends can go to war!'

But, I argued, surely he ached under the weight of political rhetoric and American scorn?

'In boxing, one fight can make a big difference and turn everything around for you,' he insisted. 'The win over Golota definitely earned me more respect over here in the States. That was the most satisfying win recently, because a lot of people thought I was going to lose that fight. I am the man who brought down Golota! And it felt good, especially after those empty victories over McCall and Akinwande.

'Like I said, I will always be the last one standing, whether it is against Briggs, Holyfield, Tyson or whoever. Once his family members stop beating him up, Riddick Bowe can get to fight me if he wants to. The most important thing for me is to know that I'm the best heavyweight on the planet, and I will be for quite a while. I'm the sleeper of the bunch, but when I wake up – *boom!*'

Forgotten, perhaps, amidst America's indifference towards Lewis and disdain for the questionable resolve of Briggs, was the fact that the two would be meeting not only for the British fighter's WBC championship, but the historically important linear title being worn by Briggs.

Later on, the fighters spilled onto Times Square to pose for shots in front of the twinkling lights, the neon Coca-Cola signs and the grandiose billboards advertising the latest TV sitcom hits and Broadway musicals. Passers-by asked the reporters who the two men were. Lewis remained unrecognised in the bustling surroundings, but this had always been something he had felt comfortable with. More damning to his pride would have been the giant poster unrolled along the width of a building, purporting to boast 'Boxing's Best' in the eyes of HBO. One British fighter was included alongside Roy Jones and Oscar De La Hoya, and it wasn't Lewis.

So the underlying feeling continued that Lewis was an unwanted champion in the eyes of many of those who were supposedly in his corner. Jones and De La Hoya were superstars, and if Jones lacked De La Hoya's marketing skills, he more than made up for that with his unique talents. He appeared to be the most naturally gifted non-heavyweight since Sugar Ray Robinson, while De La Hoya's mass crossover appeal between the hispanic and white communities produced extraordinary results at the box office.

Lewis, conversely, could generate only a tepid response from the pay-per-view market and inside the ring his accomplishments were often dismissed. America questioned the validity of his opponents and pondered whether perhaps it was the Brit's fault that the big matches with the likes of Holyfield, Bowe, Moorer and Tyson had all failed to come off. Wins over Razor Ruddock, Tony Tucker, Ray Mercer, Oliver McCall, Henry Akinwande and Andrzej Golota would not suffice; Ruddock's resolve had been crushed by his two bruising encounters with Tyson; Tucker was a washed up drug-addict; Mercer should have won the decision in their fight; McCall was in the midst of an emotional breakdown; Akinwande had never achieved anything in the first place; and Golota was pumped full of pain-killing medication the night he collapsed in a round against the WBC champion.

Of course, as with most things in life, it was all about perception. A defender of Lewis's record could have argued that America regarded Ruddock as the best heavyweight in the world the moment Tyson was incarcerated in 1992. In forty-six fights Tucker had only ever lost to Tyson, and there was no evidence to suggest Lewis should have knocked him cold early, as he had done with Ruddock. Against Mercer, Lewis had proven his heart and willingness to gut it out when things became rough. He had overcome McCall's psychological edge in their rematch. Akinwande was uninspired but undoubtedly one of the most awkward men to tackle in the division. And Golota ruined the career of the man America was certain would one day stand over a fallen Lewis, Riddick Bowe.

Briggs was far more up for a confrontation than Golota had been five months beforehand. He sneered at Lewis as the referee spoke to them in the centre of the ring, calling him a 'snotty-nosed Englishman', and then proceeded to blast away at the taller champion. A sweeping left hook caught Lewis and launched him back into the ropes, which prevented him from hitting the deck. Upon unsteady feet, the Briton sought to recover, eager to wash away his initial embarrassment and correct the poor balance which had led to this mini-crisis.

Briggs troubled Lewis again in the fight, and showed resilience and heart to those who had felt he was lacking in such attributes after the loss to Wilson. But a man could only take so much punishment. Soon, it seemed as though Briggs's only intent was to rebuke his critics and leave his head unprotected against the Lewis right hand in a bold but ill-advised attempt to cover his durability in glory. By the fifth round, the referee had seen enough.

CHAPTER TEN

King Solomon

Madison Square Garden. Back to the mecca, the world's most celebrated, nostalgic venue for a big fight. It was here that Muhammad Ali and Joe Frazier had engaged in what had simply been called 'The Fight'. This was where the greats all fought: Ali, Frazier, Roberto Duran, Sugar Ray Leonard, Emile Griffith, Jose Napoles, Dick Tiger.

Depression with the way heavyweight boxing was going at the upper echelon was therefore compounded when it was announced that Evander Holyfield's first defence of his unified WBA and IBF titles was to come against Henry Akinwande, the man who had disgraced himself against Lewis. It sounded faintly ridiculous when compared to the other matches which had taken place at the Garden: Ali v Frazier, Duran v Buchanan . . . Holyfield v Akinwande?

The negotiations for Holyfield v Lewis were stumbling and stalling. Each time one side appeared close to being satisfied with the financial arrangements, the other baulked at certain contractual obligations. There were the purses to be paid to both fighters, but the likes of Don King, the Duva family at Main Events, and Lewis's British handlers were also struggling to get their top dollar. To complicate matters further were the cable channels competing to stage the showdown, Lewis being tied exclusively to HBO, while Holyfield (through a contract negotiated by King) pretty well obligated to appear on Showtime.

Another factor to take into consideration were the preposterous mandatory challengers waiting for their own WBA, WBC and IBF title shots. So it was that a trio of thoroughly unwarranted challenges were due to be made by the commissions' number-one contenders, Akinwande (WBA), Zel'jko Mavrovic of Croatia (WBC) and Vaughn Bean (IBF). Seldom before had the three major governing bodies allowed themselves to be seen to be so obviously inept as they were at this time. For years they had faced allegations of managers and promoters lining the head honchos' pockets in order for completely undeserving fighters to receive grossly inflated ratings. Often it had taken only a little spin-doctoring or a thick smokescreen to cover up the accusations of impropriety. On this occasion, however, what little faith the boxing fan had in the sport's 'level playing-field' was being seriously threatened.

Mavrovic and Bean had excellent records on paper, but neither had ever defeated an opponent who could be ranked in the top thirty, let alone the top ten. Usually it was fighters promoted by King who were the recipients of such extraordinarily good tidings, but Mavrovic (the European champion) and Bean were linked to German promoter Wilfred Sauerland and Butch Lewis respectively.

Akinwande's instatement as the WBA number-one contender at least had legal backing, the result of an indirect twist of fate which was supposed to have punished rather than assisted King's manipulations. After Holyfield's second victory over Mike Tyson, another King heavyweight – Orlin Norris – left the promoter with some difficulty and signed up with Frank Warren. Incredibly, the WBA promptly saw fit to drop Norris from their ratings, despite the fact he had not lost a fight in the interim, and both they and Don King were taken to court in Philadelphia. The judge decided that Norris had been unfairly treated, and ordered that the veteran be matched in a final eliminator, with the winner to receive a title shot within six months of that fight taking place.

This had not been quite what Norris and his management had had in mind, seeing as they felt they held the mandatory position in the first place. King laughed all the way back to his offices in Florida, and very quickly sealed a match between the short, chunky Norris and the six-foot-six Akinwande at a local arena in Pompano Beach. Stylistically, the match was a terrible one for Norris, who was completely unable to bore his way through his opponent's long-armed reach, and lost a wide decision. Five months after effectively giving up against Lewis, and doing so with almost zero effort and in one of the worst title fights ever, Akinwande was now in line to challenge once more for what was fast ceasing to be sport's greatest prize.

It was a fight nobody wanted to see. It had very little box-office appeal, even if Holyfield had proven to be the most outstanding champion of the decade. Boxing interest was waning in the Big Apple; people there had become despondent with the lack of major events and an influx of second-rate packages passed off as masterpieces. Ticket prices were going to be astronomical, and the best King's promotional machine could come up with in order to spark some much needed interest in the fight was along the lines of 'Ooh, won't it be tricky for Holyfield to reach the chin of such a tall challenger?' Scintillating stuff.

Still, as uninspiring as the match was, the opportunity to talk to Evander Holyfield was not one to be passed over, especially as it didn't require a long bus journey to get there – the Garden was only a matter of minutes away on the train from where I was staying.

I arrived at the Garden a full hour before the press conference to announce the fight was to start. Gradually, the seats around me filled up and so did those behind the long black podium at the head of the meeting room, with the Garden executives and the TV men from Showtime, the managers and lawyers, the trainers, and eventually the two fighters and Don King.

Despite his impending retrial for defrauding Lloyd's of London, King was bright and chirpy, gleaming merrily around him, and dominating the room with his presence. As the old saying went, if you lied often enough, people would soon start to believe you. And so it was, that the more King acted like a big, friendly – if somewhat unhinged – giant, the closer you edged towards believing that he was not such an unreasonable fellow after all. After all, his work ethic coupled with an ability to come back from the gravest of legal woes was quite possibly the most potent combination in the business. He was not purely a boxing man, he would tell an audience, but he was above everything else a humanitarian, a man who just loved to pay his taxes when he was not funding the restoration of mosques and synagogues across the country in an effort to bring about religious harmony and understanding among the people. Even his fiercest critics could be made to smile or even laugh out loud.

'This is so great,' shrieked King at the conference, noticing the names of those surrounding him at the dais on that hot Monday afternoon. 'We have the Holy Warrior Evander Holyfield here, and we have all of the Apostles, too – Matthew, Mark, Luke and John, not to mention King David!' David Checketts of the Garden's sports department turned pink and held his head in his hands. Holyfield laughed, and his trainer Don Turner looked per- plexed as he shook his head resignedly from side to side.

King was a master of rhetoric. He raped the English language, revised history and drowned those around him in the false belief that he was a literary academic. Certainly, while imprisoned in the 1960s, endless hours had been spent in the company of Tolstoy, Shakespeare and Nietzsche, poring over the works of these writers. Rather than devouring their masterpieces, though, he had picked at the flesh and extracted anecdotes which could be readily stored away in his mind and later used as metaphors for the world of boxing and all of the broken loyalties which came with it. Mike Tyson had tried to pull the same trick himself, reading while imprisoned in Indiana, where he likened Hemingway's short bursts of prose to sharp combinations to the body. However, while Tyson's reported re-acquaintance with the classroom failed to result in his passing any exams, King could carry the charade off – insanely aware, as he was, of all the traps which his many enemies plotted to lay before him.

He raised his voice, allowed his words to tumble over one another to form sentences within sentences, shrieked, and even on the odd occasion indulged in self-effacement with arms opened wide in a stature of innocence. And then he would ambush – distort the deal, raise his price, bully his victims now caught off guard. He was a tactical genius.

'Now we have David and we have Goliath – my very own Zulu warrior, Henry Akinwande!' King shouted, affording just a cursory glance at the challenger, before ploughing ahead with his biblical references.

'Now Don Turner trains both fighters,' he continued conspiratorially. 'And it was cause of some consternation to these parties as to where Don would go, and I thought I might have to do a King Solomon, who, I must add is my favourite King from the Bible. God, I love King Solomon! And I thought I was gonna have to cut Don Turner in half, and offer part of him to Henry and part of him to Evander!'

And so on, and so on. It was King's stage, and he would talk well into the evening if he felt it could have sold more tickets and boost the practically non-existent pay-per-view interest.

The good news for those waiting patiently for Holyfield v Lewis, was that King took the unusual step of refraining from pouring cold water on the proposed clash of champions. Efforts, apparently, were being made to arrange the fight, and the shock-haired promoter did not even mention Frank Maloney's name when asked who or what had been stalling the match.

'It's HBO,' he replied. 'They have stopped the fight from taking place for two reasons. Number one: they do not want me involved; and number two: they do not have the money to pay for it. So, like I said after I made Larry Holmes against Mike Weaver – when they felt they did not have the money to show the fight – let me handle it, I'll always find a way.'

Despite the recent problems plaguing him and driving his express train of plans and propaganda into thick treacle, King did not have the look of a man on the slide. His rivals had been whispering wishfully amongst each other, but although their optimism that King was heading for a fall seemed premature, these were troubled times for the promoter.

Tyson had fled for the cover provided by new manager Shelly Finkel and promoters America Presents, and was now in the process of annulling all his and King's existing contracts. This left King's deal with Showtime looking distinctly unattractive. His trump card had been the delivery of Tyson onto the cable screens, but now all he had to offer was Holyfield v Akinwande and a series of mismatches between some of his lighter weight champions and deplorable opposition.

King had also been spending as much time before judges and lawyers as he had been with the sports media, entering courts across the US and Britain in order to duel with the likes of one-time business partner Frank Warren – who had feared King was squeezing him out of the Prince Naseem Hamed picture – Lloyd's of London and the FBI.

These were all subjects, however, which King was happy to address head on, his demonic Cheshire cat smile broadening, and his cold, dark eyes twinkling for a while. 'Mike Tyson is the best-paid sportsman in history, when you look at the deals I got him, in relation to the actual amount of time he spent fighting in the ring,' he argued.

And he scoffed at the idea that anyone else could garner the fighter a bigger slice of the cake, saying, 'I would very much like to see if they can come close to matching what I did for him; I don't even want to dignify this episode. It's nothing, nothing at all. We'll have it all worked out before you know it.'

As for the disputes with Warren, King commanded a pair of his cronies to hand out copies of a draft judgement made the previous week by the Hon. Justice Lightman in the High Court in London. The case had been brought by King's lawyers after Warren had signed a deal with HBO which gave the station the broadcast rights for Naseem Hamed, and a say in the fighter's future. This had left King fuming; not only did he resent HBO, but he claimed to have a contract which handed him the rights to promote Hamed's fights in the US.

The judgement had ruled in favour of Don King Productions over Warren, declaring that 'since the date of the First Agreement the successive Hamed Agreements have been held by Mr Warren as a trustee for the partnership and his entry in the Multi Fight Agreement in his own name and on his own account was in breach of the duties which he owed DKP'.

Attached to the judgement, King had made the following statement: 'The judge today sent out a message of support and hope to everyone in British boxing. For the first time in years, the future of British boxing looks bright. For too long, British boxing has been dominated by Frank Warren. Few trusted him; most feared him. This has meant that young boxers have not had a fair deal, and have not been able to develop their full potential either in the UK or around the world. My partnership with Warren was designed to make the most of the global potential for British and other European boxers. But partnerships must be based on trust and, as the judge pointed out today, Warren could not be trusted. He was more interested in himself than his boxers.'

There was always some amusement to be gained from the sight of one promoter trying to claim the moral high ground over another, but for King to talk so heartily of trust was unabashed hypocrisy. I thought of Muhammad Ali getting robbed out of $1 million after being hammered by Larry Holmes, and of similar transgressions suffered by Holmes himself, Tim Witherspoon, Greg Page and all the others.

Still, before the crowds, King's charade was impenetrable. His enemies were moving in for the kill, but even in reference to the Lloyd's case – where the feeling was that the FBI were finally going to nail him with some hard evidence of wrongdoing – he claimed to be 'totally confident at being utterly vindicated of any improprieties'.

He was on a roll now, enjoying the chance to amuse and defy simultaneously. With a microphone dividing him from his captive audience, he could happily play the part of the falsely accused, honest worker, the showman with the cigar clamped between his teeth, or the nutcase with the fountain of hair and manic laugh. Suddenly he roared in his high-pitched squeal like a Mariachi singer on acid: 'Roberto! Roberto! Manos de Piedra! Oh, Roberto,' as he spied the form of the great Roberto Duran.

Here, in this room, and on this occasion, he was the entertainer, the comedian, the larger-than-life eccentric. We laughed as he persisted in cramming excessively lengthy words into never-ending sentences, as he praised the Queen and the British legal system. He implored the assorted press to speak up, to shout their names, and then described each of them as 'a dear friend' or 'a legend'. We eventually departed from our seats so that the photographers had a clear view of the fighters trying to look mean, and we all had smiles on our faces.

It was predictable, however, that away from the tape-recorders, the TV cameras and the more recognisable scribes, King's façade would drop. It did so, momentarily, thanks to the presence of a fighter named Iran Barkley.

Between 1989 and 1993, Barkley, 'The Blade', had terrorised middle-weights and higher with his Bronx-raised mean streak, unrelenting scowl and burning aggression. He beat the odds by decisively defeating Thomas 'The Hitman' Hearns twice and capturing three world titles. He had been outfoxed by cute boxers, bombed out even by Britain's Nigel Benn, but he had kept crawling back for more. By 1994 he was well on the way to physical ruin, as the likes of James Toney and Adolpho Washington pulverised his features for round after gruesome round.

Barkley had fallen prey to the curse which dictated a fighter always had an excuse for a defeat, always a reason to try again. Only with Barkley it seemed as though his answer to all of these problems was a steady increase in weight.

I had met him before, thumping at a heavy bag in the Blue Velvet gym, a dark frown on his face. It was a strange place for him to be working out – a definitive blue-collar fighter training in a renowned white-collar establishment, where supermodels and thespians came to pose. On that particular day it had been another promoter, Bob Arum, who weighed heavily on Barkley's mind. His career as a world-class boxer over, and with Arum's new wave of hispanic stars and the riches they were earning giving The Blade fits of jealousy, the veteran who now struggled to feed his family had been in the most sombre of moods.

'What was Arum doing all the time I was with him?' he growled, the lids of his eyes drooping, hinting at the fact that he was now half-blind. 'These days, Bob Arum won't even speak to me. I want to fight as a heavyweight, but he's been telling people that I should retire and that I'm endangering my health fighting heavyweights. He's saying I should get out of the game. Here's this man telling me to get out of the game – a man that I gave so much to, and now he's concerned? If he's so concerned, why didn't he give me the sort of money he's giving De La Hoya today? He won't even return my calls. He wants me to say, "Oh, I had a good career. I made a little money. That's it for me." All because De La Hoya wins a gold medal, he gets this treatment, but I gave Arum ten hard years of my life. I fought hard fights, back to back, consistently for years, and De La Hoya goes and makes $9 million for the first real fight of his career against Chavez. Arum's a shrewd businessman and quietly humble, but I've learnt that his humility is a front. I've learnt, and now I know the deal.'

While Barkley was undoubtedly endangering himself by continuing to fight, especially at heavyweight, and while he was not taking any of the blame, his plight was a depressing counterbalance to the starry success stories of men like Oscar De La Hoya and Roy Jones. Unfortunately, while Barkley possessed a fierce spirit and immense toughness, he could not match these attributes with the smooth looks and business acumen of De La Hoya, nor the independent nature and calculated intelligence of Jones. De La Hoya negotiated on an equal-footing with Arum, while Jones effectively made an employee of his own promoter, Murad Muhammad. Barkley had always been content to toil away on the factory floor. He had few aspirations beyond tomorrow, whereas De La Hoya and Jones had long made preparations for the years ahead without the sport which presently lined their pockets.

I had noticed Barkley earlier on that afternoon at the back of the conference room. He stood there with shoulders sloped, mottled skin on his face, a scruffy bomber jacket held across folded arms. With the speeches over and Holyfield and Akinwande taking part in individual interviews with reporters, King wandered slowly about the room, cigar in mouth, readily enthusiastic to feed the hacks with quotes for the morrow's papers. Behind him ambled Barkley, once a terrifying middleweight but now just a pitiful heavyweight.

Each time Barkley dared step ever nearer to King's formidable form, the promoter executed tiny about-turns and deft mini-roundabouts, leaving Barkley chasing behind him like a lost puppy which had attached itself to a stranger. Barkley had stalked Hearns and Toney with unfaltering bravery in the ring, yet in his efforts to grab King's attention he displayed the timidity of a vole.

The Bronx Blade trudged along hesitantly behind the Colossus from Cleveland. He wanted to secure a fight on Holyfield's undercard. He needed the work. He did not care to raise his voice or to tap King's shoulder, instead mumbling intermittently an appeal for a moment of King's time. King was refusing to acknowledge Barkley's presence, and he continued to manoeuvre his large frame from one sharp angle to another. He carried on playing deaf until Showtime boss Jay Larkin unwittingly brought the two men together.

King chewed hard on his cigar, stared through Barkley from behind dark glasses and cried out; 'The Blade! The Blade!'

And with that, he turned his back once more on the bemused fighter and vanished, proving yet again that a clown was not nearly so amusing when away from the circus.

CHAPTER ELEVEN

Semper Fi

Michael Grant's apprenticeship under Holyfield seemed a strange exercise, even if the two were so friendly that Grant would one day extend an invitation for Holyfield to serve as an usher at his wedding. Many fighters wound up meeting old gym mates and even long-time friends in the ring, but in this instance people were led to believe that Holyfield was grooming Grant for success. He was, according to some reports, nurturing Grant as though he were regent to a child king. Grant was Holyfield's spiritual protégé, the chosen one who would continue the Christian Warrior's legacy into the twenty-first century.

It seemed an improbable idea, even though the two were obviously close pals. Don Turner – trainer to both – had already declared that in the event the pair ever met, he would position himself in the younger man's corner. Holyfield had admitted with a shrug that while Grant confessed to some considerable reluctance ever to face his mentor, the master himself would have few qualms of his own. It was nothing personal.

HBO, however, were solid believers in Grant's potential to assume the world championship, and he was soon signed to an exclusive deal with the station. This was, HBO claimed, the man to watch, the heavyweight champion of the next millennium.

After Grant's fifth-round pounding of Nigeria's David Izonritei, he was lined up to face Obed Sullivan (who had lost to Hasim Rahman six months previously) in May '98. This was a classic case of two men meeting each other whilst their careers headed in opposite directions, for while Grant's celebrity status was increasing with his newly signed television contract, Sullivan's private life was falling apart.

In the build-up to his fight with Rahman, Sullivan's wife had filed for divorce, and the joys of partying over a few beers had developed into a heavy alcoholic dependency. Sullivan was a happy drunk, not a violent one.

Swept up by the notorious Phoenix nightlife, with all its late-night bars and gentlemen's clubs, the fighter would rub shoulders with young actresses and basketball stars into the early hours. From there they would all move on to someone's apartment for more drinks, where Sullivan would position himself comfortably in the corner of a sofa, laugh along heartily with his new-found friends, and then drift off to sleep. Seldom did he recognise his surroundings when he awoke.

When I came across Sullivan in an Atlantic City press-room the day before his fight with Grant, he looked doleful and subdued. This was in stark contrast to the designer-suited main attraction who had addressed us all at the Crowne Plaza hotel six months before. Now, his face looked craggy and his eyes sad, and instead of the spotlight being shone upon him, he and his team were shrouded in the room's dim glaze.

Slighted by the rapid swing in media popularity towards Grant, Sullivan had become lonely and morose. The defeat to Rahman had knocked him down a couple of pegs, but more damning to his psyche was the separation from his wife and the steady realisation that he had a problem with the booze.

That afternoon, the fighters were all brought together for the final press conference. Grant kept everyone waiting for ten minutes and then strode in to claps on the back, his looming form giving the rest of us the impression that we were at an assembly in Lilliput. The other fighters, their wives and their entourages waited for the big man to take his seat at the podium. The contestants in the co-feature, Chris Byrd and a Cuban exile named Eliecer Castillo, joined him. Byrd had been sitting cheerily next to his wife Tracy, and younger brother Patrick, looking for all the world like they belonged on the set of *Happy Days*, in their pastel-coloured T-shirts and satchels slung across shoulders. Castillo was accompanied by a large, bearded gentleman and others in white baseball hats, shades and thick, unlit cigars. This was the group known as 'Team Freedom', a contingent of former amateur stars from Havana who had sailed across the Gulf of Mexico to Miami in a bid to escape the Castro regime and turn professional in America. Castillo looked naïvely content in this environment, posing for the cameras in his bodybuilder's singlet and cascades of fake gold jewellery down his chest. The story went that he had fled the shores of Cuba on a makeshift raft with his brother Eliseo and two companions, existing only on a pitcher of honey as sustenance. The sharks had claimed one of his friends during the ten-day voyage across hellish waters, and here, in the land of the free, he was all but assured of bumping into the predators' human counterparts.

Sullivan still looked glum, in the midst of his lonely descent into obscurity. In his own mind he held steadfastly to the belief that he would turn his situation around, but the feeling against such an outcome was overwhelming. On the left-hand side of the podium stood the favourites to win the next evening's battles – Grant, Byrd, and the stocky Samoan David Tua who was all but assured of victory over the hapless Nate Tubbs. To the right sat the opponents – Tubbs, Castillo and Sullivan.

'Oh, okay,' sneered Sullivan in displeasure. 'I get it. I know what this is all about. You've got those guys there, and we're over here, and . . .' He looked either side of him and shrugged. 'Well, that's okay, because I haven't come here to lie down.'

It was the same mantra opponents of Tyson from the 1980s used to repeat over and over to themselves before being hurled into the maelstrom of the Iron Man's unbridled violence, and it sounded equally defeatist even now. Sullivan had not come to lose, of that one could be certain, but merely uttering those words confirmed his position as the man who did not have the word 'victory' included in this latest script. A winner does not come to town and tell people he does not intend to lose.

By now Grant had despatched his long-time manager Bill Cayton. Cayton's continued insistence that the big man follow the blueprint laid down for Tyson over ten years earlier finally convinced the six-foot-seven-inch apprentice that he had had enough. 'We just grew apart, and there's no way of rebuilding that,' said Grant.

Otherwise, things were going well for the man from Norristown. He had the backing of HBO, the media's annointment as 'the next big thing', and its growing respect after his wins over Alfred Cole and Izonritei. He stood next to Sullivan, towered over him, and smiled long and wide as his opponent stared morosely up into the giant's eyes. This was just the next step towards stardom for Grant, a modest obstacle in his path, the second in what would surely be a lucrative line of HBO fights. For Sullivan, it was his career on the line. Outside the ring his happiness with life had been devalued by wine and women, but inside it, as many before him had experienced, there was the possibility of achieving sanctity.

Chris Byrd faced an altogether different set of problems. He was a defensive wizard, an intelligent tactician, a slick contortionist whose skills were obvious only to those with the patience to appreciate the subtler qualities of the art of war. Byrd did not set most boxing fans on fire and he didn't bring to the battleground a promise of blood and mayhem. He did not intimidate like Tyson, nor delight with his flamboyance like Ali. His effect on the TV ratings was, in fact, poisonous, and the fight with Castillo was to prove to be the catalyst for the negativity the critics around him had espied.

I thought Byrd had exceptional skills and the potential to become a perfect ambassador for boxing. He was one of the most articulate fighters I had ever met, and together with his wife Tracy and three cherubic kids, he belonged on *TwoPointFour Children* rather than inside the boxing ring. In a tribute to his defensive expertise, his cunning skills of self-preservation and his guile, Byrd's speech was completely untainted by his profession, as were his smooth, friendly features. Ironically, he was more entrenched in the world of boxing than most of his peers. Grant had wanted to be a pianist and a chorister, Sullivan was in love with the marines and Rahman watched his family members attend religious seminaries in Vancouver and medical college in Washington DC. Byrd, on the other hand, was brought up around boxing; his father, Joe, had been his Olympic team coach in 1992, most of his brothers were professional fighters, his sister was a women's world champion and even his mother worked his corner. It was truly a family affair when the Byrds hit town.

I was surprised by the television commentators' disdain for Byrd. Surely, amidst all the blood-and-guts wars waged by lighter weight swashbucklers like Arturo Gatti and Kostya Tszyu, there remained room for the sweet scientists to display their wares. But, no: Byrd turned the lowest common denominator off with his elusiveness and aversion to mayhem.

There was a definite undercurrent of feeling that the fight with Castillo was Byrd's last chance to alter his approach to a degree, to take the fight to an opponent and face the risks which came with doing so. The risks presented by Castillo were fairly moderate, even though the shaven-skulled Central American sported an undefeated record and a rough past.

Attempting to convert Byrd from a wily cloud of confusion into an all-out entertainer seemed to me to be an unfortunate exercise. Its intention highlighted the trend towards making fights which on an entertainment level were a huge success, but which detracted from the sport's core appeal – the moves and techniques which distinguished it from scrapping in alley-ways and pubs.

'Professional prize-fighting is all about putting asses on seats,' HBO's commentator Larry Merchant told me during one of our lengthy discussions about Byrd. 'Boxing is about entertainment, and HBO is in the business of staging major events. Chris Byrd does not fit into either category. He's turning the whole concept of the idea of hitting and not being hit around, and making it his priority not to get hit before he even considers attacking an opponent. The logical conclusion to all this is that he'll end up fighting on his own in a studio, with only his family and best friends bothering to tune in!'

Byrd was more concerned with securing a meaningful fight with a fellow top contender, but so frustrating was his style that none of his potential rivals had yet deemed it the right moment to step forward and attempt to erase him from the race to the world title. I thought of all the young heavyweights I had spoken to in recent times, and one of the few questions I had asked of all of them was 'Would you fight Chris Byrd?'.

'No,' Grant had replied. 'Chris needs to get himself a title first, and then I'll fight him.'

'I don't want a guy who's gonna run away from me,' Rahman had complained. 'I want to fight a heavyweight who thinks he can come and knock me out.'

By May the list of fighters who had reportedly turned Byrd down also included Tua, Andrzej Golota and Sullivan, and Byrd found himself in an age-old dilemma. Did he expose himself on purpose against Castillo and increase the likelihood of a major fight before the end of the year, or did he stick to what he knew best – thwart Castillo's one-dimensional offensive moves and risk being avoided for eternity?

Byrd stayed with what he knew best, smacking and cuffing at the advancing Castillo as though he were slapping paint nonchalantly upon canvas, and displaying reflexes which were virtually unimaginable, albeit against a limited foe. He ducked, swayed, pirouetted, spun and recoiled, making Castillo's desperate charges and swings look painfully amateurish but also inducing howls of derision from the stands. This wasn't the type of heavyweight action that the fans and HBO had hoped to see.

Castillo's eye swelled up and his face became marked and stung, but Byrd was happy to continue his merry dance and box rings around his opponent's feet, without ever exposing himself to any risk of getting caught by a sucker punch. Ten repetitive rounds passed by, with Byrd not willing to press the issue for a much-needed knockout, but at the end it was his hands which were raised in victory.

As the ring was cleared, a large figure in a white shirt and tracksuit pants moved closer towards the HBO commentary position, and took pictures of Roy Jones – working behind a microphone that evening – with a disposable camera. I recognised the man as Nate Tubbs, the podgy brawler who had been destroyed by Tua before the Byrd fight, sent skittering to the floor after shipping a vicious array of hooks and right crosses. His execution had been brief, but having showered and changed, here he was, just another fan taking shots of the world's best fighter. A companion threw him a clean towel, and as he dabbed away at his wet face, he drank from a bottle of mineral water. He lifted the bottle to his lips, tilted his head back, and opened his mouth, but as he did so his hands shook uncontrollably, and the water spilled down his chest.

Ten minutes later, Obed Sullivan was escorted to the ring by a phalanx of marines in parade dress, hoisting military ensigns in the air. They marched him to war in their white hats, brilliant navy tunics and gleaming boots, the Stars and Stripes flying above their heads as they stood to attention in the ring centre. Sullivan looked troubled and hard-bitten, soft mounds of grease peaking across his face, his brow deeply furrowed. He wandered purposefully around the ring in his golden shorts emblazoned with the marine motto 'Semper Fi' – 'Always Faithful' – and paced whilst he waited for the emergence of the giant.

When Grant left his dressing-room and entered the arena, it was as though the Cyclops had come prowling out of his cave in search of dinner, and despite the hulking contender's gentlemanly manner and interest in fair play, one knew that such sentiments did not necessarily allow mercy in the middle of combat.

Grant towered above his own escort as he made his way to the ring, and a rush of applause and shrieks stretched across the Convention Centre as he ducked his mighty form between the ropes and raised his arms aloft in acknowledgement. As Sullivan paced past him, it looked like a match between a heavyweight and a middleweight, and I felt certain that Sullivan would not be let off the hook this time, as he had been when fighting Rahman a month before Christmas.

Sullivan was heart-wrenchingly brave, taking the fight to Grant at stages, and snapping the bigger man's head back with tidy jabs and straight right hands. He took Grant's opening combinations and kept firing back, at times doing so with more precision and success, but always with that sad visage, always looking as though this all meant too much to him, that he had been slighted by the sport and was now bitterly, yet futilely, fighting to prove us all wrong.

In the eighth round, Sullivan took an enormous right cross to the chin. He absorbed the shot well, but was stopped in his tracks, frozen by its impact. The bell rang several seconds later, and as he trudged back to his corner, his trainer Chuck McGregor berated him for letting his defences slip. 'That was a bone-shattering shot!' yelled McGregor. 'You cannot let yourself take those kinds of shots! Keep your hands up, 'Bed. Keep your damned hands up!'

McGregor applied more grease to the fighter's creased head, and the folds in his eyebrows, and splashed his chest with cool water.

'They ain't that hard,' Sullivan muttered. 'He doesn't hit that hard. They're not hurting!'

'I don't care what you say, keep your hands up. Stop taking those punches. I'm telling you, 'Bed, stop doing it!' McGregor yelled into his ear.

But the failure of Grant's previous assault to end matters had lulled the fighting marine into believing that he had taken the best Grant had to offer. He trooped back out into the fray, leaving his bunker with a new sense of security, and kept up his deployment of jabs into Grant's jaw. Grant attempted some pivots and subtle moves, but Sullivan was too knowledge-able to fall for them, and kept the jab pumping.

A momentary look of annoyance crept across Grant's face as Sullivan's problematic challenge refused to subside. Grant breathed in deeply, his huge chest expanding further still, and as he did so, Sullivan moved in again, his hands slipping to waist level as he prepared to launch his power shots.

Grant beat him to it, rushing his opponent with a battering-ram charge that sent Sullivan reeling around the ring, sickening punches ramming holes into his stomach and sides. Sullivan winced, and his arms dropped, and a left hook floored him by the ropes. The crowd rose to its feet, as the soldier struggled back into a vertical position.

I felt then that there could not have been a lonelier place in the world for Sullivan, with the crowd baying for his blood and imploring Grant to finish the job. Sullivan lurched upwards, one arm grabbed by the referee, but he did not turn to face his aggressor immediately, instead swivelling to meet the hostile wave of emotion descending from the spectator stands.

He looked up at the audience through cut eyes and swelling brows, and thumped his heart. He sneered and rubbed at his naked chest, and then he was turned by the referee, turned to look darkly into the eyes of the giant. It was like the Spartan army's stand against the Persian archers at Thermo-pylae: courageous, miserable and doomed. Grant ripped into him, with power shots to the body and head, forcing him back into the ropes until Sullivan's legs caved in and his body lurched against the strands behind him.

The referee rushed to stop the fight, holding Sullivan compassionately as his body shuddered and his face bled and his eyes dimmed. Grant whooped with delight, performed a hastily aborted semi-somersault in the ring and dropped to his knees in prayer, elation written on his face.

Sullivan needed to have too many stitches applied to his wounds to be able to attend the early-morning post-fight conference. Castillo sat several rows back from the podium and held a towel packed with ice to his blazing eyes. Grant sat smiling at his seat, butterfly stitches already sealing the nick above his eye which had been caused by a head-butt, while his trainer Don Turner feigned boredom.

Grant was congratulated on his performance, and HBO's senior vice-president of sports programming, Lou Di Bella, announced that he wanted the fighter to meet an opponent such as Kirk Johnson or Larry Donald next. Someone suggested Byrd, but Grant laughed, shook his head and muttered, 'Oh no, we're going there again!'

Byrd said he had been disappointed with his own performance. 'You were right to be disappointed,' said Di Bella when the conference was over, guiding the young heavyweight into a corner of the room where I sat and eavesdropped. 'That kind of style is not going to work. I'm not saying you have to get the knockout, but ...'

Byrd listened to the programmer and nodded, his face showing displeasure with himself, but also a hint of irritation. I sympathised with him, feeling this was a classic case of the TV execs overstepping their boundaries in an effort to dictate what was expected of the fighters they showcased. It was surely inappropriate to urge a boxer to change his approach in the ring. A decision to stand toe to toe and slug it out with opponents would clearly not serve Byrd's interests at all well, even if such a strategy may have rewarded Di Bella and his company with better viewing figures.

'So how do you feel about that?' I asked Byrd, once Di Bella had moved on. 'It can't feel great being asked to change your natural style.'

Byrd leaned back against the wall and raised his eyes to the ceiling. 'Well, I can understand their sentiments,' he replied. 'I wasn't pleased with what happened tonight. I feel I could have done a lot better, and so in a sense I can understand how HBO feel.'

'So what can you do about it?' I asked. 'Is it possible to improve your lack of power significantly, or is it always going to be a hindrance?'

'I've been working on the power,' he replied. 'I've been working a little more with weights, and trying to adapt my style a little to make it more crowd-pleasing. I thought I had achieved that, but I know I need to work on it some more.'

'But Chris,' I continued, feeling strangely depressed that the fighter appeared willing to make changes because of the pressure brought to bear by forces who did not know what it was like to be in the ring, 'does this mean you move away from your natural style?'

Byrd shook his head and rolled his eyes. 'No, I can change a few things without actually compromising my style, but this way of fighting has been so good to me for years. I'm not about to change it now.'

As I walked out of the Convention Center, I felt relieved that Byrd was not about to submit to corporate demands, but Sullivan's noble stand against Grant occupied my thoughts far more as I neared the Hilton bus terminal.

My lasting memory of that evening was that ghastly look on Sullivan's face as he had stared impassively at the crowd before his defeat. I had looked hard at his face, reading into his expression as much as I could, and I had seen a man prepared to die rather than surrender. And when I left Atlantic City that night, I felt a lingering sense of guilt that Sullivan's defiance had not moved me as much at the time as it should have done.

CHAPTER TWELVE

Dreams of Replenishment

In the land of the King, a fresh disaster was unfolding. Two days before the scheduled Evander Holyfield v Henry Akinwande fight, the atmosphere inside the huge domain of Madison Square Garden was depressingly bland. Public interest in the main event was almost non-existent, although the barman at my local pub had told me a week earlier that he was going to go with his girlfriend, 'just to see how Holyfield chops down that tall guy'. The King propaganda machine had worked wonders on at least two people, it seemed.

The build-up to the show was as stale as some of the fighters scheduled to appear in the ring that Saturday night – heavyweight Ray Mercer, still recovering from a broken neck, alcoholism and virtually two years of inactivity; the aged Roberto Duran, puffy and grey and bloated, yet still fooling some into believing he had a chance of unseating the slick WBA middleweight champ, William Joppy. Nowhere on the card did there appear to be the whiff of a potentially entertaining fight; there was Johnny Tapia, a highly regarded super-flyweight champion, but he was to be pitted against a bashful youngster without a hint of promise. Finally, there was King's female 'attraction', Christy Martin, 'The Coalminer's Daughter', whose opponent sported the unremarkable record of two victories and one defeat.

I arrived at the Garden shortly after breakfast the following morning, and everything seemed as bland as the day before. Holyfield was performing some callisthenics in the middle of a ring with his conditioner Tim Hallmark, and a sprinkling of journalists were gazing at him without much interest.

'Have you heard?' Claude Abrams, the editor of *Boxing News*, asked me.

'Yeah, Christy Martin's opponent is pregnant,' I responded. 'I read it in the paper this morning. She's claiming it's a miracle! And I also heard Mercer's been tested positive for hepatitis.'

'Not just that,' said Claude. 'The whole show's off. Akinwande's tested positive too. He's got hepatitis B!'

The news was confirmed later by David Checketts, and there was a particularly loud groan from the reporters who had travelled from as far away as Japan and Australia to cover the event. A doctor provided the media with a few details about the strain of hepatitis which Akinwande was suffering from and added that Mercer had contracted the 'C' version of the illness.

Don King's statement was shockingly brief for his standards, as he spent thirty seconds expressing his sympathy for Akinwande and the fighter's missed opportunity, before hurrying away. He was chased by the hordes, their microphones and cameras hovering around his cloudy shock of hair. The rumours had surfaced abruptly after the announcement that the show had been scrapped. Joppy against Duran could not be elevated to main event status, because a) it was a cruddy co-feature anyway, and b) Duran's purse was already under threat because it seemed he owed more than twice the total amount to an ex-wife in alimony payments.

It was a PR disaster, and the story doing the rounds was an altogether believable one: pay-per-view interest was low, ticket sales even more so. The show was heading for financial turmoil and no one was going to come out of it any richer. Whether the Garden, which had pumped several million dollars already into advertising the show, had been inclined to accept Johnny Ruiz as a substitute opponent for Akinwande or not, King claimed to have no alternative but to pull the plug.

As he retreated into the confines of the Garden, his stepson Carl King swaggered by his side in a skintight, sleeveless red top, a look of angst on his face. 'We'll answer more questions later,' he snapped at inquisitive reporters, but it was a nameless fighter who was prodding him for his attention the most. 'No, man, now is not a good time,' he barked again, fingering his spectacles as his stepfather slipped away from him.

The fighter tutted and stopped following the problem-plagued Kings, but Carl had heard the man's displeasure and turned back. He walked over to the fighter, rotated his shoulders and rubbed his mouth with the palm of his hand.

'Listen, man, I said I'm fucking busy,' King said harshly. '*Now is not a fucking good time!*' He stared at the fighter, and the man visibly shrunk, his expression dropping into a childish sulk as King glared at him once more and then returned to his master.

Out of such a mess, however, the Kings found some reward. The day before the cancellation, the weigh-in for Holyfield and Akinwande had been held in the Garden's foyer and among the crowd of spectators had been Hasim Rahman. I watched as Rahman concentrated on the proceedings, and then searched for the eye of his trainer Tommy Brooks who was Turner's assistant in Holyfield's corner. When their eyes met, the two saluted each other with their fists and Rahman edged closer. He was distracted by Carl King, who motioned for him to move closer in his direction. They leaned towards each other, over the cordon which separated the crowd from the Holyfield and Akinwande camps. They pressed heads against ears, whispered, nodded to each other, exchanged pieces of paper and said their goodbyes. I watched this brief interlude, and sensed a small conspiracy passing before my eyes, then wondered if it were too obvious.

But it made a lot of sense. The Kings did not mould potential talent; they watched it grow in the hands of their rivals, and then they pounced upon it with lucrative deals and tempting offers, luring it away from its source. And the heavyweight division was the most fertile of breeding grounds for kidnapping such talent.

A week after Carl King had whispered into Rahman's ear, it was revealed that Larry Donald, a friend of Rahman's, had ditched his and Rahman's promoter, Cedric Kushner, and signed with King. It seemed only a matter of time before Rahman followed suit.

★

Fortunes changed drastically in the world of prize-fighting. Just as it was a thin line which divided the lucky winner from the more common loser at the blackjack tables and slot-machine halls of Vegas and Atlantic City, so it was with the line which criss-crossed the paths of fighting men. Few characterised this more than Evander Holyfield, God's warrior with the pagan first name.

When I first came face to face with Holyfield, it was a dark, wet evening at the start of 1996. Roy Jones had just put on a virtuoso performance before an appreciative Madison Square Garden crowd. In a ringside seat, Holyfield had sat quietly under a tan cap, hardly noticed until announced by the MC. Later on, with most of New York huddling under umbrellas, an anonymous figure stood stoically by one of the Garden's side exits. There Holyfield waited, with a suited gentleman by his side, looking out for a limo which would not arrive. He stood there, hands in leather overcoat pockets, teardrops of rain slipping from the peak of his cap and onto the bridge of his nose. Only several feet away, Manhattan rushed by, oblivious to the unobtrusive presence of a two-time world heavyweight champion.

He waited a while longer before venturing out into the open, and headed towards Macy's department store, God's warrior without a chariot. And still he had remained unrecognised – just another person in the crowd, shielding himself from the spattering rain.

Back then, I recalled as I waited to meet Holyfield at the Garden, he had been considered – after a long and prestigious career – to be washed up. Ten months later he had knocked out Mike Tyson, and now, seated before me in a chocolate-brown pinstripe suit, he was back on top. He was at the height of his game, the magic behind his legend ever expanding.

Holyfield sat in his chair, hands clasped together in front of him as he looked at me from under protruding brows which looked like they had been etched with eye-brow liner, his Clark Gable moustache betraying the hint of a sneer. This was a fighter who had taken the long route towards public acclaim, winning a professional title before Tyson had, but waiting far longer to reap the rewards. He was the Tyson antidote: a strategic boxer with an underestimated punch, the grafter who would punish himself in order to get the maximum output from his aching body. Some reckoned Holyfield's mental strength bordered on the impenetrable, matched only by his ego and the notoriously competitive spirit which made an appearance everywhere from the pool hall to the bowling alley.

His successes may have come from a bottomless pit of competitive spirit, but it was always his god that he thanked first after conquering each goal. I wondered aloud whether he was aware of the snipers' remarks that this was all for show – that it was arrogance on his part to suggest that God could side against another man in something which in its basest terms was just a fight.

'But that's what having the faith is all about,' Holyfield argued. 'It's all about speaking from your heart. When you pray for something, and work hard to achieve something and you succeed, your thanks should be to God. You should let people know about it. Why keep it quiet? Why keep it a secret? I believe. But it's no good me just believing and then not doing anything about it. It's my duty to tell everyone about the Lord's good work.'

I knew the Bible was a violent book, full of conflicts between siblings and armies and opposing religious factions, but I remained fascinated nonetheless by the contradictory nature of preaching a gospel of peace and goodwill and then tormenting a rival with your fists for a living.

'I'm a professional,' responded Holyfield. 'I'm a professional fighter. That's my job. I love people and I feel in my heart a sense of wanting to help people who need help, but when it comes to my job I don't love anyone so much that I wanna give them an advantage over me! The Bible teaches us about working hard and living cleanly. It teaches us about respecting one another and conducting ourselves in a righteous way, and the thing is – do you live by that word or not? I have never strayed from those teachings.'

I was not surprised by Holyfield's lucidity, but there was something to be said for the transformation he had made from the fighter who had clashed on three occasions with Riddick Bowe, and emerged from each utterly violent confrontation with a distracted glaze about him and stumbling speech. This was not the finished fighter of three years ago.

He looked at me when he spoke, and though his sentences occasionally became disjointed, his vocabulary was precise and laced with a humour I had not noticed before.

His successes against Tyson and Michael Moorer had replenished him. His nemesis, Bowe, was meanwhile drowning in his own social short-comings, and once more I shook my head at the insanely unpredictable way in which professional boxers' fortunes fluctuated. I felt that Holyfield, more than any champion since Muhammad Ali, had proven to be the exception to so many rules, rules which dictated that a good, small heavyweight would always lose to a good, big heavyweight. That they never came back. That nice guys finished last. I didn't see Holyfield as a martyr, but, yes, he was inspirational, and there was an inherent goodness about him, even if he did make as many mistakes in life as the next man.

But beyond the spirituality of the man and the sense of goodwill and belief in himself as a God-fearing, clean-living human being, there was still a substantial amount of sporting pride. He was a businessman, as astute in that field as he was competent at his sport, but he knew that in the shape of Lennox Lewis there remained some unfinished business to attend to.

The making of the fight with Lewis would prove to be one of the clearest examples of the problems which needed to be negotiated in modern-day championship boxing. The actual fighting itself, as so many of its practitioners would explain, was the easy part, the athletic release after months of legal wrangling and economic forecasts. The hard part was get-ting past the negotiating tables and vaulting over the contrived principles of the deal-brokers.

King was claiming that HBO were trying to freeze him out of the promotional equation. In turn, HBO were claiming that Holyfield was pricing himself out of the market after his recent coup in getting paid a grossly disproportionate $20 million for meeting Moorer, a purse which had seriously burnt the fingers of the treasurers at Showtime, HBO's arch rivals.

Holyfield had reasoned at one of the Akinwande conferences that 'if Lennox is so sure he can beat me, then he should be prepared to take the short end of the purse, beat me, and then be in a position to demand more money in the future'. Lewis and his manager Frank Maloney argued that they had already agreed to $5 million less than their original asking price, but that Holyfield still baulked at making the deal. There was a pot of $20 million available, but Holyfield was refusing to fight Lewis for anything less than that exact amount as his end of the purse.

'Look, Lennox has built his whole career around two men who made their names in defeat – Razor Ruddock and Andrzej Golota,' argued Holyfield. 'Lennox ain't never beaten a champion in the ring, but I've beaten Bowe, Tyson, Moorer, all of the great heavyweights of my era. Lennox and his people have been calling me out and that doesn't bother me at all, but I don't have to bring somebody down to be made to feel higher. I don't need to go out there saying anyone's ducking me. If a fight can't be made, it can't be made. The fact is that a fight comes up when it's time for it to happen. I never told anybody Tyson ducked me, even though I was his number-one contender for two years. In the meantime Lennox should have respect, because you know what? When he gets the dog whupped out of him by me, it's gonna make him look awful silly after telling everyone I ducked him!'

Holyfield smiled beneath his moustache, replacing the faint sneer which swept across his lips whenever he entered the ring, and which did so now as he got into his stride and spoke more about his British rival. There seemed to be an underlying sense of personal hostility towards Lewis, as though Holyfield, too, had become embroiled in America's distaste for a fighter they felt was overly concerned with self-preservation and chess strategy. For someone who had so recently protested that 'if I never get to fight Lennox Lewis, it won't matter', Holyfield displayed an unexpected eagerness now to disprove the idea that Lewis's threat was anywhere near as formidable as the ones presented to him in the past.

'I know boxing styles,' he said emphatically, leaning towards me slightly. 'Lennox has the style which will allow me to hit him whenever I want to. Guys with brute strength like him don't think about nothing else except clobbering somebody. Every time he takes a swing at me, he's gonna miss and I'll counter him. I'm not the kind of fighter who feels he has to take you out straight away.'

'The last big guy you fought was Riddick Bowe,' I said. 'How do you compare Lewis to Bowe? Bowe was a big guy with power, and he hurt you.

PENNSYLVANIA - SEPTEMBER 1997
Former two-time heavyweight champion Tim
Witherspoon takes a break from training for yet
another comeback. He would lose five of his next six
contests.

NEW YORK - NOVEMBER 1997
Nigerian contender David Izonritei is congratulated
by round-card girls after knocking out Lou Savarese
at the Apollo Theater in Harlem.

NEW YORK - NOVEMBER 1997
Hasim 'The Rock' Rahman wears USBA and IBF
intercontinental title belts after defeating
Obed Sullivan by a decision
at the Apollo Theater.

NEW YORK - NOVEMBER 1997
Monte Barrett (left) squares up to opponent
Val Smith at the Apollo Theater.

ATLANTIC CITY - MAY 1998
From left to right: Chris Byrd, Michael Grant, David
Tua, Obed Sullivan and Eliecer Castillo face the press
before a 'Night of the Young Heavyweights' show at
the Convention Center. Grant would later fall to world
champion Lennox Lewis in two rounds, while Tua
would soon earn a shot at Lewis himself.

NEW YORK
In the summer of 1998, veteran former heavyweight champions Larry Holmes (left) and George
Foreman publicise a proposed January 1999 match-up
of golden oldies. The promotion collapsed, but while
Foreman remained inactive, Holmes continued to
chase another world title fight.

NEW YORK - JUNE 1998
Tim Witherspoon and Andrzej Golota pose for pictures
at the Polish consulate before their September '98
fight in Wroclaw. Eight months earlier, Golota had
been knocked out in a round by Lennox Lewis, but he
still had more than enough to beat Witherspoon easily.

NEW YORK - JULY 1998
Monte Barrett is making the transition from prospect to contender, but still feels like he's not being moved fast enough. At the Queens Police Athletic League (PAL), he hits the speed ball before a bout in Atlantic City.

ATLANTIC CITY - SEPTEMBER 1998
Ike 'The President' Ibeabuchi, before weighing in for a fight with Everton Davis. In June '97 the Nigerian beat David Tua, but legal troubles soon doomed his career. Today, Ibeabuchi faces years behind bars for sexual assault. Left to right: assistant trainer Jay Wilson, Ibeabuchi, head trainer and former world welterweight champion Curtis Cokes and manager Stephen Munisteri.

DELAWARE - SEPTEMBER 1998
A week before challenging Evander Holyfield for the
WBA/IBF world titles, Vaughn Bean is flanked by a pair
of boxing legends - Michael Spinks (left) and Smokin'
Joe Frazier. Bean surpassed expectations, making his
fight with Holyfield a competitive one before losing a
unanimous decision.

NEW YORK - MARCH 1999
Promoter Don King raises the hands of rival world
champions Lennox Lewis and Evander Holyfield [left]
before their first unification clash, held at Madison
Square Garden. In a fight which Lewis appeared to
control with ease, the judges rendered a widely-
condemned 'draw' verdict.

EVANDER 'THE REAL DEAL' HOLYFIELD
After losing a decision in the rematch with Lennox Lewis, Holyfield defeated John Ruiz for the WBA championship. This made Holyfield the sport's first-ever four-time heavyweight champion, although Lewis's loss of the WBA title had been a result of political wranglings.

ATLANTIC CITY - NOVEMBER 1999
Hasim Rahman wrestles with trainer Chuck McGregor, days before his showdown with former Russian army officer Oleg Maskaev. In a big upset, Rahman would be knocked clean out of the ring in the eighth round and counted out.

LENNOX LEWIS
After winning the decision in a second fight with
Evander Holyfield, Lennox Lewis at long last became
the undisputed heavyweight champion of the world.
In 2000, Lewis scored second-round knockouts over
Michael Grant and François Botha, leaving only David
Tua to stand in the way of a titanic confrontation
with Mike Tyson.

Aren't you at all worried that Lewis might be able to inflict the same punishment on you?'

'Bowe was the best big guy I've ever fought, as far as skills are concerned,' said Holyfield, shrugging dismissively at the mention of Lewis's power. 'Bowe could hurt you coming forward and he could hurt you going back. He could fight you on the inside and the outside. Comparing him to Lennox is . . . No, Lewis is nowhere near the fighter Bowe was. Bowe threw combinations and created chances and openings for himself. Lewis is what I call an "ABC fighter". He follows the same patterns, just tries to run you over. I don't beat people through physical strength. Everyone knows that most of the guys I've fought are much bigger than me, but you know what? I've been fighting at this level for years; the pressures no longer affect me the same way they used to, and mentally I am scared of no man. Some of those guys may hit a little harder than me, but they can't out-think me. Anyone can fight tough for two rounds, but does Lennox have the skills and the heart to continue in the sixth and seventh rounds, when his arms are tiring and his heart is beating hard? Will he start to question whether he can continue?'

'But if the desire to fight Lewis is there, aren't these political and financial deals which need to be sorted out first just a secondary distraction?' I asked. 'If two fighters want to fight, then surely they can bring pressure to bear?'

'Well, I believe in rules and regulations, and the rules say that I had to fight Henry Akinwande first, and then Vaughn Bean,' replied Holyfield truthfully. 'Some people may say, "Forget about the belts and fight Lewis for the glory," but I want all three belts – one for the Father, one for the Son, and one for the Holy Spirit. What's the point in me taking Lennox's belt for the Holy Spirit, if I've got nothing to give the Father or Jesus?'

★

On a bright June morning, the Polish Consulate in New York hosted a conference to announce the return to the ring of its nation's most famous fighter, Andrzej Golota. In a reception room decorated in tapestries and murals, Golota stood behind rows of bottled Polish lager and before posters advertising Polsat TV, the channel which had arranged to transmit his continuing US campaign back home. He was his usual restless and fidgety self, constantly rubbing at his pockmarked face and chewing hard on his gum, stepping from foot to foot in his tight black jeans and ostrich-skin boots. The fuss boiled down to Main Events' decision to announce a two-fight deal which would match their heavyweight liability with a journeyman named Corey 'T-Rex' Sanders, and for Golota then to return home (for the first time since being found guilty of kidnapping), where he would perform for a partisan audience against Tim Witherspoon.

At the back of the reception room, a huddle of Russian and Slavic promoters watched the proceedings, taking notes as Dino Duva formally announced that the Sanders fight would take place in Atlantic City and the Witherspoon match would be staged in Wroclaw.

I hadn't really come to watch Golota pose restlessly for the cameras, unsmiling and impatient, scratching his nose, chewing his gum, banging his hands together and pleading with everyone around him to 'Come on, come on. Let's go!'. It was Witherspoon I wanted to talk to, there being only so much interest one could take in hearing Golota and his promoters bang on about how his defeat to Lewis eight months previously had been solely down to some medication for a knee injury. So upset was Golota about this injection administered to him before the Lewis fight that he even announced an intention to sue the doctor responsible.

Witherspoon arrived late, with a chubby young daughter, Tom Moran and Country in tow. He seemed to have aged since our time together in the Poconos. His body looked flaccid and weak, as though starved for some time, although a crease of flab was still visibly flowing over his waistline. His shoulders looked shrunken, and so did the sockets of his eyes. There were not going to be any miracles this time, I felt certain. His loss to Mercer had been debatable, the defeat to Donald the predictable result of a slow, old heavyweight trying to keep up with a mobile, young one. But losing so convincingly to Jimmy Thunder had been the final nail in the coffin of Witherspoon's career. And now that to defeat Witherspoon was almost a given as opposed to the uphill task it would have been deemed only two years earlier, everyone wanted a piece of his name before it became forever consigned to the dustbin of past champions.

'I've had a few things go wrong recently and my performances haven't been good,' Witherspoon said to me as he sat by a stairwell eating his lunch and keeping an eye on his daughter. 'I really wasn't able to train the way I had wanted to for Thunder, and Donald was a change of opponent at the last minute. I'll be ready for Golota come September. I'm grateful for this chance, I just don't want the Polish fans to attack me when I've knocked Andrew out!'

It was sad listening to the man try to bolster himself with such brave talk. It hadn't been that long since he had been justifiably regarded as a threat to any heavyweight on the planet, but the psychological distress of defeat had clearly taken so much out of Witherspoon's drive. At times, as I watched him play with his daughter and chat to a beautiful reporter from Polsat who was wearing a trendy suit of burgundy velvet, he looked more like fifty than forty. I turned back towards the physically ripped form of Golota, all pale and spotted with acne, and still pacing irritably from side to side, his steel-blue eyes looking completely devoid of compassion, and I shuddered at the kind of torture he had in store for the veteran.

'I'm telling you, Tim did not train one bit for Thunder,' said Moran quietly, as I tried to fathom exactly how Tom saw any chance of success for his friend. 'People keep telling me Tim's too old, and that he's past it, but that's just not true. He's lazy. I'll admit it. Sometimes I have to go knocking on his door in the mornings and physically get him out of bed, because he doesn't want to go running, but it's not down to his age. I still believe he can win a world title and I know he can win this fight. But I also know this is our last chance. This is what we've been asking for, and now we have it. I believe Tim can do it, I just don't know if he's going to exert himself enough to carry it off.'

'I feel so happy with this promotion,' Witherspoon said later on, as the Polsat cameras rolled. 'I've known the Duvas for a long time. Lou's like a father to me.'

The Duva patriarch smiled happily at these words and seemed genuinely touched, but he did so as he sat next to the man whose job it would be in September to pummel the mouth from where these compliments had come. The father figure would be doing his damnedest to make sure Witherspoon was knocked out in Poland, and then he would give the vanquished a hug and congratulate the old pro on his grizzled effort.

The Polsat beauty interviewed Witherspoon another time, and on this occasion her subject's daughter scraped her knees across the carpet in an effort to admire more closely the lady's snazzy footwear. Miss Witherspoon told the reporter that her attire reminded her of something from a Spice Girl's wardrobe, but as she hovered closer towards Baltic Spice her form blocked the TV lens and she was scooped up by Golota's manager, Ziggy Rowalski. He lifted Witherspoon's daughter gently away, plopped her on the carpet, ruffled her hair and spoke to her kindly. He failed to mention that he oversaw the career of a man who was months away from an attempt to destroy her father's will with his fists.

Several nights later, Witherspoon may have seen another example of the fate of a former champion when he fails to heed the early-warning signs of tainted victories and questionable motivation, and continues his ill-advised pursuit of lost glory. On 26 June, another former champ was cast upon the scrapheap of men from the 'Lost Generation', Witherspoon's old gang; men like Leon Spinks, who wound up scratching a living as a doorman in Las Vegas, or poor John Tate, whose senses were distorted by cocaine in April, as he rammed his pick-up truck head-first into a telephone pylon, and died as a result.

A week before Buster Douglas's fight with Lou Savarese, my early arrival at the HBO studios in Manhattan presented me with a chance to talk to the former champion in a room to ourselves before the rest of the media pack arrived.

Eight years had passed since Douglas's titanic win over Tyson, and much had changed in his world. After submitting in abject surrender to Holyfield in his first defence, Douglas's life had plummeted downhill. He had returned to his hometown of Columbus, Ohio, with pockets stuffed with money. Here, he had fattened his body with junk-food, dulled his mind with marathon video sessions and tinkered forlornly with his Harley Davidson. This was the life for Buster Douglas, until it almost became his death.

He slipped into a diabetic coma in 1994. Weighing in at an unimaginably grotesque thirty stone, he was knocking loudly on death's door. Somehow, he had survived, and in the previous summer had embarked on a comeback which had wider odds of success than the 42/1 offered against him defeating Tyson on a sterile February night in Tokyo.

An hour before he was to be summoned to the conference theatre, Douglas gazed absently around him in our assigned interview room, sipping water and quietly waiting for my questions. Tufts of hair sprouted from his usually clean-shaven dome, and after a knock on the door he was joined by his father Billy, son Lamar and manager John Russell.

I remembered Lamar as the young, admiring son who had looked up in awed delight at his father after the defeat of Tyson. It was a picture reproduced on the sports pages of newspapers around the world, with Douglas eyeing the heavens and reaching for the air with a triumphant fist.

'I'm feeling good,' said Douglas, with little animation. 'I've been working really hard, and I'm just glad I'll be fighting for a title once more, after I've beaten Savarese. I feel so close to a chance of redemption, this is gonna be a great year for me.'

'Some people would say this is a strange way of aiding your recovery from the coma, though,' I suggested. 'Why is returning to the ring the best way for you to get your life back together again?'

'Look at the shape I'm in now,' replied Douglas, but with that same empty expression on his face. 'I've come back with more determination and more focus. I want to be champion of the world again, and now that I've been given a second chance at life, I'm not going to waste it. I almost died, but when I woke up I realised that I had to get back into the game of life. For me, the game of life is this – the game of boxing. I'm very happy now,' he insisted, though he barely showed it. His eyes looked dead and his skin sagging and worn. He had the same expression which Witherspoon could not disguise.

'I've made a 360-degree turn,' he said. 'I took a lot of things for granted when I became ill.'

'What things?'

'Life in general,' he said quietly. 'I have a different outlook now. I'm so much more appreciative of each and every day. Now I want them all. Tyson, Holyfield, Lewis . . . all of them. I had so many distractions after I beat Tyson. It was like a whirlwind following me around, and I allowed myself to get swayed away from the main goal.'

'And what was that?' I asked him.

'To stay the champion of the world,' he replied. 'I can't make that same mistake again and let that whirlwind catch up with me.'

A week later, Douglas was knocked to the ground three times by Savarese in the first and final round. His punch resistance looked non-existent, his heart never truly in the fight and his face conjuring up all those terrible images of his forebears' similar struggles to find themselves outside of boxing.

While Savarese collapsed to his knees and cried tears of joy into his mother Carol's neck, Douglas stepped wearily down from the ring and returned to his locker-room. His face looked no different in remorseless defeat than it had on the afternoon he described his plan to rule as heavyweight champ once more.

'What can I say?' he muttered quietly. 'Shit happens.'

Douglas did not retire after the loss to Savarese. Not long afterwards, his brother Robert was killed in a drive-by shooting, and his father developed and later died from cancer of the colon.

CHAPTER THIRTEEN

Frustrations

Hollis Avenue in Queens was about a thirty-minute walk further from the nearest subway station than Monte Barrett had led me to believe. I bought myself a bottle of Snapple at a Lotto stand, and then started the long trek to the local Police Athletic League (PAL) building.

Barrett and I had kept in touch regularly since our initial get-together in May '97, when he had been a novice pro with ten fights under his belt. Then, he had liked to create the impression of a man whose whole career was mapped out before him, and that any outside forces which would dare to attempt to re-route him would be dealt with immediately. By now, the transition to prospect status was under way, while men like Rahman, Tua, Byrd and Grant had reached solid positions in the top tens of the various commissions. These men were now one or two steps away from title contention, while Barrett was in need of a breakthrough bout just to put himself into their bracket.

He was, I felt, close to following in the footsteps of men like Tyson, Bowe and Briggs, and emerging as the latest in a long line of heavyweight talents from the Big Apple. He was Monte '2GUNZ' Barrett, the fighter described in some quarters as 'the man' for the future, New York's latest offering to the heavyweight equation.

This was a fighter more aware of the mental conditioning necessary to reach and stay at the top than Bowe, but with the street edge obvious in Tyson. He could punch with either hand, but he was not a concussive hitter like Tyson, nor as physically imposing as Bowe. He was versatile, though; a boxer and a banger – a keen and mobile strategist, possessor of an impressive arsenal of shots, from a whipping uppercut to an improving left hook to the body.

I found Monte to be a pleasant enough person, though he could be as vain and intimidating at times as he could be approachable and humorous. With a chip on his shoulder and tattoos across his biceps, he always looked capable of dishing out punishment with a dash of nastiness for good measure, though he always assured me — as all the others did — that he did not take his fights personally.

He had a following by now, of cousins and brothers and homeboys from his neighbourhood in Jamaica, Queens. He was the pack leader — a veteran of wars on the pavements and back alleys and the gyms, where the big shots from across the five boroughs came to gain reputations and usually ended up humiliated if not just beaten.

I arrived five minutes earlier than Barrett, and was made to wait in a tiny foyer by a security guard before the fighter arrived with Old Timer. Barrett showed up in his Phat Farm and Fubu street gear, while Davis was in baggy pants and denim shirt.

'Wassup?' Barrett asked me, as he signed a register and gave Old Timer and his twisted legs a head start on him to reach the top of the stairs and enter the gym on the third floor. As his aged trainer struggled up the steps, Barrett slung his gym bags across his shoulders and tipped his baseball hat back. 'Time for things to start moving in my career,' he said ruefully. 'I'm getting tired of waiting for my chance to shine, you know what I'm sayin'?'

I followed him into the gym, where another of his assistants, Artie Cintron, sat beside the ring eating peanuts with Davis. The windows were opened slightly to relieve the close heat of the training room, the rap music was turned on and the training commenced.

On the floor of the ring, Barrett performed push-ups and stretching exercises before shadow-boxing. He fired power shots at an imaginary rival, held the top rope, shuffled and winked at us. Above his head was a blackboard with words of wisdom scribbled upon it in white chalk: 'You are not beaten when you suffer a defeat. You are beaten when you quit. Never give up.'

The fighter pummelled the heavy bag for four rounds, and then the speedball, interrupting to goad his mentors and pull faces at a girl nearby, who sat smirking in the background, examining her long, silver fingernails. Barrett joked, smiled, relaxed, closed his eyes and struck the speedball with unerring accuracy, but his laid-back demeanour did not disguise a simmering undercurrent of discontent.

During a fifteen-minute interval between exercises, he prowled the gym floor and wiped at his face with a towel. 'I'm a patient person, and I understand this business, but I'm not happy at all with a lot of things, especially the way I've been treated by the TV companies. They're putting hasbeens ahead of me on their schedules. Guys like Greg Page and Phil

Jackson are yesterday's news, and I would take them tomorrow. Why don't they put me in there against them?'

He paced up and down, as Cintron jotted down some notes on a pad of paper, and the girl shrugged the leather jacket off her back. Barrett was displaying more of the anger he had shown in Foxwoods the year before when his fight had been cancelled at short notice.

'Do you feel like you're ready now to take that step up in competition?' I asked him.

'Of course, I'd take them tomorrow,' he insisted. 'I am the future of the heavyweight division. Why don't they put me in there against this kind of opponent? I realise that a lot of people have a financial interest in me and I need to be moved right, but if I'm a phoney then let it be known. I train hard and stay focused, no matter what adversity I go through in life, so put me in there and test me, because I know I'm ready.'

'Maybe they feel like you need some more experience first,' I ventured.

'But that's how I get the experience, by fighting these guys. I'm still a few fights away from the top, I know that, but this is the fight game – they should put some of us less experienced guys in together, and then after that I'll be ready for someone like Tua or Rahman.'

'You know Rahman well?' I asked.

'Not real well, but I know him. I would like to fight him – he's big and strong and I respect him for what he's done, but I really don't like him personally.'

'Why's that?'

'He talks a lot of junk,' replied Barrett. 'I was sparring with Larry Donald one day, and he was mouthing off and saying things to distract me. Tommy Brooks had to tell him to shut up. Maybe he's jealous of my crossover appeal – my good looks, my sociable nature. Damn . . .'

His sense of frustration was tangible. I thought of the relaxed individual I had first met at the Starrett City gym a year earlier, and of the tirade at Foxwoods. Now, as Barrett carefully tried to forge his way towards contender status, he discovered the traffic at the top was clogged, with little prospect of an imminent breakthrough.

'The thing is, I have these qualities, and the bullshit TV organisations aren't letting the public know,' Barrett complained. 'My manager's not doing his fucking job – and you can tell him that – and the TV people aren't doing shit. The only ones doing their job are me and Al. Al's preparing me to win the fights, and I'm winning them, but everybody else is failing to keep their side of the deal.'

'Boxing and my kids are the only civilisation I have left in this life,' he announced, almost reading my mind. 'Being messed around by people is all part of the process, I know that. I will come through it all.'

He began to dance and reel off seven-punch combinations at the mirror in front of him. 'Maybe I need a different nickname to get people more interested.'

'What's wrong with "2GUNZ"?' I asked.

'Nothing, but maybe I can do better than that – name myself after a superhero or something . . . '

'Monte "Batman" Barrett?' I jokingly suggested.

The girl laughed, and I was glad to see Barrett didn't think I was taking the piss out of him.

'I've already come into the ring as Superman,' he replied. 'Maybe I should take on one of those names that they have on *Return to Oz*.'

I hadn't seen the programme, but it was advertised on billboards around the city's subways and bus-stops – a high-budget cable series set in a maximum security prison full of gangsters, psychopaths, young Mafioso-types and hard nuts from the 'hood.

'I haven't seen it,' I said.

'You know who Run DMC are, right?'

'Right.'

'Take a look at this, then – a gift to me from Darryl McDaniels. He came to see me after one of my fights.'

Barrett flashed his wrist in front of me and showed off a gold Rolex chunkier than a Yorkie bar.

'Looks like you're catching someone's eye,' I said cheerily. 'But you know there's a big enough queue of fighters waiting for a crack at the title, and you've got some way to go before you deserve your chance.'

'Sure, I know that. But I'm not asking for a world-title shot. I realise I have to wait my turn. What I'm asking for is a chance to prove myself. I want to fight Shannon Briggs on HBO, because that would be a real local war right there. I've torn up his picture at press conferences, called him out, done everything I should do to create interest in the fight, but HBO still won't use me.'

We were only a week away from Barrett's next bout – a ten-rounder in Atlantic City against one Derek Amos, which was to be followed quickly by a fight at the Yonkers racetrack in the Bronx before his homeboys and local fans.

'Amos is a step up, isn't he?' asked Barrett.

'He's a step up,' I replied. 'He's cagey and experienced, but he's not that powerful or strong, and he doesn't have the look or ambition of a young, fresh fighter either.'

'Who's he fought?'

'Well, he got knocked out quickly by a British heavyweight called Danny Williams,' I said. 'Does that make you want to go out there and end things even quicker?'

Barrett shook his head and shuffled again, as he began his skipping exercises. 'Any man over 14 stone has the power to knock someone out. I feel real strong, but I don't want to get cocky and feel I can just walk right through someone. Speed is power, but I have both, so who would really have an advantage between me and a big hitter like Riddick Bowe or Lennox Lewis?'

It was a rhetorical question, and as I sat back against the window-ledge watching the aspiring champion complete Cintron's exercise schedule, I found myself comparing Barrett with Chris Byrd. Both had below-average heavyweight power, but there was one glaring difference. Byrd was a complete non-hitter, but acted accordingly and had shaped himself into a defensive magician. Barrett believed he was a puncher, and always tried his damnedest to prove it.

'You sometimes look like you're trying to prove too much, like you're trying to be all things to all people,' I commented as we clambered into his four-wheel drive at the end of the afternoon.

'I know,' he replied. 'I've let myself get carried away in the past, but it's because I don't want people to see me as just another heavyweight who can bang a little bit. I want to show people that I can move well, throw double right hands, triple left hooks to the body. I can do so many different things in there. I never want another fighter to be able to look at a tape of me and know what to expect.'

'But you would agree that sometimes it's as though you're trying too hard?'

'Sure, give it to me raw and give me the truth. I don't want yes-men surrounding me. I expect more from myself, because I'm a perfectionist. But I know this much – I can't wait to be in the driving seat. It's like Evander Holyfield once told me: "Once you're the champ, you'll be able to steer things your way." I'm so tuned in to what it takes to become champion that I still do not accept the possibility of defeat.'

He opened a can of orange juice and veered the vehicle right and towards the subway station.

'The way I feel right now, and you can tell I'm not happy – I just wanna get to the stage where I'm calling the shots, and then I'm gonna shit on people from a great height!'

'That's not a very positive attitude . . .'

'Maybe not, but I'm not ever gonna let people get away with messing me around.'

'But there's always a degree of that in this business,' I argued. 'You can't avoid it completely.'

He half-heartedly agreed with me, and pondered the traffic in front of him.

'When you said you wanted to be matched with another guy in your situation, who did you have in mind?' I asked.

'Any of those guys,' he replied. 'Lance Whitaker, Lawrence Clay-Bey, Nate Jones, Lamon Brewster . . .'

'But you're friends with Brewster.'

'Yeah, we were all pretty cool with each other in the amateurs, too,' Barrett said. 'We would sit next to each other at tournaments one day, fight the next, and then in the evening go out for dinner or to the movies with our wives and girlfriends. That's the way it was then. It's the same now.'

'But it's more personal, though, isn't it?' I pursued. 'No head-guards, no vests, a lot of money on the table, a lot more risk. It can't get more personal than that.'

'It's nothing personal,' replied Barrett.

I couldn't accept that. Few things in life could have been deemed more personal than the physical challenge and the very real threats presented by professional boxing.

'Hey, look, don't get me wrong,' Barrett said as we halted on the street and I let myself out onto the sidewalk. 'I'm not surprised by any of this. My patience is being tested, but I will prevail. These two fights I'm about to have are both steps up, and then everything's gonna start looking up.'

★

It was already dark at six o'clock as the subway train chattered through the Bronx suburbs and deeper into the borough's core. I looked out of my window at the winking lights surrounding Yankee Stadium and at the grim-looking projects which stretched from the shoreline to the border with Westchester.

A month before, Barrett had leapt into the ring with Derek Amos. He had worn his Superman outfit again, but his performance had been less than extraordinary against a man with little desire and much mileage on the clock. Amos had been cuffed and pounded, but Barrett had again struggled to find the range for his booming right hands, and it had taken eight rounds before the referee had been convinced to call a halt. Even then Amos had protested.

Tonight, Barrett was to battle the veteran Bryant 'Special K' Smith at the Yonkers racetrack. It was a rare opportunity for his neighbourhood friends to see him in action within easy travelling distance from their homes. The budget for the show was not huge, and the site not glamorous – a sprinkling of bedraggled punters dotted the stands next door to watch the evening races – but the makeshift arena was filled to capacity.

A bus dropped me off at the entrance to the racetrack, and I had to walk across a carpark and a field to get to the venue. Outside the front doors, small pockets of men and women had gathered together for swigs of beer and puffs of marijuana. Inside, the air was filled with the pungent smell of acrid grease and boiled hotdogs.

As the undercard bouts passed by, the arena filled up and the mass of young fans at the burger grill moved towards their seats in anticipation of seeing their local hero in action.

Smith was first to the ring, walking wearily from the back of the hall and past the hordes screaming abuse at him. He wore a tatty pair of shorts and worn-out boots and a 'Stone Cold' Steve Austin T-shirt. His seconds wore faded denims and scuffed shoes.

Barrett's appearance was greeted with a flood of applause. The homeboys pumped their fists in the air and shouted expletives at the poker-faced Smith. The girls shrieked approvingly at Barrett's Zorro costume. The home-town boy wore a black mask, cape and matching satin shorts with an emblem of two crossed, scarlet muskets embroidered upon them.

Brooklyn's answer to Antonio Banderas stood steadfastly in his corner as Smith went for a nervous stroll around the ring. Barrett stared coldly at his opponent through the gaps in his mask, his feet kicking air, his arms hanging loosely by his sides.

'Man, you gonna get fucked up!' yelped a youth at ringside, leaning over the metal barricades, and waving his hands frantically to grab Smith's attention. Smith paced past him, ignoring the copycat outbursts, which now did a Mexican wave around the hall.

Barrett's robes were removed ceremoniously from him by one of his team, while Smith's wrestling T-shirt was yanked off his back by an assistant trainer. The men were brought to the centre of the ring. They eyeballed one another, ground their teeth, bumped each other's fists and turned back to their corners.

Barrett beat on Smith for three rounds, hurting him, rocking him, forcing him back. Pinprick trails of blood started to seep down from the older man's eyelids, and onto his neatly trimmed moustache. Soon the trails became dark rivers of gore, and the two fighters' trunks were splashed and stained with the wounded man's blood.

Barrett tore into him, sending raindrops of blood onto the scorecards of the judges and the notepads of the ringside reporters. The crowd roared, the homeboys continued their incessant volley of insults in order to distract Smith – as if he didn't have enough problems already – and the girl with the silver fingernails rushed to the front of the crowd and waved Monte forward, urging him to gun for the knockout.

By the middle rounds, Barrett tired and Smith began to ignore the blood and concentrate more on his counter-strikes. Barrett grabbed and trotted out of trouble for a round or two, then punched back, countering Smith's stabbing jabs with lunging right hands. Smith ducked and staggered back as Barrett advanced with chin held high, and the two men swiped and leaned.

Smith lasted the distance and lost a unanimous decision, but beyond the wounds to his eyes and the emotional trauma of listening to a thousand strangers demanding his execution, he had succeeded in a victory of sorts by avoiding the knockout against the heavily favoured Barrett.

Barrett was applauded by his fans, but I could see the displeasure on his face. I walked past the ring on my way towards the exit, and caught Barrett's eyes as Old Timer and co-trainer Jimmy Glenn removed his thick, red gloves. He edged towards the ropes and stretched out his hands. I shook his taped palm, now coated in grime and sweat.

'You don't look happy,' I said above the noise.

'You know me,' he replied, bending at his knees and looking through the bottom rope. He wiped some sweat from his forehead, and glanced at the inky red blots on the canvas. 'I'm never truly satisfied.'

CHAPTER FOURTEEN

Shake'n'Bake

*Vaughn Bean is my guy. It's me who's spent years investing in his
career and guiding him to the title. It's me who's risked everything,
so tell me why the fuck it is that I'm supposed to hand him over to
HBO or anyone else for that matter, just so's they can get an
audience and put him in with one of their fighters? This whole
game's full of cliques, and if I don't wanna be part of those cliques,
then the fuck I won't!*
BUTCH LEWIS, JANUARY 2000

*I know how good my guy is. But I also know that if I can keep
him busy and away from trouble, and that if the world champion
comes knockin' on my door, askin' for my guy's availability for a
title defence, I'm sure as hell not gonna say, 'Well, actually, fellas, I
wanna put him in with a contender first, just so he deserves the
opportunity you're offering!'*
FARID AHMED, CO-MANAGER OF
VAUGHN BEAN, JANUARY 2000

Towards the end of a frustrating summer, Don King breathed a sigh of relief
as, once again, prosecutors failed to convict him of insurance fraud. This
time a jury had come to the unanimous conclusion that the FBI had failed
to bring forth enough evidence with which to send the promoter to jail.

King, who had been remarkably restrained at Madison Square Garden
when it was announced that Akinwande had tested positive for hepatitis,
was back to his old rambunctious self on leaving court. He shook hands
with and signed autographs for the jurors, gabbled away at reporters and
promised to 'come out with all guns blazing' at his numerous rivals.
Prematurely, it transpired, many of King's adversaries had made solid

preparations to take advantage of his crumbling empire, in the expectation of the Don being put away for an anticipated six-year stretch.

Although King's businesses had taken some direct hits in the preceding months, most destructively the loss of Mike Tyson, the promoter had proven to the world over and over again that he was the Grand Master of the comeback. He was called the 'Teflon Don' by the US media, the man with the eternal ability to keep re-emerging as the primary player in boxing.

Of course, snatching a dull heavyweight like Larry Donald away from a rival promoter was a trivial affair. In fact, Donald's own manager admitted he would stand to profit more from suing King than he would have done from the fighter's career. But what Donald's promotional hopscotch did show was that while there were some fighters jumping his ship, others still felt that there was no better way to secure a title shot than to sign up with Don King.

King was also supremely confident in his ability to woo Tyson back, but it was going to be a hard task even for him to achieve. Tyson had not fled without support. He had the backing of some astute businessmen, and a team of lawyers who had thrown the book at King.

In the third week of July, Tyson surprised observers when he applied for a licence not back in Las Vegas where he had originally been suspended for biting Evander Holyfield's ears but in New Jersey. His advisor, Shelly Finkel, felt that the Nevada Commission was in two minds about reinstating the boxer, and that New Jersey – who had not suspended him in the first place – would be more sympathetic to a Tyson hearing.

The New Jersey commissioner, Larry Hazard, had been on friendly terms with Tyson for some time, and he surely knew that the state he presided over, which had temporarily swept aside Vegas as the premier fight location in the world, would have this position bolstered should Tyson's return take place along the Atlantic City shores. Tyson had knocked out Tyrell Biggs, Larry Holmes, Michael Spinks and Carl Williams in Atlantic City, in world-title defences, but had not fought there since 1990, when he had demolished Alex Stewart in one round. When Tyson had been released from prison, King had signed a contract which gave the MGM Grand in Las Vegas exclusive rights to Tyson's return, and Atlantic City venues never received a look in.

'To the best of my knowledge, Mike Tyson has acted very well during his one-year suspension, so I believe he should come before the [Nevada] commission,' said the NSAC head commissioner, Marc Ratner, on learning of Finkel's intent to head for New Jersey.

Finkel and Tyson did not want to take too many chances. Were they to be rejected by Nevada, the other state commissions would be under pressure to continue their compliance with the original ban. Going directly to New Jersey circumnavigated some of the red tape which lay in the path of Tyson's return.

Unfortunately for Tyson and his revamped management team, the anger still pounded away behind those hooded eyes of the former heavyweight champion. After some inane character references from former boxers Bobby Czyz and Chuck Wepner, Tyson was asked if he could assure the commissioners that a repeat of the ear-biting episode was unthinkable.

Tyson responded with a series of expletives before his lawyer, Tony Fusco, jumped forward, put a reassuring arm around his client's back and pleaded for calm. Two days before New Jersey was due to give its answer, Tyson withdrew his application and decided it would be in his best interests to return to Las Vegas.

Meanwhile, Evander Holyfield and Lennox Lewis were approaching mandatory defences – the final obstacles blocking them from a unification contest in 1999. Lewis was scheduled to face the Croatian Zel'jko Mavrovic on 26 September in Connecticut, while a week earlier Holyfield was to meet the irrepressible 'Vicious' Vaughn Bean.

The Holyfield v Bean fight was set for the champion's hometown of Atlanta, Georgia. The champion had high hopes that local businessmen would put up enough money for seats to be sold at refreshingly low prices in order to 'allow the kids of Atlanta the chance to see a heavyweight champion of the world defend his titles in their own city'. The businessmen did not share Holyfield's enthusiasm for the event, perhaps as a result of Bean's weak public profile, and so Holyfield himself ended up injecting money of his own into the promotion.

As a non-casino venue, the Georgia Dome in Atlanta could not and would not have been able to pay King an extortionate site fee for the purpose of hosting an Evander Holyfield fight. Even though Holyfield had been treated to a ticker-tape parade in the city after his initial destruction of Tyson, no one claimed he had suddenly acquired the Midas touch.

Vaughn Bean did not stand out from the heavyweight pack in any way, shape or form. He was a small heavyweight, at just six foot and fifteen and a half stone. His only defeat had been the decision loss to Michael Moorer eighteen months earlier, so while everyone knew he was no world beater, no one really knew quite how good he was either – especially since the majority of his victims were a decidedly unimpressive bunch.

Bean's major strength, all agreed, was his promoter Butch Lewis. Lewis had last been seen in heavyweight championship boxing the night Michael Spinks was rolled over by a marauding Tyson, but his biggest critics had to concede that he was nothing if not shrewd. Lewis did not carry the sledgehammer vocabulary of King, nor did he run an efficient promotional machine like Top Rank, but he was a second-division player who occasionally upset the best-laid plans of the big shots.

Since Spinks's retirement, Butch Lewis's meal ticket had been the IBF middleweight champion Bernard 'The Executioner' Hopkins, a throwback Philly fighter with a sharp tongue and sound skills. Lewis had taken Hopkins into fights against Roy Jones and cities like Quito in Ecuador and sent him into the ring with an escort of bare-chested axe-carriers. Hopkins had decided to terminate their relationship when his own investigations into Lewis's business practices revealed his total purse for the Jones fight had been twice what he had been told.

'Butch goes there to HBO and negotiates supposedly on my behalf, but he's not doing that, he's negotiating for Butch Lewis,' said a smarting Hopkins. 'The TV corporations? They're in it to get the best deal possible for themselves, what do they care?'

Hopkins successfully sued Lewis in a Pennsylvania courthouse, but Lewis simply turned to Bean as his next project, and through means which would later become clear, the heavyweight rapidly ascended the ratings to become the number-one contender in 1996. After losing to Moorer, his lofty position had remained inexplicably intact.

It took me well over a year to arrange to meet Bean, which was certainly an inordinate amount of time to wait before being granted an audience with a moderate heavyweight of dubious distinction. I'd called Butch Lewis's New York offices on so many occasions that I almost felt like celebrating the first anniversary of my initial attempt to make contact with 'Vicious' Vaughn by inviting the weary voice on the other end of the line to join me for a drink. Lewis appeared to have two staff answering his calls – a woman named 'Squeak' who grew gradually more exasperated with my persistence, and a man who sounded like Samuel L. Jackson in *Pulp Fiction*. Calls would be diverted to Lewis's limousine carphone, messages would be left, excuses would be made. It was trickier than trying to catch hold of Riddick Bowe between arrests, but from all that I had heard Bean was no Chicago bad boy, and from what I had seen, he wasn't quite the enigmatic figure Bowe was.

'You wanna speak to Bean!' a disbelieving Lewis yelped on one of the rare occasions he answered my call. 'What for?'

'Well, he is Evander Holyfield's mandatory challenger,' I replied as innocently as I could.

'Uh-huh,' grunted Lewis unconvinced, sensing an ulterior motive to my request. I chose not to mention the fact I had listened to Hopkins ranting and raving about him only several days earlier. 'He's like that guy played by Al Pacino in *Devil's Advocate*,' Hopkins had advised me. 'Butch looks after Butch – that's all Butch does. The man is a snake!'

'Well, see, Dominic, I'm gonna do all that I can to get you and Bean together, an' I'm sorry that you've been kept waiting so long. I appreciate you've been waiting all this time, so here's what I'm gonna do – I'm gonna see Bean in Chicago next week, and then why don't you give me a call after that?'

I did, but Butch was out of the office – on holiday in the Caribbean, in fact – so I would have to wait another fortnight. Shortly after Lewis's return from vacation, the Akinwande v Holyfield fight was called off, and Bean's challenge was confirmed. I called Butch's press officer, Kelly Swanson.

'They're in Wilmington,' she told me. 'Just get on a bus, and when you reach the terminal, give me a call back.'

Wilmington, Delaware, was not a major fight town, that much was clear. Small-time shows had been staged at a club called The Kahuna, but this was no Philadelphia- or Brooklyn-based hotbed for up-and-coming fighters, even if several of the sport's world champions had chosen to move there after winning their crowns.

The town was like a second home to Butch Lewis. Michael Spinks had moved there, and Lewis had promoted some of Bean's mismatches at The Kahuna. Hopkins may not have been overly impressed with Butch's business acumen, but Spinks remained a loyal supporter of his one-time promoter, and now helped work Bean's corner.

I called Kelly when I arrived at the bus stop in Wilmington, and she arranged for me to be collected by one of Bean's co-managers, a bespectacled gentleman named Greg Miller. He drove us a mile out of the town centre, turned right off Maryland Avenue and into a scrapyard full of rusted machinery congealed with treacly oil.

Outside one of the metal units, a man in a white hat and dark shades approached us and extended his hand. 'What's your name again?' Butch Lewis asked. 'Sure, sure, Dominic . . . I should have remembered that by now, the number of times we've spoken on the phone.'

We went inside. A thick-set man rested his pained legs upon some stained matting in the converted garage, his solid chin resting upon the heel of his hand. It had been more than a quarter of a century since, but once this man boasted ownership of the sporting world's most coveted prize, the heavyweight championship. To this day, he could still make grown men waver in their boots as they watched him beat the heavy bag.

Smokin' Joe Frazier was a week away from stepping into an Atlanta boxing ring for a world-championship fight. Across from him would stand Evander Holyfield. Frazier wished it were him in there instead of Bean, wished he could have met Holyfield in '71, the year he had cut the wings off the Butterfly. Frazier would not be trading shots with Holyfield, but Ali's former rival was to join Spinks in the Bean corner, along with the less familiar head trainer, Nelson Brison.

Frazier used to come out smoking, Holyfield preferred to sway his head to the sounds of his beloved gospel music. These days, Frazier liked to scoff at the notion that Holyfield belonged up there with him in the pantheon of heavyweight greats. At times, he had even hinted that there was still enough juice remaining in his left hook to handle 'The Real Deal', if it weren't for those darned ankles of his.

As I moved closer into the small gym, everyone gathered around the ring, watching Bean pummel the large set of mitts being held before him by Brison. They all had the same T-shirts on, dark garments with the legend 'World Heavyweight Champion – Vaughn "Shake'n'Bake" Bean' printed across the chest; Bean himself, his three sparring partners, Frazier, Spinks, Brison and Lewis. Only Miller and I broke this sartorial pact.

I smiled at the slight absurdity of seeing Frazier and Spinks dressed in Vaughn Bean T-shirts. Here was one of the greatest heavyweight champs of all-time, alongside quite possibly the best light-heavyweight ever, and they were both playing a minor role in the training camp of an altogether ordinary and unproven contender like Bean.

Frazier and Spinks leaned closer to the ring ropes as Brison moved deftly around the ring, with the pear-shaped Bean in close pursuit, winging shots at the opened mitts. Spinks, whom Butch still called 'Slim', looked at Bean through his shades and from under his pale-blue sun hat, and shouted advice from the corner of the ring. 'Never take your eyes off him,' he called out. 'Keep your eyes on him all the time. Never lose concentration.'

I stood closer to the ropes, and when the timer rang for a minute's break, Frazier turned to me and smiled. 'Hello, son, my name's Joe,' he said.

'I spent some time with your son recently,' I said.

'Marvis? He's a great kid,' Frazier's smile broadened now, and he stooped to massage his aching legs. 'He's turned out real good. A gentleman.'

'He told me he's not going to fight again,' I said.

'No, he won't fight again. He's done fighting. He's doing real well for himself training the kids in the gym, and working with the Lord. He has different things in his life now. Marvis don't need the boxing game for himself no more.'

Bean had moved out of the ring by now, and had changed gloves before setting about the heavy bag. He moved steadily forward as his hands beat against the bag's sides, bumping the contraption with his shoulders, nuzzling it with his chin, and whipping the shots harder and harder as his audience muttered its approval.

'So does he have it?' I asked Frazier. 'Can he beat Holyfield?'

Smokin' Joe whistled softly under his breath, his large, bearded face breaking into another grin as he patted Spinks on the back. 'Our guy punches good, and he's got fast hands,' he said.

'But he doesn't punch like Smokin' Joe, does he?'

His eyes looked startled. 'Ain't no way you can compare no one out there to me!' he growled, only half-jokingly. 'None of 'em! I still consider myself no worse than the third greatest heavyweight champion of all time, so how can any of those other so-called contenders be anywhere near my level? Ain't no comparison!'

'So what does Bean have to make the great Joe Frazier work with him?' I asked, knowing that Frazier's and Spinks's close ties with Butch were the dominant reasons behind such a formidable alliance.

'The thing he's got going for him the best is that he sees openings real well,' said Frazier. 'When a fighter sees well, that's almost as good as being able to punch well.'

The approval was rising by now as Bean took another step forward, so that the bag was almost being carried between his chin and collarbone. The sweat poured and the challenger's T-shirt clung to his skin. He was not an extraordinary sight to behold, and nor was it easy to ascertain whether he was looking ahead to the fight with Holyfield with any great degree of relish. The fighter's stomach was soft, and leaned over the top of his shorts, but he wasn't quite up to the levels of porkiness attained by the likes of Tony Tubbs and Greg Page before him. He stuck his chin down and fixed a baleful gaze on the bag as the seconds ticked by and Brison and Butch fingered their stopwatches.

'Ten more seconds!' called out Butch, who was pleased to see his fighter react with further grunts and heaves of breath as the bag was sent flying at haphazard angles towards the end of the exercise. I suspected then that Bean was coming to fight, and that if Holyfield expected a quick knockout before his fellow Atlantans, he was in for something of a surprise.

Butch and Frazier both looked enormously satisfied with proceedings. Spinks walked past Frazier, and then, noticing the comical sight of the former heavyweight terror wearing a pair of shorts with some immaculately polished lace-up shoes, remarked, 'Nice legs, Joe. Real nice!'

'Thank you so much, Michael,' replied Frazier, trying his best to sound effeminate.

I asked Spinks why it was that he had never put the gloves back on after his loss to Tyson, and he replied with a resigned smile that he had wanted to, but that with each step he took towards launching a comeback, he was many miles away – in his own mind – from actually doing so. He said he had had the style to contain Holyfield, and that while Roy Jones was fairly recognised as being one of the fastest light-heavyweights in history, he too had been no slouch himself.

While Bean headed for the shower, Butch led me into a weight-training room with Frazier and Spinks. The men sat down in front of me, below an illustration on the wall of Holyfield battering Tyson, and I felt a faint twist of nerves as two of history's greatest fighters watched me and waited.

'Are there any advantages that Bean can take in with him against a champion like Holyfield?' I asked them all, but I knew it would be Butch who would leap in first.

'We have to take advantage of the youth factor,' he said, his mauve tongue clicking against small, yellowed teeth, his eyes still invisible behind his dark glasses. 'Holyfield – as good as he is, and the arsenal that I know he does have – is thirty-six. But I don't want it said at the end of the day, when we upset him, that he got old. We're gonna make him *feel* old. He's gonna be in a real fight, for however long it lasts.'

'But he's enjoying the best form of his career,' I argued. 'He's coming off two wins over Tyson, and he's got revenge over Moorer. How can Bean prepare himself for that kind of a challenge?'

'He's prepared,' insisted Butch. 'Look, people laughed when I took Leon Spinks, after only seven fights, to challenge Muhammad Ali, and they did it again when I got the Larry Holmes fight for Slim. Both times they said we didn't have a chance, but we did it twice, and we're about to do it again.'

The three trainers nodded, and I could hear from next door Bean on his way in to join us stopping briefly to chat to the three sparring partners, Terry Porter, James Stanton and Faruq Saleem.

'We know what we're up against,' said Butch. 'One time, I was genuinely concerned for Holyfield. I was concerned for his health when he signed to fight Tyson the first time. I know now what a great fighter he is, no doubt about it.'

'So how can Bean put a loss to Moorer behind him, and get the mental edge necessary to beat someone even better in the form of Holyfield?' I asked.

'Well, he knows this is his last chance,' replied Butch. 'He knows he didn't take full advantage of the Moorer fight, when he should have made sure of the win, rather than leave it in the judges' hands – even if I do believe he won that fight. He's got a break now, because he's still the number-one contender and he's got this fight with Evander. I don't see another chance like this coming around.'

Bean sat himself down between Spinks and Frazier, and looked at me through large, dark, almond eyes and introduced himself shyly.

'When I watch tapes of the Moorer fight, I see a lot of things I could have done better, and I'm taking all that knowledge into the Holyfield fight,' he said softly, looking like a schoolboy about to be scolded in the headmaster's study. 'I was worried about Moorer's southpaw style. I decided to move a lot and react off what he did, when I really should have pressured him more. He ended up doing nothing, so there was nothing for me to react to! If I had poured it on over the last couple of rounds, I would have pulled it off.'

I knew he would have plenty to react to against Holyfield, who was a supreme pressure fighter and probably the best counter-puncher in the business. I looked at Bean, and wondered where his window of opportunity would come from. He was the kind of fighter Butch liked to work with best. He was quiet and humble, though not dull, and he didn't look like he rocked too many boats – unlike Hopkins, who was confrontational and fiercely suspicious. Bean at first preferred Butch to do the talking for him. I thought of his amateur pedigree, his five Chicago Golden Glove championships and his knockout of Maurice Harris, a young heavyweight who was now really coming into his own.

'Holyfield's title is up for grabs,' Frazier chipped in. 'He's been ready to go for a while now, and Bean's the man to do it.'

'I think Holyfield's gonna come out to win quick, but we're coming to take the title,' added Brison.

Bean smiled, rested his head back against the wall and the caricature of Holyfield, relaxing more now, and looking comfortable in his soft, yellow T-shirt. 'Joe's inspired me to fight this fight with a lot of heart,' he said happily. 'Mike's showing me some boxing moves. I'm gonna mix my boxing with my brawling for this fight. I think Holyfield's expecting me to do a lot of holding and standing off, but it ain't gonna be that kind of party.'

'So what kind of party is it going to be?'

'It's gonna be straight up, slammin', head-banging, nose-breaking, jaw-taking action!' Bean sang out loud. He slapped his chest twice, and smiled at me again. 'There's no fear here. None. The fight is within yourself, and I fight that fight every day.'

'Where does that belief come from?' I asked.

'I prepare for something like this by calling upon my religion, Islam, and going into myself,' he replied. 'Islam is my strength.'

'In the same way Holyfield's god gives him strength?'

'I can't speak for Holyfield and his god,' said Bean. 'But I can tell you what Islam has done for me. I know I've already won this fight, it's just that now I've got to turn up to see how I did it. I'm looking at Holyfield as just another guy – that's all he is. This is all easy to do when I call upon my beliefs.'

'Yeah, when the bell rings, the referee had better watch out,' mumbled Frazier. 'Holyfield's up against it now!'

'But we're expecting Holyfield to be at his best,' said Butch. 'That's all we want from him, his very best. He's at home, I know he wants to be impressive at home, but we would fight him in one of those thirty-six bedrooms of his if he wanted. But you know that a man can only take so much, and for Holyfield to keep training his body the way he does, and then go through the emotional let-down of what happened with the Akinwande fight, that takes a toll, man.'

Greg Miller agreed to give me a lift back to the bus terminal that afternoon. Before we departed, I watched Butch hand out flight tickets to Bean and his three sparring partners, warning them at the same time to get to the airport two hours before take-off time or else they wouldn't be going to Atlanta. The fighters trooped into a minibus and set off for their temporary accommodation, while Frazier and Spinks loaded up their own cars with holdalls. As the van drove away, I watched Bean through the rear window and saw him rest his jaw thoughtfully on the palms of his hands.

I believed him when he had said there was 'no fear' there, but I wondered why. He was a man with a humble training camp – a mucky old garage and a rusty old van to take him there. I thought of Holyfield in the corrugated-iron splendour of the House of Pain Gym in Houston, and of the limos and modish trucks he used for transportation. I pictured Holyfield captaining his own private jet onto the runway in Atlanta, and of Bean all scrunched up in the economy class section of a cheap flight from Wilmington.

'I know what you're thinking,' said Miller, as he drove me to the bus depot. 'But I'm telling you, Bean's ready for this fight. I would say he's in the best shape of his life, and don't be fooled by his physique – he's never gonna be built like Holyfield. But he can beat him.'

I pictured the gargantuan spanner which would be thrown into the works were Bean to spring the upset. 'I suppose most of us are hoping Holyfield will win, so that we can get to the unification with Lewis,' I admitted. 'How does Butch feel about Bean fighting Lewis if he wins?'

'We could fight Lennox Lewis,' said Miller, with the emphasis on 'could'. 'Believe it or not, Bean likes fighting bigger guys, because he can just chop them down. He and Michael Grant fought on the same show at The Kahuna once, and Grant refused to spar with him beforehand. They all think Bean doesn't look like much, but once they get into the ring with him, they don't want anything to do with him again!'

When Bean flew off to Atlanta, he carried with him the hopes of Frazier and Spinks too, for his pair of former heavyweight champs-turned-trainers still smiled at the buzz created by a championship bout.

'They're talking about Roy Jones as the greatest light-heavyweight that ever lived because he's so fast,' Spinks had whispered to me during Bean's workout. 'But I was pretty fast too, you know?'

'They're talking about Holyfield going down as one of the greatest heavyweights ever now, but I think I could have taken him up until a couple of years ago, when the desire had gone.'

'They kept telling us you were coming back, Michael,' I said. 'But you never did. You lost to Tyson in '88, your knee still had problems, and even though you kept suggesting you'd come back you never did.'

'I know, I know,' Spinks said quietly, and with a smile on his face. 'But each time I started to really think about it, I was one step further and further away from actually being able to do it.'

★

Much to Don King's delight, forty thousand people proved the doubters wrong and filled the Georgia Dome to capacity on 19 September. Such an audience restored a dose of optimism into the hearts of those who felt that boxing could never again draw such numbers.

The ball parks of San Francisco, New York and Chicago had long finished doing business with boxing promoters as the sport lost its mainstream appeal. In Britain, arenas which were once filled to capacity for a ten-round international heavyweight contest, would struggle to attract a third of the business for a championship match with local favourites.

Somehow, Holyfield – never a major draw – had managed to attract forty thousand to watch him beat up Vaughn. Actually, those who had come in expectation of a slaughter were instead made to eat humble pie for their jokes, which had referred to the challenger as anything from a 'hasbeen', to 'Mr Bean' and 'Broad Bean'.

For two rounds, it seemed as though Holyfield was going to achieve the quick win, as he lambasted his squat opponent without fear of any return fire. But Bean, who had amused people in the days leading up to the fight by wandering around Atlanta in a Moroccan Berber's hat, took Holyfield's punches and started dishing out some bombs of his own, sweeping the fifth and sixth rounds.

Somehow, he had Holyfield wobbling at one stage, but a knockdown in the tenth put Bean flat on his back courtesy of an uppercut thrown a split second before the two were separated for mauling by the referee. Bean shut his eyes tight, and it looked like the referee could have counted all the way to a hundred. Butch screamed blue murder at the referee, insisting the knockdown was a foul, and calling the official a racist.

Halfway through the count, Bean hauled himself to his feet, and fought on. He confused Holyfield, being so bold as to charge at the champion with uppercuts thrown from the outside and right hands which looped errati-cally in the air yet managed to hit their target with unthinkable precision. It was a surprisingly entertaining match. Bean had come to fight after all, and somehow he had hurt Holyfield, had more success against him and made him move back and cover up more than Mike Tyson and Michael Moorer had ever been able to do.

'I didn't know what he was gonna do next,' admitted Holyfield wearily after the fight. 'But, then again, I don't think even Bean knew what Bean was gonna do next!'

'Same old song,' Vaughn sighed despondently afterwards, in the belief that he had taken enough rounds off Holyfield to have won. 'I felt I won the fight. I'm not happy, but I'm coming back. I proved I could beat the best in the world, given the opportunity. I don't fear nobody – Evander Holyfield or Lennox Lewis, it really doesn't matter to me.'

CHAPTER FIFTEEN

Flirtations and Titillations

A week after Evander Holyfield's tepid showing against Bean, Lennox Lewis failed to ram home a clear message that he was the best heavyweight champion in the world when he was extended to the full twelve-round distance in his fight with Zel'jko Mavrovic.

Lewis hammered the Croatian, but the Eastern European's chin stood up to the test. Lewis left the ring at the Mohegan Sun Casino with no more respect than he already commanded in America, while Mavrovic – his face a swathe of blisters and welts – returned to the arms of his stunning girl-friend, Jelena, and the credit warranted for his resilient efforts.

'Someone had better convince Holyfield and Lewis to finally get together in the ring, before someone else gets to them first,' said HBO's Lou Di Bella.

While Holyfield v Bean had been mildly absorbing and Lewis v Mavrovic a fine match of wills, I was more intrigued by an event which had occurred shortly before the WBC championship fight took place. As was customary for the majority of HBO and Showtime telecasts, main events were usually backed up by a televised chief support bout, and for Lewis v Mavrovic, a potential thriller had been made, with Hasim Rahman pitted against David Tua.

During conversations with both men over the previous twelve months, it had been clear that each saw the other as the perfect foil to prove himself as the outstanding contender in the division. Their trainers at the time, Lou Duva and Tommy Brooks respectively, saw it as the fight of their dreams, pitting father and son-in-law's strategies against each other for the very first time. A week before the fight, however, Rahman pulled out, and the news-paper reports stated that he had jumped ship and signed with Don King. This was the confirmation, I believed, that the brief exchange between Carl King and Rahman at Madison Square Garden had been one of the final phases of King's latest conspiracy.

The attraction of joining King's empire was obvious. Fighters who linked up with him were being rewarded with almost embarrassingly high world rankings, virtually guaranteeing them world-title shots. One heavyweight, Jade 'The Jewel' Scott, had lost twice as a cruiserweight, signed with King, seen himself ranked as high as number four with the WBA, only to lose a warm-up contest with the poorly regarded Melvin Foster. Despite this loss, Scott remained ranked, while Foster was squeezed below him at number twelve. The fact that Rahman had already travelled all the way to Russia to dispose of Foster in two rounds indicated the difference in political leverage being accorded between himself and Scott.

It sounded like Rahman's world was being turned upside down by this latest decision of his. Di Bella announced that the fighter would never appear on HBO again, and Rahman's erstwhile promoter, Cedric Kushner, threatened to sue him for breach of contract. I wondered whether Rahman fully appreciated the implications of what he just had done: it soon became clear that not only had he signed with King, but that he had days beforehand accepted a $250,000 cash advance on a fresh contract extension with Kushner. In a way, perhaps Rahman thought he was cunningly playing the promoters at what was considered to be their game.

Instead of fighting Rahman, Tua tore apart the gargantuan Eric 'The Whip' Curry in two rounds. Rahman wasn't answering any telephone calls, and neither was Don King Productions, which wasn't in the least bit surprising.

The Monday after the Lewis v Mavrovic fight, I received a call from Greg Juckett, Kushner's PR man, to tell me that the promoter had called a lunch meeting in Manhattan for the next day. Rahman would be present and an announcement of legal proceedings against King would be made.

The following afternoon, I took the subway to Times Square and walked several blocks uptown to Gallagher's steak-house. It was growing colder, and the air was filled with the smell of chestnuts being roasted by street vendors. Gallagher's was opulent and warm. The waiters hovered by the front door with sombre looks on their faces. Portraits of Mickey Mantle and Babe Ruth adorned the walls. Businessmen tucked into fillet steaks and bottles of rich red wine.

At the head of a table the ample form of Kushner held court. On either side of him sat Rahman and the fighter's uncle, Haleem Ali. Clearly Rahman had decided it best to stick to his original contract extension, but it was going to be interesting to see how King would react to this turn of events.

Kushner's lawyer was introduced to the media guests, who included the sports writers from the tabloids as well as the *New York Times*. An aide handed each of us a file which provided details of a $12 million lawsuit Kushner had launched as plaintiff against the defendants, Don King Productions. The legal jargon was rambling and raised several issues which were not directly concerned with the attempted seduction of Rahman, but it was King's recent deals with the heavyweight which had clearly driven Kushner towards taking these measures.

Rahman looked sheepish sitting next to his promoter, nodding curtly in my direction, but for the most part looking as though he would rather be back home in Baltimore. Kushner made his formal introduction and told everyone that 90 per cent of boxing's woes would evaporate if Don King did likewise. It was generally considered that Kushner was one of the more personable of boxing promoters, though to praise him as a moral giant in an otherwise seedy business would have been going too far. Knowing that Kushner, like most of his peers, had a considerable axe to grind with King, his philosophy on his formidable rival was not a particularly reasoned one.

But just as Main Events' excuses for Andrzej Golota's capitulation against Lewis had been of negligible interest to me at the Polish Consulate in June, so too was Kushner's introductory tirade against King on this chilly September afternoon. Of far more relevance, I thought, was the reasoning behind the decision Rahman had made. It soon emerged that the financial lure had been just one of several factors inducing the fighter to take the course of action he had made.

'I was originally contacted by Carl King, who introduced me to Don,' said Rahman. 'From then on, my conversations were either with King directly, or through his lawyers.'

King had arranged for Rahman to fly to Las Vegas the previous month, where the promoter was staying at the Hilton for a rescheduled middle-weight championship fight between William Joppy and Roberto Duran.

'When we met in Vegas, he told me that there was a conspiracy going on between the Duvas [Main Events] and Cedric. He said that it had been arranged for me to lose the decision to David Tua if I couldn't knock him out.'

Rahman had suspected there was some truth in what King was saying. His trainer, Tommy Brooks, was married to Lou Duva's daughter, Donna. The Duvas promoted Tua, and Rahman was distressed at the conflict of interest this presented for Brooks. In addition, Kushner had enjoyed an excellent relationship with the Duva clan for many years. Each Christmas Eve, he had once told me, he was the only outside guest invited to dinner at the Duva family home in New Jersey. 'As a member of the Jewish persuasion, being welcomed into an Italian home for Christmas was most flattering', he had said.

Kushner dismissed the allegations of any unscrupulous deal-making with the Duvas, and defied King to come up with any evidence to substantiate his claims. What could not be questioned was the fact that Rahman had accepted $200,000 as a signing bonus for extending his contract with Kushner in June, coupled with a personal loan of $50,000.

Shortly after the initial meeting with King in Vegas, Rahman was summoned to an hotel room in New York on King's only day off during his fraud trial. In Vegas, Rahman had been paid $35,000 cash not to take any warm-up fights until the New York meeting. In New York, he was given a further $100,000 not to fight Tua, and his friend Winky was also given a cash sum of $25,000.

'King told me he controlled the ratings,' said Rahman. 'He said to me, "How do you think Henry Akinwande can look so bad against Lennox Lewis, and then I still go and get him a shot at Evander Holyfield?" I believed King had the power to do everything he said he could do, and so I accepted the $100,000 not to fight Tua. I believed him when he said Cedric and the Duvas were in cahoots together.'

'There have been reports that you've got yourself into serious debt gambling,' said one reporter, 'and that this was the reason you took King's money.'

Kushner's lawyer looked a little jumpy and tried to interject, but Rahman was quick to answer. 'That's just not true,' he said. 'I don't know where those rumours come from, but it is true that I had some financial worries. I took the initial payment from King because I had just been served a lawsuit by my first trainer, Janks Morton. By my understanding, all of the matters with Janks had been solved, so I was concerned when that situation came up again. It had nothing to do with gambling at all, and I'm perfectly willing to give back the $25,000 they gave me.'

When word had eventually reached King that Rahman was beginning to have second thoughts about their deal, telephone calls were made to Rahman's home and also to his relatives. King even sent some Baltimore attorneys to pay him a visit, having tracked down the fighter's residence on the Internet. The lawyers tried to cajole Rahman away from Kushner again. Rahman refused, and King sent him a message.

'He said that if Hasim continued his career with another promoter, that his career would be fucked,' said Rahman's uncle. 'He made it very clear to us that he controlled the heavyweight title absolutely. If we signed with him, he would set up a match with Holyfield. If Hasim came back to Cedric, he would be fucked. They were his words. He said he would fix it so Hasim would never get a major fight again. He told us that he always delivered on his word, and that Cedric was stealing money from us.'

'He's been trying to call me all this week,' said Rahman. 'He's been saying that if I didn't believe he had the power to do what he said he could do, he could get Bob Lee [the president of the IBF] over for dinner, and that Lee could let me know what the score was.'

As Kushner feasted on his lunch, the whole scene was that of a prodigal son returning home, with Rahman sitting meekly by, uncomfortable with the legal implications involved and the controversial nature of the meeting. It was unlikely that a great bond of trust could be restored between promoter and fighter. It should have been Rahman's time to break into popular recognition, but instead he was left disturbed and chastened by this interlude with King.

I didn't feel strongly that Rahman was a victim in the whole affair. In fact, as it later transpired, he had come out of the whole debacle $125,000 better off and without any obligation to King whatsoever, so he was hardly in a position to complain about lost earnings, even if HBO were threatening a boycott. 'I'm not portraying myself as a victim,' said the fighter. 'I don't want any pity, and I don't want the finger of blame pointed at anyone else. What I want to do is get back in the picture again by fighting. I would like to fight Tua as soon as I can, and I'll be ready to do so before the end of the year if they let me.'

They did let him. A rescheduled contest with Tua was set for 18 December at the Miccosukee Gaming Reservation in Miami. Just as his career had seemed to run into a lengthy crisis, Rahman now found himself closing in on the fight which would bridge the gap between being a contender and a confirmed world-title challenger.

The IBF announced that the fight was to be sanctioned as an official eliminator, with the winner guaranteed a crack at Evander Holyfield's world title within twelve months.

★

At the end of November, it was formally announced that Evander Holyfield and Lennox Lewis had signed to fight each other for the undisputed championship of the world. It was a financial gamble, but Madison Square Garden won the bids to stage the fight.

A thousand miles away in Las Vegas, as King played host to the world's media with barely contained delight, Mike Tyson was issued with a licence to box again by the NSAC. The countdown was soon under way for Tyson's comeback bout with Francois Botha, but on his return from exile, he could not resist a snipe at the Holyfield v Lewis fight. 'They can't sell out the Garden, but I could just by masturbating,' he sneered.

While Tyson had little good to say about the two men who now stood under the spotlight which had once been his own private domain during the 1980s, Lewis and Holyfield were hardly enveloped in a mutual admiration society themselves. Shortly before their match was announced, Lewis labelled Holyfield 'a hypocrite' for not practising what he preached and fathering numerous children out of wedlock. 'He's got to learn a little more respect, that's what it is,' reasoned Holyfield. 'You know, I want to get out of this game just as fast as he wants to get out of it. He wants to get out of it with a good name, by beating me. That's what it is. But I want to unify and then get out, too. He's just another guy that I have to get, that's all. We all at some time need to open our mouths and speak, but history shows that I have always done what I said I will do. I said that I would be heavyweight champion of the world, and I did. I told people that I would whup Mike Tyson. Everybody I whupped, I told people I was gonna whup.'

The battleground had been established. The principal soldiers, as well as the generals and quartermasters in the various guises of promoters, lawyers, managers, TV executives, trainers and other minions, were all in attendance for a revelatory morning at the Garden to announce the fight formally.

Getting access into the Garden was, at the best of times, a difficult task, and so I could only imagine the kind of restraints being enforced now that the superfight was to be proclaimed to the world. I thought of the many infuriating moments recounted to me by others or actually experienced by myself spent trying to make plain English understood by the Garden's celebrated gatekeepers.

'You can't go in there, sir, without any credentials.'

'I'm going in to collect my credentials.'

'Well, you still need some form of credentials to get in, sir.'

'I see. I need credentials which qualify me to collect other credentials,' the victim would reply.

'That's right, sir, that's exactly right.'

'Look, I am here to collect my credentials. I have not been supplied with any credentials or other forms of identification in order to get these credentials, so can I please come inside?'

'Not unless you have some form of ID, sir,' the gatekeeper would bark with a growing venom injected into the word 'sir'.

'Will a passport do?'

'Yes, sir.'

Not that a passport would prove the slightest corroboration that any individual had any business whatsoever entering the premises on any given morning. America's obsession with carrying ID at all times had driven me up the wall on many occasions in the past. It seemed as though you had to be in the throes of mid-life crisis before beer could be purchased without having to go through some kind of totalitarian security check. The Garden's customer relations department had adopted a similar procedure.

Not that any such traumatic small-talk was necessary on the morning I arrived for the grand announcement, for it happened that my arrival at the VIP entrance coincided with that of Lennox Lewis and his small entourage of family members and old friends from the 'hills of Jamaica or from whence he came', as King often teased. I was ushered through into the elevator by one of the gatekeepers, who simply asked me if I was 'with them', to which I nodded rather condescendingly – which seemed to work wonders. I think it could have been safely discounted that I was a relative of Lewis, and next to the PR suits with six jars of gel slicked into their blast-proof hairdos I looked like a scruffy sod, but I wasn't going to start complaining.

We all crammed into the small lift. There was Lewis, his brother Denis and their sweetly smiling and serene mother Violet. The six lieutenants from HBO and the Garden's PR machine glanced at their reflections in the metallic doors. At the fifth floor I swooped out behind the whole ensemble, and swished into the arena half-imagining that the turning heads of the sound recorders and cameramen all strained to catch a glimpse of my arrival. I plonked myself down on a third-row aisle seat.

Behind a large screen, Lewis and Holyfield started to rehearse their walk-on roles for the promotional film, which would be televised on the late-afternoon newscasts. The 'players' hovered around the arena: Dino Duva from Main Events looking shell-shocked after the exhaustive negotiations. Lewis's co-promoter, the Greek-Cypriot liquidator Panos Eliades, sitting in a front-row seat, watching events unfold before him with the contented smile of a man who has made a deal which would perhaps leave others uncertain of a financial windfall, but not he. Frank Maloney, pasty-faced and irritable, Violet clutching her handbag tightly in her lap, smiling benignly and rising to her feet every few minutes to scan the auditorium.

Before the hordes were allowed in, Lewis and then Holyfield practised their walks from behind the curtain and onto the ring, which had been elevated from the arena floor. Lewis emerged rather awkwardly in his double-breasted suit at the command of a female producer, and as he did so, sparks from the pyrotechnics' latest contraptions flew perilously close to his face. He stopped for a moment, and then continued his walk to the ring, where he waited for Holyfield with arms folded.

When the rehearsal was over, Lewis approached the ropes first and parted them for Holyfield. Holyfield thanked him, but there was no eye contact, no chit-chat as there had been before Holyfield fought Riddick Bowe, nor any overwhelming sense of mutual respect as had existed before the Atlantan challenged Buster Douglas in 1990 and then defended against George Foreman six months later.

King relished every moment of his role as master of ceremonies, spending almost two hours addressing the press with outrageous analogies and self-promotion. He talked about the Queen and Sir Winston Churchill and the beauty of the British legal system which had ruled on his behalf against an Englishman (Frank Warren) earlier in the year.

'I am dedicating this fight, this fight which I am calling "King's Crowning Glory", to the women of the world,' King announced. He trumpeted the causes and historical legacies of the civil-rights campaigner Dorothy Haight and of Eleanor Roosevelt, Margaret Thatcher and Helen McDougal, the former White House secretary serving time for perjury related to the Whitewater scandal which had threatened the political lives of Bill and Hillary Clinton.

'I've been waiting a long time for this moment to happen,' said Lewis, shaking his dreadlocks and turning to face Holyfield. 'I've been waiting a very long time, Evander. Too long.'

'Well, it's like they say, you had better be careful for what you wish for, because one day you might just get it,' replied Holyfield.

When the rhetoric and verbal posturing and one-upmanship were over, the fighters posed and the reporters bundled in closer. I moved in the opposite direction, away from the chaos and into the peaceful periphery, where I watched the Mexicans and Bob Lee's New Jersey contingent hold court at their assigned tables, and the Venezuelans from the WBA storm out in a huff after being omitted from the earlier formal introductions.

In the thick of it all, I watched as King was fêted by boxing's integral figures – the moneymen, the media, the political cohorts, the commissions' lieutenants, the captains of industry, the mobsters of the day and the bankrollers. Then, in a moment of great irony, I watched as he exchanged greetings with a large man with an enormous moustache. The two men laughed uproariously, held arms and hands firmly and talked to each other for several minutes. I remembered Cedric Kushner's stated belief that Don King was like a cancer to boxing, and so I wondered to myself on the way back home, why it was that he had welcomed the cancer into his arms so effortlessly that cold November morning.

★

The fact that King had told me he would be 'honoured' to grant me an interview in Atlantic City the following week did not inspire me with any great degree of confidence. Instead, I felt as though I had just received a circular through the door from a double-glazing sales company, informing me that I had won £75 million tax-free, but that there were certain conditions in minuscule print which I had to accept first.

It came as some surprise, therefore, when one of the few employees of his who seemed to have a grasp of what was required from a media-relations department, Greg Fritz, called a day later to confirm that a meeting had been arranged between the King and I for 11 a.m. in an Atlantic City hotel that Friday. King was to be on the shore to promote a WBA welterweight title fight between his champion James Page and Main Events' Jose Luis Lopez, but the hyping of the Holyfield v Lewis showdown remained his primary concern.

I returned to Atlantic City once again, this time as dawn broke, but eleven o'clock soon passed. For more than four hours I sat and drank coffee with the technicians from Showtime and some of King's foot soldiers.

'He still hasn't arrived yet,' said Fritz. 'We're expecting him to arrive in time for the weigh-in, but right now he's still in the Knicks' jet with Holyfield and Lewis.'

New York's basketball team had lent its private plane to King, and with both heavyweight champions and their entourages safely on board, the craft had jetted to cities across America on a whistlestop tour to promote the unification of their titles. According to one of the techs, Holyfield kept himself at the front of the plane, with Lewis staying put in the back, even though their companions mingled with each other and watched cities like Los Angeles, Chicago and Washington DC drift by beneath them.

Come the weigh-in, King still hadn't appeared. I returned to the coffee percolator and reams of photocopied material in the press-room, and waited for another four hours. At 8 p.m. Fritz told me to continue my wait in a suite on the top floor of the hotel. The Eagle had landed.

Fritz returned with his boss an hour later. I stood up to greet King, expecting to see him dressed in his familiar tuxedo and spectacles, but instead he was casually attired and grubby. The man looked tired, the strain of the tour already telling in the bagginess around his eyes, and the creeping huskiness in his throat.

He shook my hand softly, excused himself, and slunk into the bathroom next door to urinate. I was glad we had shaken hands already, remembering that he had once remarked to George Foreman at an airport bathroom in Caracas that, unlike most people, he washed his hands before he touched his dick.

I feared that the onset of fatigue would discount the possibility of any serious interrogation, that with Fritz hot-stepping it around us like a referee overseeing a rugby scrum my time would be extremely limited, as well as heavily censored.

'Can I just get a drink of water?' King croaked. I didn't consider it appropriate to refuse, and anyway, Fritz was at his side in a second, with a tumbler in his hands.

King sipped the water, licked his lips and ducked his face into the palms of his hands. He rubbed at his eyes and massaged his cheeks, and when he reappeared it was as though some schizophrenic transformation had taken place. A joyous glaze which bordered on the unhinged had replaced the weariness. The eyes sparkled, as did the now more noticeable diamond cubes of ice on his fingers, and in his teeth he chewed on a cigar bigger than a snooker cue. Goodbye, lonely old man; welcome back, Mr King.

I asked him what the Holyfield v Lewis fight meant to him personally, knowing his response would give me the time to prioritise my remaining questions. The response was rehearsed and revealed nothing new. In fact, it was a carbon copy of the speech he had given that afternoon at the Garden.

'Each of the fights I did in the past was a classic in its own realm, but they were just building stones to this fight I'm doing with Lewis and Holyfield,' he said. 'This fight is my crowning glory. All the other fights have been like staircases to me.'

'You're dedicating this fight to the women of the world,' I continued. 'Included in that description, you singled out Margaret Thatcher. Did her government's policies strike a chord with you?'

And he was away, in his element, reeling off one cliché after another, but none so drab that it threatened to dull the edge of his interminable repartee.

'Margaret Thatcher was the first prime minister in 10 Downing Street who ran the government, who stepped into the shoes of the incomparable voice of liberation for Europe and the world: Winston Churchill. She has set the tone for others to come!' His voice grew louder, and my pen scribbled faster. 'We have also invited the Queen!' he sang, using the royal 'we' to talk about himself. 'The Queen is the symbol of the monarchy of the UK – long live the Queen!'

I started on my next question, but he interrupted me again.

'Long live the Queen!' he called out. 'God save the gracious Queen, long live your noble Queen, God save the Queen, man! This is so great, I mean, God save the Queen!'

When King had completed his conversion into an unadulterated Anglophile, he went back to panning the professional progress of Lewis, accusing Eliades and Maloney of gravely mismanaging the Briton's career.

'I think it's self-evident that things would have turned out for the better if Lennox Lewis had come to me as his promoter from the very beginning,' said King modestly, rolling his eyes and wriggling his head playfully. 'The fact is that he's had to come to me for every big pay-day he's had. From the time of Tony Tucker – you know, $9.5 million for Tucker – all the way through to the $4 million we offered for him to step aside so that Mike Tyson could fight Bruce Seldon. Then the $18 million that they didn't take, even though I put a $2 million clause in there for tardiness. Have you ever heard of anything like that? If we are tardy and the fight don't happen on the date that it's supposed to be, due to no fault of his own, then he would have received a $2 million kiss for tardiness.'

King talked long and hard, seldom drawing breath, and always with a dark glint in his eye, a glint which promised mischief but also cold reprisals against those who crossed him. He gave the impression that he was willing to speak deeply on any chosen subject, but it was futile trying to penetrate what Americans called 'chutzpah', his mixture of grit and bullshit. I asked him if he wanted to spend some time alone with Tyson, some time to ask the fighter why their relationship had soured. It was one of the few subjects King did not wish to dwell on, replying as he did, that he didn't 'really wanna speak on Mike Tyson. Let the record speak for itself. I wish him well. I would say to the people – *you* be the judge. You know how the world will turn for him in the absence of me. I hope Mike Tyson gets everything coming to him that he truly deserves, I really do.'

There was an ill-disguised menace in his last sentence, but he looked at me innocently as though he had offered nothing but goodwill towards all men this Christmas, and that included Tyson. The tobacco-filled snooker cue danced through a series of wild twists and turns in King's lips, and the lights cast a shining shroud on the top of his grey and pampered crown, giving him a disturbingly ecclesiastical aura which he probably sensed himself.

'It's ironic, really, with you now promoting Holyfield, and Tyson being on the outside,' I said. 'Ten years ago, you and Tyson were intrinsically linked and Holyfield was a Main Events man. You even described him as being "a pious schoolboy who couldn't draw flies to a dump". Has he become more marketable since then?'

I hadn't set out to shock King or lay any petty traps for him to fall into, but, as I suspected, the derogatory remark brought back to haunt did not faze him in the slightest.

'He has become more marketable since then, because now he has me,' King said immediately. 'I mean, you be the judge.' He stopped talking and sucked at the cigar, glaring at me now a little, not so much embarrassed by my recollection, but challenging me to try harder if I wanted to unsettle him.

'And are you having a similar effect on Lennox Lewis?' I continued.

'Watch what I'm doing for Lennox Lewis!' he exclaimed. 'This is a new Lennox Lewis, and you know it. Everyone knows it! When you see me at the helm, Lennox Lewis is not this normal, pious, benign man that they made him out to be. He is not a chess master. A chess master cannot relate to the 'hood, or the hills of Jamaica, or the ghetto, you know . . . I'm changing that and embellishing upon that. Before, you would have heard him say, "I'm gonna get in there and give it my all." Give it your all? Losers give it their all! He has said that he will go in with Evander Holyfield, and he will come out with all three belts. No prevarication or second-guessing. This is not a chess player. This is the heavyweight champion of the world! Let us not be so benign!'

As he rambled on, I thought of his attempts to lure Rahman away from Kushner and then of his embrace with Kushner at the Garden. I wondered why it was that he, more than any other promoter, was able to entice fighters away so easily from their existing contracts. Then I remembered Larry Holmes drinking his Coke at John Henry's in Easton, and explaining how the majority of fighters would always plump for $150,000 cash over legitimate contracts which assured millions of dollars over the course of several years.

My mind went back to the exchange of greetings between King and

Kushner. Kushner had told me it was 'another spoke in the wheel, another kink in the armour. These legal proceedings don't usually go anywhere, but it never stops becoming an inconvenience,' he had remarked. 'I am sure that Don King would like to find better ways of spending his money than hiring lawyers to respond to my lawyers, but that doesn't mean to say that we have to stop doing business together.'

'First he's suing you for stealing one of his fighters, then you're hugging each other like the best of friends. Do you find that kind of situation strange?' I asked King, interrupting one of his lengthy discourses on the wonders he had worked with Holyfield's career.

King paused for a moment, mulling the question over in his mind, nibbling at the root of his cigar. Fritz was performing miniature leaps in the background, pointing at his wristwatch and then pacing between the suite I had been assigned, and the one next door where a gaggle of television crews had converged.

'I would say that I'm titillated,' he replied, rolling the eyes and wobbling the head again. 'It entertains my fancy. Surprised? No.'

There were only a few occasions when King elected to complete his response before I had to butt in. On these occasions, I quickly gathered my cue, as he would abruptly recline in his seat, bite down on the cigar and crack one of his wicked grins.

I asked him about the cheating and the stealing, the soiled contracts and the poaching of fighters, and all he did was snap the cigar from his lips, and shake his head as though it were a rubber ball attached to a spring.

'I play the game by the rules which were laid out long before Don King ever came into this world,' he protested. 'I've had the wolves attacking my hen house. They've had a free-for-all, and in the past they've managed to escape with a few chickens. In the trauma of my trial, in which I was found innocent, contracts became irrelevant and immaterial. The presumption of innocence was cast asunder. I created the largest purses in the history of the world, yet ironically they would try to say that I'm the one who would rob the guys. One of the guys, Larry Holmes, said, "If he robbed me, then I'm getting paid more being robbed by him than if I was getting 100 per cent from another promoter." They have to find some way to defeat me or try to stop me, but they can't defeat me. I've totally eradicated the word "failure" from my vocabulary. I have a setback every now and then. Failure? Never. But then, how do you combat a force like this, that's coming down on me like a juggernaut on a super-highway? How do you stand by righteousness and make things happen in spite of the insurmountable difficulties and impediments that they put in my path? I knew that it was inevitable that my innocence would be pronounced and that justice would come, because first of all I had never done anything wrong, yet the FBI persisted with their investigations. Now that doesn't take the word "frame" out, and that's why you frame pictures – to make them look better. You frame situations and you make whatever you want to happen, happen. I've said from the very beginning that the only way they could convict me of something that don't exist is to frame me.'

He talked about Rahman, of how he had been there in the fighter's hour of need, to assist him financially and to take another look at the direction his career should have been going. He talked of his times in Britain, quoting from Dickens this time, on how he found his journeys to the island to be 'the best of times, the worst of times'.

When the interview was over, he sat back wearily, removed his spectacles and rubbed his eyes pink. He sipped his water again, and muttered 'You're welcome' as I thanked him for his time. We shook hands, and his grip was soft, but not so weak that it couldn't have taken the lives of two men.

CHAPTER SIXTEEN

War Chorus

Christmas was approaching, and New York was alive with shoppers scouring grocers' stores for Brazil nuts and Moroccan dates. Santa's helpers waded along dirty, rain-soaked sidewalks and the ice-rink outside the Rockefeller Center was opened for the season.

As the end of the year loomed ever closer, there was a sense of rejuvenation permeating the cynical armour of heavyweight boxing. Mike Tyson was looking for a New Year return after the lifting of his suspension. Evander Holyfield and Lennox Lewis were heading for a coronation of sorts in 'King's Crowning Glory'. Elsewhere, Monte Barrett continued to tiptoe his way carefully towards contender status while Tim Witherspoon's descent accelerated. In his most recent fight, Barrett had strode to the ring in a ten-gallon hat with a pistol-wielding trio of scantily clad cowgirls and bombarded old Greg Page for ten rounds.

A month beforehand, Page's old friend Tim Witherspoon had taken a miserable beating at the hands of Andrzej Golota in Poland. Golota had jabbed and speared and lashed, and Witherspoon had prodded tentatively with a dying jab and a reserve of strength and spirit, which had almost run completely dry. Tom Moran told me it was the same story over again – that Terrible Tim had not trained properly – and I tried to argue that Witherspoon was simply too old, too weather-beaten and too uninterested. It was time to start making those videos, I suggested. It was time to start hunting for that musical talent in Philadelphia, as the two of them had planned to do when the boxing journey was over. I knew it would never be over. Escaping from boxing was as problematic as reversing a pact with the Cosa Nostra.

Even Moran was beginning to see his close friendship with Witherspoon under threat. During their time in Wroclaw, Moran had grown to trust Golota's manager, Ziggy Rowalski. Witherspoon's financial problems were no secret, and Rowalski offered to have the veteran back in Poland for some less demanding fights against weaker European opposition. Moran liked the idea, seeing a chance for his friend to make a little money with a minimal risk to his health. Witherspoon's back spasms had worsened, and the chances of him actually being physically crippled had become a morbid reality.

Rowalski proposed a fight against another Pole, Przemyslaw Saleta. Saleta was a former cruiserweight whose chin had not stood up to the test against heavyweights. Moran was offered $40,000 on Witherspoon's behalf and accepted, but Tim wanted to get back in the ring as soon as possible, and instead took up Danish promoter Mogens Palle's offer of $250,000 to fight the undefeated Brian Nielsen in Copenhagen. It didn't matter that fighting Saleta would be less hazardous, Witherspoon was broke again and in desperate need of a pay-day.

Nielsen lacked innate skill, but he was burly and strong and on a roll of forty-eight wins, and he saw Witherspoon as the perfect opponent for him to overcome in order to 'match' Rocky Marciano's world record unbeaten streak of forty-nine victories in the 1950s. Nielsen knocked Witherspoon to the floor five times, and in the fourth round the American stayed down, the pain searing through his back, his pride dashed and his reputation floundering.

It was all so depressing, really, the unsympathetic nature of the sport. But it would have been too easy to blame outside forces for Witherspoon's predicament rather than place a large degree of the responsibility on the former world champion's own shoulders.

A few months earlier, as I walked to the Roseland Ballroom, a block or two away from Gallagher's, I thought of the beauty of boxing and the bleak fascination which constricted those who lived in its strange world. I thought of its ugliness, the callous roar of a crowd appealing with mass hysteria for their fighter to 'fuck him up, fuck him up'. And while the packs of predators salivated at the sight of another man being driven to concussion, we, the media, remained an abstract presence.

The Roseland was playing host to another of Cedric Kushner's 'Heavyweight Explosion' cards, with a Canadian named Kirk Johnson facing Alfred 'Ice' Cole in the main event. Obed Sullivan fought earlier in the evening, losing a decision to the journeyman Jesse Ferguson, and then disappearing into the dark hallways to sit on his own and lightly brush at the stitches which closed the cuts above his eyes.

Neither Johnson nor Cole was a bad soul, but they brought out the animal in each other when they stood face to face inside the rectangle of light which hovered above the ring like a vacuum sucking prey into the bowels of a space ship. Johnson, with his doe-eyed, teddy bear looks and smooth vanity, rubbed his nose in Cole's face, and the pro-Cole hordes screamed.

I sat in between two reporters, Jack and Scoop, and waited for the first round. Johnson steamed into Cole, releasing blows to the body, which looked like they had been intended to drive through Cole's torso and into the ropes behind him. Cole survived, and his fans growled for Johnson to be punished. Jack thought Johnson had the fastest hands in the division. Scoop told me he was interviewing porn stars now, bolstering the meagre income he received from his biofiles. I was beginning to get a headache.

Johnson slipped in the second round, but the referee ruled it a knockdown and the Cole fans erupted in delight. 'Fuck him up!' they urged Cole. 'Fuck him up! Fuck him up!' Johnson, the teddy bear, was docked three points for three low blows, and a shift in momentum soon swung in Cole's favour. 'Fuck him up!' they chanted. 'Fuck him up!'

At the end of the sixth round, a peroxide blonde with silicon implants slithered around the rectangle, and as her arms lifted the ring card, her pink PVC mini-skirt rode up to her armpits. 'Take'em off! Take'em off!' screamed a group edging disturbingly closer to Johnson's corner.

At the end of the seventh, another ring-card girl was told to 'get da fuck outta there and get your friend'. The brunette's face dropped, and she looked like she was on the verge of tears, and I wondered why she was disappointed not to have gained approval from her detractors in the first place.

My head pounded now, while the action inside the ropes intensified. Johnson and Cole were trading viciously. This was what Vaughn Bean would have described as 'head-banging, nose-slamming, jaw-taking action'.

'Hey, you, Johnson!' called out one of the men in the crowd. 'Hey, hey, Johnson, over here!'

Johnson and Cole grabbed each other, and Johnson locked his muscled arms around Cole's ribs. Cole tried to wrench himself free, but Johnson needed the rest to catch his breath.

'Hey, hey . . . Johnson, look this way man, look this way!'

They spun into the ropes, and the referee intervened, breaking the two apart and then motioning for them to engage once again.

'Here, Johnson, down here . . . Johnson . . .' the voice persisted.

Johnson's bear eyes glanced away from Cole and down towards the man at ringside. He looked at him with a quizzical look.

'Man, you gonna get fucked up!' screeched the man. 'I mean, truly fucked up!'

Johnson looked back at Cole, but he had momentarily lost his concentration, and a second later a right hand gave him spaghetti legs, and the bear eyes clouded. He buckled, tottered, stumbled forward slightly and grabbed Cole again, and the crowd noise swelled like a raging fever around the ballroom. 'Fuck him up! Fuck him up! Fuck him up!'

At the end of the round, Johnson's trainer slipped while climbing the corner steps and briefly passed out in a drunken stupor, the numerous shots of Jack Daniel's having taken their toll. When he came to, he spent the rest of the evening perched on the floor, looking sickly and lost.

Cole thundered into Johnson again at the bell, striking Johnson's friendly, child-like features with another right hand, and again Johnson lurched and survived. The result was a draw, and the crowd screamed abuse at the judges and Johnson. Both fighters' faces were lumpy and raw, their foreheads and eyes swelling and marked with the wounds of their own private war. They embraced each other briefly, spoke to one another, the one nodding as the other spoke, and then they parted.

★

Six days before Christmas, Hasim Rahman fought David Tua in Miami. It had been three months since the match had originally been intended to take place, and there was a lingering displeasure on the part of Tua's handlers at Main Events towards Rahman's initial cancellation. With the prize being a fight with Evander Holyfield, the stakes were very high for both parties.

Rahman was calmly confident about his chances. Tommy Brooks had departed, and in his place Rahman had hired Chuck McGregor, who had worked against him the night he fought Obed Sullivan at the Apollo in Harlem. 'I fully expect to knock him out,' Rahman told me. 'I've had enough distance fights now. There's gonna be no more decisions. I'm knocking them all out, believe me.'

But Tua was a quiet assassin, a Samoan who spoke in disarming whispers about economic hardships during his upbringing in Auckland. During our various conversations he had talked about gods and giants, of fighting grown men in the back room of his father's sweet shop and being strapped if he lost. He talked about being beaten by an elder sister, of wanting to hurt any man who didn't shrink away from his cold eyes, and about how he missed playing rugby and cricket in the streets back home in New Zealand.

Although he was quiet to the point of being shy, I reminded myself after our first meeting that Mike Tyson had once been this way too, moving from bouts of lisping courtesy to pure venom in the ring. Tua had looked like a young Tyson on his HBO début, destroying Johnny Ruiz with a ruthless animal instinct in no more than nineteen seconds. He had performed a similar execution upon the previously unbeaten Darroll 'Doin' Damage' Wilson six months later.

Yet since then, a basic flaw had been exposed by fighters who had boxed from long range with Tua. Opponents had become wise to his thunderous left hook, and so were retreating to their left, nullifying his major strength and scoring points with tidy jabs to the listless expression on the chunky battler's face. Tua caught up with most of these men in the late rounds, but the previous summer he had lost for the first time – a tight decision to the ill-tempered Nigerian Ike Ibeabuchi.

I felt that Rahman had long been uncertain as to what style of fighting suited him best. He always looked as though he were torn between becoming an out-and-out bomber with his right hand, or else developing into a textbook boxer. According to men who had fought him, his jab was a far more effective weapon than his right cross. It was a steady, thumping jab which kept opponents leery of wanting to take him on at close range, but the right hand had also masterminded several highlight-reel destructions which Rahman took more pleasure from.

'I'm knockin' them all out from now on', he had said, but had he ever encountered a chin as solid as Tua's? A chin, which had stood up to Ibeabuchi for twelve rounds so hard-fought that they had broken the CompuBox computer-count records for volume of punches thrown and landed in a fight – a record previously held by Muhammad Ali and Joe Frazier's third and final set-to, 'The Thrilla in Manila'.

A tent was constructed to stage the fight. HBO's commentator, Larry Merchant, described the match as the most significant of the year, bringing together two live and viable contenders for Holyfield's and Lennox Lewis's world titles.

Tua walked to the ring with his trainers and uncle, coral necklaces of orange and copper hung ceremoniously around his square neck, his head shorn to the bone, save for a tiara of dyed gold around his forehead.

The steady Queen drumbeat reverberated around the tent, heralding Rahman's emergence from his dressing-room. He emerged into view, his face gleaming with perspiration. Onlookers reached out past the cordon of security officers, and he banged the tops of their fists with his gloves.

'My time,' he had told me. 'My chance to shine. No more decisions. I'm knockin' them all out.'

He smiled arrogantly, nodded at his friends in the crowd, walked in time to the sound of his battle song. *Boom-boom-ksshh. Boom-boom-kshh. Boom-boom-kshh. Boom-boom-kshh.*

In the ring, Tua stalked his own shadow, while his uncle and Rahman's pal Winky exchanged trash talk. Winky was huge, lolloping around his temporary stage in a Denver Broncos top so big it could have housed the whole event on its own. Rahman slid through the ropes. The music began to fade. *Boom-boom-kshh. Boom-boom-kshh.*

They met in the middle, the two contenders so close to the prize, so near to the sport's Holy Grail. They stared at each other, Tua betraying no emotion, Rahman looking equally impassive as he gazed down at the shorter man. Tua was squat and massive, built like a sawn-off shotgun. Rahman was a little looser, rolling his shoulders, imposing his height advantage over Tua, glowering at him with the hint of a smirk on his face, resigned to whatever fate would befall the two.

From the first bell, Rahman dominated with his left hand. The jab punctured Tua's guard and struck the top of his head like a ramrod, simultaneously notching up points on the judges' cards and holding his opponent's left hook at bay. Tua timed the right hand well, ducking it or negating its effect by rolling his head from side to side as it swiped at him, but the Samoan's own attacks proved fruitless.

Rahman rattled him. Tattoos of jabs were followed up with big right hands, each one steadily gaining strength and sharpening in accuracy. By the third round, Rahman had almost mastered his foe completely. By the fourth, Tua's eyes puffed and reddened. In the fifth, his icy demeanour began to melt, the frustration telling in his wild leaps to connect with Rahman's chin, only to find the American's right glove superglued to that part of his face.

At the end of the sixth round, Lou Duva screamed at his charge, while towels were whipped in the air to add a cool breeze, and water was sprayed down the fighter's chest and stomach, and under the waistband of his shorts.

'You're going to lose this fight!' Duva screamed. 'There's no way you're getting the decision!'

Tua grunted, spat water into his bucket and looked through darkened, arched eyes at Rahman.

'Keep firing the jab, all night long. Bing-bing! Don't stop using it,' McGregor urged Rahman.

Tua waded in and Rahman waved an uppercut through his short-armed defences. Tua stalled for a moment and then resumed his chugging motion. Rahman boxed and moved, his right-hand bazooka now redundant while it protected his jaw from any hooks, but his jab carving a way towards victory with precision.

Tua had become painfully one-dimensional. Drumbeats and tribal instruments sounded in support of the two fighters. *Boom-boom-kshh. Boom-boom-kshh. You've got blood on your face, you big disgrace . . . boom-boom-kshh . . . boom-boom-kshh.*

Towards the end of the ninth, Tua stepped face first into a rare right cross, and was rapped on the jaw by a short hook. He stalled again, his feet holding firm for a second as he gathered himself, and then he moved forward. Rahman moved back, threw the jab. Tua walked into it, inviting the shot again and again, as if he were a man willing to brave the rain just to get somewhere special. The prize. The world title. The heavyweight championship of the world.

'You've got to knock this guy out!' screamed Lou Duva. 'There's no way you're getting the decision.'

The audience responded to the impassioned plea, urging Tua forward in some quarters, pleading for Rahman's caution in others. Rahman was still the master, boxing at a distance so exact it could have been calculated by a machine. The jab was perfect, the defensive mechanism impervious to Tua's hook. The hook was launched again, and missed. It sailed past Rahman's face as he manoeuvred into a tidy little retreat and then tormented again with the jab.

A rare glimmer of hope for Tua as the left hand, tiring slightly from its use, fell an inch lower than the closeness maintained for most of the fight. The opening. The one chance permitted, or so it could have been. The shark sensed blood. Tua exploded. *Bang!* The hook was driven home. It crashed into the side of Rahman's jaw, flinging him against the ropes near Tua's corner.

A second passed. Mount Duva erupted. Rahman reeled backwards, his shoulders sagging, Tua barracking in for the kill, the referee jolting into action. The bell sounded to end the round. At its first ring, Rahman's arms dropped to his sides. Tua exploded with another hook. The referee rushed to pry him off the wounded Rahman. Duva raced into the ring and screamed.

Rahman rolled against the ropes, his eyes momentarily blank, his legs dancing. Duva screamed at the referee as McGregor joined the fray.

'What the fuck do you think you're fucking doing?' Duva screamed.

''We need more time, ref,' said McGregor. 'That last shot was after the bell. It was an illegal blow. Five minutes, right?'

'Right,' said the referee.

Rahman grabbed the top rope and guided himself back to his corner as though he was playing a one-man game of tug-of-war, his feet treading awkwardly like they were stepping through a series of tyres.

The referee forgot about his promise of an extra two minutes' recovery time, and Rahman looked dazed as he rose to his feet for the tenth round. Dazed, wounded, fucked, however the crowds at the Roseland would have put it. If they wanted 'fucked', this was 'fucked'.

Rahman tried to give himself a kick-start, bouncing on his toes in an attempt to pump energy back into his shaken limbs. Tua bulldozed him, driving him back into his own corner and unleashing a torrent of hooks and swinging right hands. Rahman bobbed and weaved against the ropes, his senses gradually coming back to him.

He ducked a shot, he took a shot. Ducked one, took one. He peered through his guard at Tua. The referee moved in closer, leaned in and tried to get a look at Rahman's eyes through the gloved fortress which attempted to prevent the Tua battering ram. The ref moved back out and hovered. Tua fired, missed. He fired again, hit. The ref jumped in as Tua fired twice and missed twice. The ref jumped in and waved his arms across Rahman's chest, signalling the end.

Tua cannoned himself into the air in jubilation. Rahman shoved at the referee. 'No!' he protested, his eyes awash with anger. 'No!'

Duva hoisted Tua into the air, dropped him, hugged him, punched his fists triumphantly. Tua wailed and shouted his praise. He hugged his trainers and his managers and his uncle, and planted kisses on their cheeks.

Winky put his hand on Rahman's shoulder. His team moved in, comforting their fighter, complaining to the officials, admonishing the referee.

'He was hurt,' said Tua. 'I knew he couldn't take it for too long. He was boxing well in the beginning, but I knew I would catch up with him eventually. When we started to fight on the inside he was doing nothing, and I could tell he had little left. Lou told me to go out there and knock him out, and I did just that.'

Rahman had an entirely different opinion of what had happened. 'As far as I see it, I'm still an unbeaten fighter,' he argued. 'I've got twenty-nine victories against one robbery. Everyone saw what happened. Someone get me that referee – he robbed me of victory. I was buzzed, it's true, but this is boxing. All fighters get buzzed at some stage, only I wasn't given the opportunity to show that I could come through. He hurt me in that ninth round, but by the tenth I was not buzzed. My head was clearing, and I was ducking his shots. I was gonna finish clearing my head and then come on in the eleventh and twelfth rounds. I deserve more respect than for an inexperienced referee to stop the fight after I duck four shots!'

It was a bitter and inconclusive end to Rahman's unbeaten record, and I thought about the psychological damage it might have on him for as long as he continued to fight for a living. Nobody had thought he could box as proficiently as he had done, and yet he had still been defeated. People could argue with some justification the nature of the defeat, but it was in the record books now. It was a cold statistic. Tua had knocked him out in ten rounds. The referee had stopped the fight.

The year had come to an end with a mixture of ugliness and controversy. The sordid memory of Johnson looking innocently out towards the lynch mob at the Roseland. The poorly fated dream of Rahman's to consolidate a world-title fight by handing Tua a beating.

The year ended. I wondered how resolute Monte Barrett remained, now that the sneaking suspicion that he lacked the firepower he believed he had, had almost become fact. Did Kirk Johnson really wish to put himself through the mental torture of listening to the hounds baying for his blood all over again? *Fuck him up! Fuck him up!* It had seemed inhuman to me, their enraged demands that a man be damaged on their behalf – or was this the raw, naked truth about boxing, that we all came to witness carnage, only some of us excused our presence with supposedly intellectual validations?

In my heart of hearts, I earnestly hoped not. I had wanted always to remain completely impartial, and in admitting this sentiment I had been warned by wiser men than myself that this would always prove to be impossible. Professionalism did not always entail impartiality. Had I, in the gloomiest corner of my heart, secretly wanted to see Rahman fuck Tua up? Definitely not. But if it had been he who had been accorded such a for-tuitous victory, would I have felt as passionately as I did the day after the fight that an injustice had been rendered in Miami? The truth is I wouldn't have done, and I could not help feeling to a small degree that there was something wrong about feeling that way.

CHAPTER SEVENTEEN

Icons

Shortly before Christmas Mike Tyson signed to fight 'The White Buffalo', Francois Botha. The match was made for 15 January in Las Vegas, with the MGM Grand holding Tyson to their existing contract, which gave them the rights to four more of his fights.

Botha was a limited but gutsy sort, with a thick Afrikaans accent and a rough, sandy head of hair. Shortly before Hallowe'en I had met him in New York, where he was in town with Frank Warren. Botha had been one of the 'chickens' Don King would refer to in Atlantic City, and Warren the wolf set to snatch him from the hen-house.

It was easy to label Botha a joke, with his mythical 'White Buffalo' gimmick and the answer-machine message at his home informing callers that they had got through to 'White Buffalo Enterprises' – as though he operated a global conglomerate of outside business interests. He was anaemic-looking and flabby, and his record had been built on such non-entities as to persuade Muhammad Ali's biographer Thomas Hauser to once demand of him in public to name one fighter he had beaten to justify his lofty ranking as the IBF's number-one contender.

Botha had only been stuck momentarily on answering that question, retorting with the perfectly legitimate excuse that although he had spent the majority of his career being spoon-fed a diet of easy victims, he had seen men such as Riddick Bowe and Evander Holyfield repeatedly pull out of fights with him. By choosing to fight Tyson, Botha risked forfeiting his mandatory rating with the IBF, but he boasted of a self-confidence that he possessed the skills not only to subdue Tyson, but Lewis and Holyfield too if given the chance. Such unwarranted optimism was par for the course, but it was during what I had thought would be little more than a mundane interview for a local paper that I stumbled across a dark sentiment which Botha harboured towards some of his rivals.

In 1995 he had briefly held the IBF title after defeating Germany's Axel Schulz in Stuttgart. Before the month was up, however, he had been stripped for testing positive for anabolic steroids. Labelled a drugs cheat, the White Buffalo had flown back to his home in Newport Beach in disgrace, hotly protesting his innocence.

'It was from some medication I had been taking for an elbow injury,' Botha told me in New York. 'They did some trials with it, and discovered that the medication contained something like a fraction of a trace of this anabolic steroid.' He stroked his stubbly chin with a hand, and looked at me with his striking, bright eyes. 'It's ridiculous to me that I should be punished and have my title taken away from me like that, especially when you look at everything else that's going on in boxing.'

'Such as?'

He looked about him and laughed scornfully. 'Look, I'm treated like that after an accident, and yet there are bigger names out there than me who are pumped full of the stuff. Come on, you know everyone in boxing talks about it. Everyone knows it's true.'

Botha took me by surprise, and I gave him the opportunity to tell me that his comments were off the record.

'You can put them on the record,' he said, 'I don't care.'

'But do you have any proof?' I asked.

'Proof?' he snorted derisively again, and chuckled. 'No, I don't have physical proof if that's what you mean, but talk to people in boxing – they'll tell you the same thing. It's the worst-kept secret in this sport.'

'So why do you believe the rumours?'

'Come on,' he sighed. 'Read between the lines.'

As the fight drew nearer, Tyson seemed keen to reinvent the dark persona which had kept crowds so captivated in the 1980s. He dispensed with the contrite and humble attitude used to help him retrieve his licence the previous summer, and spat venom at anyone who rubbed him up the wrong way whether intentionally or otherwise. NSAC officials were branded 'Nazis', an American reporter was told on air to fuck himself, and Botha was assured he would end up 'in a body bag, because that's what I do for a living'. On the week of the fight, when asked what would happen to Botha if he chose to take the fight straight to him, Tyson replied that the Afrikaner would 'die'.

Botha's soft physique and wide-eyed look convinced most people that he was unlikely to give Tyson much more trouble than he had encountered when demolishing 'Hurricane' Peter McNeeley four years earlier.

Tyson continued to play the intimidation game, stepping out of his dressing-room to the doomsday chime of his favourite rap song, his eyes as cold as dark metal, a black knitted skullcap upon his head. Botha, in contrast, looked as though he had been vomiting violently, his face pale and sweaty and his eyes watering.

Tyson came out for the opening round with his trademark skip, but from then until the fight's sudden conclusion, he looked like a very old Tyson rather than the Tyson of old. He charged in, swiping at Botha with wild, one-punch attempts to knock the Afrikaner out. There was no technical approach, no rapid-fire jab, no combinations, no strategy. Botha was made to look exceptional by Tyson's foolish rushes. The underdog may have had jiggling breasts and an unsightly paunch, but against the predictable mono-tony of Tyson it was as though he had acquired the foot movement and subtle grace of Nureyev. For five rounds Botha handed Tyson a boxing lesson, smiling and taunting as he did so.

'I'm gonna give you a beating, white boy!' Tyson sneered at one stage.

'Well, you'd better get started,' fired back Botha, 'because all of America is watching you, and you're losing!'

In the fifth round a perfect right hand from Tyson ended Botha's hopes of a huge upset. The shot rocketed into the South African's face, landing between Botha's nose and mouth and sending him to the floor with absolute conclusion. Botha attempted to rise twice. He pitched face first on the canvas at the initial attempt, and then stumbled back into the ring ropes as the referee's count reached 'ten'.

Once victory was his, Tyson the humanitarian appeared, rushing to help his beaten opponent from falling out of the ring, and kissing the man on his head.

★

The Mike Tyson of old would never return. It had been thirteen years since he had so ruthlessly taken apart the usually durable Trevor Berbick, but now all that remained of the once 'unbeatable' champion was his power, an explosive arsenal with a rusty mechanism and unreliable trigger. The Tyson of old was gone. So too were his old mentors Cus D'Amato and Jim Jacobs. Bill Cayton remained in the business, but he had never emulated his success with Tyson. Heavyweights had signed with him, but things had always gone awry – Tommy 'The Duke' Morrison contracted the HIV virus, Michael Grant tired of being brought up 'the Tyson way', and Cisse Salif's punching prowess flattered Cayton to deception.

Tyson's relationship with trainer Kevin Rooney had always been volatile, and after Rooney's inevitable sacking in 1988 the last remaining vital member of Tyson's original core had been shut out.

Every time Tyson returned from yet another disastrous interlude in his life, the media speculated the possibility of reconciliation with Rooney. They did so after the loss to Buster Douglas, the prison sentence for the rape of Desiree Washington, the defeats by Evander Holyfield and, most recently, the return from suspension after feasting on Holyfield's ears.

A pax was never made, and Tyson went through a string of new trainers, some of whom only survived a week in the gym before despairing with the excess baggage which came with being Tyson's chief cornerman. There was Richie Giachetti, Larry Holmes's former trainer, and Don King cronies like Aaron Snowell and Stacey McKinley. Jesse Reid spent some time with Tyson in the gym, but sickened of the homeboys screeching their ill-informed words of advice and commanding more of Tyson's attention than he could. Even Tommy Brooks, who was assigned as Tyson's trainer just before the Botha fight, faced problems of his own, audaciously asking Tyson's number-one crony, Steve 'Crocodile' Fitch, to actually earn his enormous salary.

Even the cynical elements in American boxing could not help but look back on Tyson's prime years with a sense of nostalgia. Nobody felt there was 'another Tyson' on the way up, nobody could point at an emerging prospect and claim that he was setting heavyweight boxing on fire the way Tyson had done.

I could never have described myself as a Tyson fan, preferring the jab and movement of men like Ali and Holmes, but Tyson reminded me of good times – of staying up into the early hours to watch him fight live on ITV. Tyson fights to me meant Dickie Davies freezing his balls off in Atlantic City, wrapped up in a sheepskin overcoat, with his badger hair being pummelled by the wind.

I was heading into what I had grown up believing to be Tyson country. At the outset of Tyson's stardom, he had been as big a marketing phenomenon as pop bands like Wham! and U2, and as recognisable as screen heroes such as Tom Cruise and Charlie Sheen. His story was serialised over the course of months by the *Daily Mirror* and the *Daily Express*, his face sold magazines, books and posters, and the sports pages carried regular updates on his projected defences.

I remembered vividly the collections of *Tyson Presents* videos, with Tyson sitting alongside the merry-faced Harry Carpenter in a BBC archive room, and the two admiring the exploits of Jersey Joe Walcott, Ezzard Charles and Jack Johnson. My outstanding memory of all these compilations was of an even younger Tyson skipping rope in his old Catskill gym, with D'Amato leaning on the ropes in the background, muttering to him and extolling his unique words of wisdom. The aura and intensity of those images had been more striking than even the most adrenaline-thumping of scenes from the *Rocky* series.

There was something unimaginably compelling about Tyson back then, and it went beyond his supposed invincibility. To me, he had been the definitive '80s icon. Watching him fight on television sent a tingle down the back of my neck, and I wasn't alone. Hardened figures from the fight game had admitted the same thing to me on numerous occasions. I didn't see Tyson as an object of sympathy. It made my stomach turn listening to the sycophants who excused him for all his sins – especially the rape of Washington, but I missed the vibrancy which he had once brought to boxing.

The train sped past lakes of thin, dirty ice and evergreen forests ascending into the skies, and as I leaned my head against the window and tried to catch some sleep, I thought of the moments from those videos which had also stood out. Of Tyson, leaning from a porch not so far from where the train was, releasing his beloved pigeons into the air. Of Tyson, rolling up to D'Amato's house after an early-morning jog, his rhinoceros body enveloped in a thickly padded tracksuit. Of Tyson, his hair unshaven and bushy, eating meatballs in Camille Ewald's kitchen, his body twice the size of the elder 'kids' sitting beside him.

Leaving the train in Hudson, I caught a cab to Catskill. The driver took us over the Rip Van Winkle Bridge, and asked me my reasons for being there.

'Well, he's still around,' he said. 'He keeps in touch with some folks around here. I know someone's still paid to look after his pigeons for him.'

'You've seen him recently?' I asked, wondering again if Tyson was seeking a friendly reunion with Kevin Rooney. It was unlikely, really, seeing as his old trainer had just successfully taken him to court and sued him for a percentage of his future earnings in the ring.

'Not personally, but I hear he's been around,' said the driver. 'People here really don't have a problem with him. He was always a good person to people in Catskill, never got himself into the kind of trouble he's been in since.'

He took me on to Main Street. I paid the five-dollar fare and watched the car disappear up the road. The air was chilly, and snow had been brushed to the sides of the sloping paths and sidewalks, which twisted in and around the almost silent neighbourhood. This was where D'Amato and Rooney had given Tyson the only education he thought would take him anywhere. This was where it all, effectively, had begun.

The gym was on Main Street, two floors above a police station and in the same building as the local courthouse. This was where the wise old man had taught the young Tyson about feeding flames and controlling fears.

There was nobody outside, and the only sound was the quiet hum of light traffic passing over the bridge. Wisps of snow fell from the greying sky, and I shook the slush from my shoes as I tapped at the entrance window by the police kiosk. The duty officer told me to walk up two flights of steps and I would be outside the gym.

I couldn't hear a sound from beyond the massive oak door which led into the gym. No beating of the heavy bag, no whirring of the speedball, no words of tuition from the crusty old trainers. I looked at a small yellow Post-It note which read: 'Kevin. I want to be a fighter. Give me a call. Joe.'

I knocked on the door, and there was no answer. I knocked again, and a voice wearily responded that someone was coming. It opened, and I looked at Kevin Rooney. He had changed, just as Tyson had changed. His face was different from the one which had worked Tyson's corner on all those distant nights in Vegas and Atlantic City.

I thought of Michael Spinks in Vaughn Bean's Wilmington garage, and of how time had treated him so kindly, and I wondered whether Tyson would ever have traded his victory over Slim for the peace Spinks had found at the end of his boxing journey.

Rooney had always been lean and clean-shaven when employed by Tyson. Having been a fighter himself (as a skinny amateur he had won the Golden Gloves welterweight title in 1975) he knew all about conditioning and fitness. On this day, his face was fleshy and speckled with grey stubble.

I sat with him in the gym for several hours. He talked about his introduction to D'Amato, the early days in the Catskill with D'Amato and Ewald, the education of Tyson and the aftermath.

'I guess you could say I'm the only guy out there who's teaching what Cus taught,' he said, threading the laces through a new pair of gloves as he awaited the arrival of his students. 'I've carried on this gym, otherwise it would have wasted away. In that sense, I feel honoured and privileged to carry on Cus's legacy.'

Tyson and Rooney had fought viciously in the early days, but all I saw of Rooney was a man battling not to be broken, a man whose sense of duty towards D'Amato's gym was filled with humility and even a strangely sweet innocence. In so many ways it appeared to have been untouched since the days of Tyson, and it looked like it hadn't been cleaned for a decade. Layers of dust covered the antiquated weight-training devices, the ring ropes and the tables. The bathroom was squalid.

'I keep Cus's name alive here,' said Rooney. 'I talk about him as much as I can. I've had the gym renamed "The Cus D'Amato Boxing Club". I feel his legacy is respected, even to this day. Even by his rivals. No one can say anything bad about him.'

The gym was filled with ghosts. The walls were covered in yellowed press clippings, exhibiting the lives of Rooney, Tyson and D'Amato and other fighters connected to the Jacobs-Cayton-D'Amato triumvirate.

I looked at the solitary, worn-out ring and thought of the image so often televised during the days of Tyson's emergence, of D'Amato telling a bothered Tyson that 'Your mind is not on your work – there's something distracting you.' It would happen many times in the future.

Behind the ring, Rooney had dedicated the wall to D'Amato's memory. On charcoal paper he had inscribed the words, 'We mourn his passing' in silver ink, and glued photos and newspaper cuttings of his old mentor beneath it.

'I knew that when I was around Cus that I was around genius,' said Rooney. 'It was the way he talked, the way he carried himself. He had a lot of character. He was there to meet me when I got off the train in Hudson when I first arrived here. Even at sixty-six years old he was a solid block of a man. He took me to the gym and talked to me. He told me his stories and his life experiences. He had a scrapbook on his life, which I read, and the story slowly unravelled. He stopped the mob's control of boxing all by himself. He was the only guy who stood up to them. If it wasn't for Cus D'Amato, the mob would probably still be controlling boxing. If it wasn't for Cus D'Amato, there would be no Bob Arum or Don King. Each one of those guys should hold a memorial for him every year for what he did to rid the sport of the mob.'

Despite the well-documented hostility which now existed between Rooney and Tyson, I could detect no hatred or vengeance in Rooney's words. He pitied Tyson to an extent, for being transformed from a man who was 'a historian who could conduct a conversation with anyone', into 'someone who acts like a rough guy and likes to demean people who want to talk to him'. But Rooney's remorse for Tyson's plight was not unequivocal. 'It's all his own fault. He allowed himself to be stolen away when he should have stayed right here at home all along.'

And so now, in the musty old museum which was the only home Rooney claimed Tyson ever had, he had set about trying to discover the Tyson of tomorrow. I had never believed that history repeated itself. I didn't imagine Rooney felt any differently, but the good times with Tyson had been too memorable to consign to the past, and handling fighters from other weight divisions – no matter how successfully or not – just didn't fill the void in Rooney's life.

Like Cayton, Rooney had yet to recreate his heavyweight dream. Hasim Rahman had once been based at Catskill, until his financial backers at the time had pulled out. Jeremy Williams had been Rahman's dormitory mate, but the warm pleasures of California and a part-time acting career had lured him away. Another fighter, Wayne Howard, had been looking good until over-confidence led him head first into a knockout loss in Miami, and he had quit the sport altogether.

Rooney was talking about his latest pupil when the door opened again and two men of contrasting appearance wandered in. The first was a wiry figure in an ill-fitting tracksuit, with an inane grin painted on his face. He asked Rooney for some Vaseline to rub into his knuckles, hit the heavy bag for all of thirty seconds and then disappeared.

'It would be hilarious, a book about the characters who come into this place,' said Rooney with a smirk, and then introduced me to the second man. This was his heavyweight hope, his 'future', as he described him.

The young man was short and stocky, with a wide, full-moon face and a slightly lazy eye. He reminded me of Tyson. His name was Jerome Tab, and he was shy and quiet and spoke awkwardly to us both. When he took off his coat and started to limber up for that morning's exercises, his unease evaporated and he relaxed into his combat rhythm.

'His parents brought him to me last year,' said Rooney, as the fighter shadow-boxed in a pair of dark leotards and white T-shirt. 'They drove all the way from Carolina, because boxing was the only thing he ever talked or knew anything about. They decided if he wanted to be a fighter, they were going to take him to someone they had heard about and trusted.'

'How can you tell if someone's got what it takes?' I asked. 'There have been too many Tyson wannabes already, haven't there?'

'I look at their attitude,' said Rooney. 'This kid Jerome comes here and wants to learn every day. He's taken some knockdowns in sparring, but he didn't quit. He just keeps getting up, coming back and learning from his mistakes. He throws punches with bad intentions, which is as it should be in heavyweight boxing. He tries things out after I've told him about them. What I look for in a fighter who's hoping to do something in his career is ring generalship. That means, I want to see someone try to control the ring and control what's going on inside it.'

As if the ghosts of the D'Amato era did not abound already, a tape cassette played during Tab's workout only served to highlight an already eerie atmosphere in the gym. The fighter leaned against a heavily padded structure beam, and waited for the cassette to begin, like an automaton holding still until being triggered into action.

Rooney pressed the 'Play' button on a battered old tape-player, and D'Amato's gravelly voice filled the room. The voice shouted out a series of digits, each of which signified a specific combination: '7, 7, 2, 5, 5, 1.' This numerical theory applied to prize-fighting had driven Michael Grant to distraction as Cayton and another former Tyson aide, Steve Lott, had attempted to manipulate the giant's progress the year before.

The formula had suited Tyson perfectly, however, and the way Tab responded to the phantom voice of D'Amato suggested that it worked well for him, too. The numbers were shouted out again when the aspiring professional entered the ring for a sparring session with a tired-looking light-heavyweight. The numbers were announced in staccato fashion, and Tab reacted with a succession of uppercuts and scything left hooks which left the sparring partner so stunned he wanted no more after the third three-minute session.

'You think you've got another Mike Tyson here?' I asked.

'Could be,' said Rooney.

'But you still think you would be the right man for Tyson, even after all that's gone on in the past?'

'Yes, that's true,' he said, searching the *Daily News* for Michael Katz's Wednesday column. 'Tommy Brooks is a good trainer, but he doesn't know the D'Amato way like I do. Mike didn't look good against Botha, and we can attribute that to ring rust, but I was there in Vegas that night, and I could see he wasn't standing in the right position.'

'So what could you do for Tyson if he ever took you on board again?' I asked.

In the background, Tab wound down his exercises for the morning beside a series of photos and clippings chronicling the Tyson era.

'I'd have him fighting twice a week in the gym,' Rooney said. 'There'd be no TV cameras. I'd sharpen up his skills, then ask for George Foreman.'

'But Foreman's hardly on the scene now,' I argued.

'But it's still a huge fight,' insisted Rooney. 'Foreman's been asking for Tyson since Mike first got out of prison. Some people think it would be Foreman against Frazier all over again, because of the size difference. But I'd say, "Okay, then, let's get them both together and then see what happens when Foreman gets hit by Mike Tyson." That's what I'd do.'

The trainer turned to stare at the pictures on the walls once more. He pointed at the framed portraits of Primo Carnera, Max Baer, James J. Braddock and Ezzard Charles, and of a poster print taken after his Golden Gloves win in '75. I gazed at a Polaroid snapshot of a teenaged Tyson playing with some young children upon the climbing frame which now stood dusty and unattended by the ring.

The voice of D'Amato continued to echo around the room, even though the tape had finished playing and Tab had departed for his lunch. The museum curator wandered past me, hands in pockets, the faint smell of whisky on his breath, and checked all of the side doors were locked.

The image of Tyson peering at his adopted father through cupped gloves flickered before my eyes once again. The legacy which Rooney had assumed weighed proudly upon his shoulders, and although the world he had immersed himself in was a solitary and in most ways graceless one, I found his dedication touching.

Whether the old Tyson ever returned for more than a quick nostalgia fix, or the 'new Tyson' – in the shape of Jerome Tab – proved to be far more than the latest in a long line of impostors, Rooney was determined to keep on feeding the flame which D'Amato had lit.

Rooney was talking still as we broke into the bright winter daylight of Main Street. I imagined he was heading to a diner for something to eat and a shot of Jack Daniel's, or perhaps home to rest before the afternoon training session. He was smiling all the time now, misty-eyed with his reminiscences.

He asked me to stay for the rest of the day, and I declined. There was a train leaving from Hudson before the hour was up, and I had work to do back in Hoboken. He shook my hand goodbye, thrust his hands back into his coat pockets and ambled up Main Street, the steam from his breath following him until he too vanished from sight.

The train trip back to New York was a poignant time for me. I wished my brother Benjamin had been there at the gym, to read the wallpaper and picture in his mind's eye the same images I had recreated for myself, images which reminded me of the many teenaged evenings we had spent together watching live televised coverage of the big fights in the early hours of the morning, back home in a converted garage. I thought of the immaculate destroyer who, through a technical proficiency which some failed to recognise, wore down and obliterated proven men like Holmes and Spinks. The Tyson of that age would have imagined an oral assault on another man's ears to be unthinkable, I was sure. What was the need when his skills and hunger, his resilience and fortitude were seemingly impenetrable?

But if defeat to Buster Douglas had done some psychological damage to Tyson, then the humbling experiences with Holyfield had caused an irreversible trauma, which by my reckoning had switched off any rationale he once had. Tyson no longer had that steely self-belief. He had become petrified of defeat, and so would respond to the simplest of adversities with yet more miniature self-destructions.

So it had been during the fight with Botha that, instead of breaking from a clinch, he had decided to try to snap the Afrikaner's arm in half. It had taken over two minutes and a dozen security staff to prise the rabid Tyson from his intended prey.

'He can be what he once was,' Rooney had said, but I felt this could never be so. I wasn't so sure that Tyson didn't want to be anything but what he had become.

'Look at what y'all made,' he had said before the Botha fight and I wondered whether he was not only talking to the media he despised so much, but also to the phantoms of his past whose memories ached as painfully as they did for Kevin Rooney.

CHAPTER EIGHTEEN

Taurus and Terronn

The man looked like a fat Salvador Dalí. He wandered around the assembly area, cornering the players and making them wince as he clasped his sweaty palms around their hands. He spoke like a man in the midst of a perverted climax, simpering and salivating, as he tried to impress upon us all a sense that he was a pivotal wheeler-dealer in heavyweight boxing.

The fighter remained close by Dalí's side, watched as golden-laminated business cards were dispensed to the world, listened as the man announced in the trickling language of a con merchant that he would volunteer his fighter's services as a replacement opponent for Evander Holyfield.

'Taurus is gonna be the first fighter to win the world title on his pro début,' he wheezed, flashing the cards and running moist, pale hands through the roots of his greyish-white ponytail. 'Pete Rademacher couldn't do it, but Taurus can.'

Taurus was a big heavyweight with wide shoulders and little ears which poked from the sides of his bullet-shaped head. I looked at him and raised my eyebrows, and he just shook his head and lifted his gaze to the ceiling.

'Let's talk,' said Dalí, grabbing me back into his lair as I attempted to recoil and spin away towards somebody – anybody – else nearby. 'You want rights to the first story on Taurus, the man who will win the world title in his first fight? Do you?'

He guided me away from the bustle of the crowd and up a hallway, and Taurus did not follow us – relieved, I imagined, to be spared the toe-curlingly awful company of the man who claimed to represent him.

'Five years ago I was running the Israeli Boxing Federation,' the man said, his piercing little eyes lying at me through thin-rimmed spectacles, his belly so bloated it looked as though he was suffering from malnutrition. 'Today, I handle the future heavyweight champion.'

'In his first fight?' I asked eventually, resigned to the fact that I had to humour him to a degree, in order to survive.

'That's right. Well – that's the offer I've made to the commission, anyway. Here, take a look at these brochures, my daughter's a movie star, you know. She's made me a proud man.'

I looked at the brochures.

'Taurus doesn't admit it to his pals, but I'm his manager. I've got a contract. If only he helped me out here and started calling Holyfield out, then maybe we could make something happen.'

This all happened back in June 1998, when Henry Akinwande had tested positive for hepatitis B only hours before he was due to challenge Holyfield. Before the show had been scrapped by Don King and Madison Square Garden, John Ruiz had been mentioned as a replacement opponent. The idea had been rejected, but Dalí wanted to get Taurus some publicity, and mistakenly thought it would do him some good to target me as his chance to tell the world about Taurus's quest to succeed where Rademacher had failed all those years ago against Floyd Patterson, and win the crown in his very first professional fight.

Now, eight months on, I sat with Claude Abrams of *Boxing News* in a dingy Italian fast-food café across the road from Macy's, and watched Taurus queue up for some food with his homeboys. It was almost one in the morning, and four big drunken blokes were kicking each other in the head on the main road outside Penn station.

'Still being managed by that nutter?' I asked Taurus.

'He was never my manager,' the fighter replied, an embarrassed smile on his face.

'He's a fucking thief, that's what that guy is,' chimed in one of the homeboys. 'He's taken so much money from other fighters, he has to staplegun all the belongings in his office to the floor, just so they don't get thrown out the window whenever fighters go in there demanding their money!'

I told Claude about Taurus and Salvador Dalí. We had just seen the IBF welterweight champion Felix Trinidad defeat one of America's best fighters of the modern era, Pernell 'Sweet Pea' Whitaker. Afterwards, we had listened to King bellow, 'Puertooooo Ricoooo! Viva Puerto Rico!'

Next to us, Michael Grant had stood stoically beside Magic Johnson, dressed in an olive-green designer suit, a diamond stud glinting from the tiny crease in his ear lobe, a baby boy slumbering in his wife's arms to their right. On the undercard, Vince Phillips – the former junkie who had collapsed the Russian Kostya Tszyu two years before – had defended his crown against an unknown named Terronn Millett.

Millett still had a bullet lodged in his spine from the day someone had tried to steal his car, but it was Phillips's health which was now question-able. He was drained and fatigued at the weigh-in, having lost almost four stone in weight since entering his training camp. 'Looks like he's got fucking AIDS,' a manager whispered in my ear when Phillips had peeled off his trousers behind the scales.

Millett cut Phillips and busted him up badly, hammering him to the floor with right-hand lightning bolts until the referee called a halt.

When I turned my attention away from Taurus, I saw another man waiting his turn to be fed. He was small with a thin moustache, and he asked for something masquerading as a veal meatball. It was Terronn Millett.

What a way to celebrate, I thought. Weren't champions supposed to rejoice with vintage champagne and extravagant feasts with their loved ones? Surely they weren't supposed to queue up with a chipped plastic tray and ask for extra ketchup with lukewarm meatballs, before sitting down with a cornerman and guessing how much of their purse they would get to see after deductions.

'It's sad really, isn't it?' said Claude.

'Yeah, it is,' I replied. 'He should be out there partying in some five-star hotel. There should be a stretch limo waiting to take him to the airport tomorrow morning. And when he gets back to St Louis they should present him with the keys to the city and name a shopping mall after him.'

Millett eventually sat down to eat, patches of moist soreness around his eyes, and outside the fighting on the street continued.

CHAPTER NINETEEN

The Thirty-million-dollar Man

Hasim Rahman's first fight back after the controversial loss to David Tua was staged the night before 'King's Crowning Glory', in another evening of boxing at the Roseland Ballroom. He had been lined up to take on a brave but limited opponent named Michael 'Gold' Rush. It wasn't destined to be a thirty-second walkover, but clearly a win for Rahman was almost a foregone conclusion, while his management sought to keep his name alive after the loss to Tua.

I had not seen Rahman since the loss of his undefeated record in Miami, and I wondered whether Don King's words were ringing loudly in his ears. 'The fight's been fixed!' the promoter had yelped. 'Only way you gonna come out of there the winner is by knocking David Tua out.'

I didn't believe King had any proof to back up these allegations, but they probably weighed heavily on Rahman's mind. He had, after all, been streets ahead of Tua when the late blow was struck, and the referee's reaction had been undeniably bumbling.

It was the night before Rahman's return, and the temperature had dipped to such an extent that the cold was biting. My lips were chapped and my eyes painful as I waited for a minicab to take me from Hoboken to Fort Lee, where the fighters were holed up in the Hilton.

Even though Rahman was favoured to resume the winning track the following night, I still felt that he had come to a crucial turning point in his career. Did he capitalise on his otherwise impressive showing against Tua and maintain his position in the pack of top contenders? Or did he fall by the wayside, his ambition extinguished, only to be replaced by the resolution which had taken over men like Tim Witherspoon and Greg Page – a desperate bid to make money, and to hell with the big prize?

His manager Steve Nelson met me in the marble hotel foyer, and we took the elevator to Rahman's room on the third floor. The fighter opened the door when we arrived, his form dwarfing his companions, Chuck McGregor, Winky, Hasim Jr – or 'Little Rock' as he was nicknamed – and one of the child's pals from Baltimore.

Inside the room, the air was stale. The days leading up to a fight were surely the most difficult for all fighters, lodged as they were in one hotel after another, with nothing but eighteen channels of shit to choose from, as Pink Floyd might have said.

'Dom-in-ique!' Rahman said, as he welcomed me into the room, forgetting once again that I was neither female nor French. 'Man, you wrote some bad things about me after the Tua fight. I know, Dominic, I know. Don't you go trying to tell me otherwise. I got told by several people, "Man, did you see what Dominic wrote about you?"'

I did tell Rahman otherwise, and I hadn't a clue which of 'my' reports he had read to make him believe that I had criticised his performance against Tua, but I was amused by his sensitivity towards his critics.

He had talked about this in the past. I knew that he analysed all the press reports of his fights, and took even the mildest of criticism very much to heart. He scanned the Internet, too, always tapping into the boxing websites and reading what people were saying about him.

He returned to the game of cards he had been playing with Winky, reminding me of the accusations that his flirtation with King had enabled him to pay off gambling debts back home. McGregor chewed on a slim, unlit cigar and Nelson sat on the corner of a bed. Little Rock and his friend watched an NBA game on the TV. Rahman only looked up when the sports reports came on and provided the updates on the Holyfield v Lewis weigh-in and final press conference.

'You comin' to see my dad fight tomorrow?' Little Rock asked me.

'Sure,' I replied. 'Are you going too?'

Little Rock nodded, giving me a wide-eyed stare.

'You like seeing your dad fight?' I asked, as Rahman and Winky slapped their cards on the table and finished another round of 'War'.

Little Rock nodded, and his friend – tipping the scales at cruiserweight before he had reached third grade – said, 'He's gonna knock him out in the fourth round.'

'That's your prediction?' I asked.

'No, mine's the third round,' replied Little Rock, who was sweet-faced and skinny and impeccably mannered.

'You want me to stop while you ask your questions?' Rahman asked me, leaning over his cards and kicking the trainers from his feet.

'No, you just carry on,' I replied.

Rahman was winning his card game, and Winky was complaining. I joked with Winky about his face-off with Tua's uncle in the Miami ring, and he looked embarrassed. I remembered how he too had benefited from the Don King episode, pocketing $25,000 cash by virtue of being the fighter's closest friend. This was another of King's little games, currying favour with the buddies, and hoping that a few good words on his behalf would exact a pay-off.

'I suppose you're tired of talking about what happened in December,' I asked Rahman.

'What happened in December?' he bluffed. 'You mean my victory over Tua? The simple answer – it's made me stronger, made me realise that I don't take nothing for granted, don't stay on the ropes when my trainer says not to, showed me that I should never relax in the ring.'

'What bothered you most?' I asked. 'The late punch or the early stoppage?'

'What bothers me most is that the late punch went by like it just didn't happen,' replied Rahman, shuffling the pack once more, and flipping a card in Winky's direction. 'It was like we had made it all up. Had he hit me with a low blow or something like that, I would have got my time. I would have got my five minutes. When somebody fouls you flagrantly, the rules state that you get up to five minutes to recuperate.'

He won another hand, gathered the cards towards him, and looked at me incredulously.

'The next thing I know, the referee's telling me I've got five seconds left in the corner! I knew I was recuperated, but I wasn't going to get in a slugfest with Tua in that tenth round. My thing was, I'm gonna lose this round because I'm not gonna be offensive-minded until the eleventh. I was just gonna stick out a few jabs. He came out and hit me with a good shot, probably his best shot of the fight apart from the one after round nine had already ended. I took the shot, and then just kept moving my hands so I wouldn't take any more cleanly. The rest of his shots were glancing blows or touching blows. Nothing else hit me hard, and then the referee stops it!'

'Deep down, did you believe you were still going to win?' I asked.

'In my heart of hearts, I know that he could not have kept that pressure up for the next three rounds solid,' he said. 'He told everyone afterwards that he thought I was weakening, but I'm telling you he really didn't think that. Where was this weakening coming from? He lost the sixth, seventh and eighth rounds easily! My jab just kept him in check. He had never been tamed like that before.'

I couldn't detect any sense of lost confidence, no sign that Rahman may have been turned gun-shy by the events in Miami, but until he stepped into the ring again it would be difficult to know for sure. For now, he appeared almost buoyed by his new-found respect in the sport, and the winning of the sympathy vote for the circumstances surrounding his defeat.

Nelson and Cedric Kushner were filing protests with the IBF, who had sanctioned the match as an official eliminator, but one thing I felt certain about was their failure to force Tua and Main Events into a rematch. HBO had already offered the money for the fight to take place that month, but it had been rejected.

'I wish Tua the best of luck for now, but when he gets in there with me again, it's gonna be a totally different fight,' added Rahman.

'Isn't the loss going to weigh on your mind, though?' I suggested. 'Is there a danger you might feel inclined not to build up a big points lead again, instead go for an early knockout and get caught cold?'

'That's just not happening,' Rahman insisted. 'I can change, but he can't change. I showed him the difference I can make in that fight. I did things in that fight that nobody's seen me do before. Look, when Tua was competing in the Olympics, I wasn't even thinking about boxing. I've already come and surpassed him within a short amount of time, so from now every day that I train, I'm getting better and better than him the whole time. He's maxed out! He don't have any more to offer.'

'Does the loss torment you?'

'No, it don't play no tricks on my mind, because I refuse to accept it as a loss. I know I won that fight, and I know I got robbed by the referee, simple as that. Tua didn't do anything to me. He didn't do anything to my career. What he did do was make me a meaner, more focused fighter and more confident. Not only am I just more confident, but I boldly predict that he won't even see the ninth round if we ever fought again. He's made an already dangerous man even more dangerous. If I don't knock a man out, I'm still gonna stay focused the whole time. Next time, it won't matter if the bell rings or not. I won't be there for that kind of thing ever to happen again, believe me. I'm gonna watch them all like they're coming into my house. Nobody will ever have that opportunity again. I mean, this is my livelihood we're talking about, and when I look at my son having to watch his father get hit after the bell like that, I just can't accept it.'

'But it's important for you to have your son and family around you at your fights?'

'Well, it is,' he replied after a short pause. 'I was seeing too much of them before the Jesse Ferguson fight, but my thing is financial security for my family.'

'Beyond anything else?'

'Well, truthfully – if I never become world champion, but I make $30 million, I'll be happy. I'd much rather have $30 million than a world title. If I can get bigger and better fights without fighting for a world title, then I'm never even gonna get involved with world titles. World championships really don't mean that much to me. If the TV corporations wanna pay me good money to fight the best, then I really don't need to pursue a belt.'

The card game was over now, and I could sense McGregor's and Nelson's surprise that their fighter was speaking so emphatically about his prime reason for fighting, dispelling the romantic notion that the drive came from an unquenchable thirst for world domination.

Mike Tyson had symbolised '80s greed and excess in many ways, but his ascent to the world title had been sparked by his hunger for success, a longing to carve a place in history beside his legendary predecessors. Evander Holyfield was certainly not frugal, but his championship dream was filled with determination and self-belief. His drive had been the consolidation of title belts, and the money was the reward for his efforts.

Rahman's attitude now echoed the sentiment of the typical '90s fighter. Money was the key purpose, because this was a business, and anyone who believed they were in it for the sport should have stuck to the amateurs and exposed themselves to all risk and no reward.

'You have to play the game, but not allow yourself to be the game,' said Rahman. 'It's naïve to assume otherwise. I've heard about the stories in professional boxing from way back when, the politics, the things you hear about this person and that person, and all of the false promises. It ain't no different from life. You gotta think of yourself as a businessman in this game, even if you're the fighter. Everything ain't always what it seems. You're fooling yourself otherwise.'

I wondered if he was really directing his words at me, scolding me for perhaps harbouring some sentimental wish that the glory of standing proud in the gleaming armour of a champion king was worth a dozen cable-TV deals. But he was contradicting himself at the same time, adding that when poetic justice arrived, he would have back the minor title he had lost to Tua, and then everything would be back to normal.

'After all,' he said, 'let me put this scenario to you: when people talk about the best heavyweights around today, they talk about Holyfield, Lewis, Grant, Tua and Hasim Rahman. Say Tua'd never hit me after the bell, and I had won. Would they be saying his name at all?'

'Are you going to miss it when they're no longer mentioning your name?' I asked sadly.

'Dom-in-ique!' he said, mockingly. 'Dom-in-ique! What makes you say something like that?'

'Because this game doesn't last forever, does it?' I replied. 'There have been hundreds of men before you who thought so, and very few seemed to know that this is the way it works out.'

'But I know, Dom-in-ique! I know. That's why I'm telling you, my number-one priority is financial stability. The glory and the title belts don't even take second or third place to me, and that's why I ain't falling in the same trap as the others did.'

Despite his nonchalant and laid-back attitude, I knew that it meant a lot to Rahman to be classified as potentially the next great thing in heavyweight boxing. The media had by and large felt he was the victim of an injustice in the Tua fight. The HBO commentary team, including the world's pound-for-pound best, Roy Jones, had thought so too, so Rahman remained a considered member of the élite young guns. But he held his place precariously, and would be the first to be demoted should another newcomer score a dramatic breakthrough victory in the meantime. That was why it was so important to get past Rush at the Roseland the following night.

Tua's defeat of Rahman may have carried an asterisk beside it, but a win was a win. That was all that mattered, really, the big 'W' next to a fighter's name. It didn't truthfully matter how it was achieved. It propelled the fighter over the next hurdle, took him into the next phase of bargaining and negotiation with extra leverage.

By now, Tua and Michael Grant were seen as the outstanding young contenders. Rahman needed a win over one or the other, while Ike Ibeabuchi, who had taken a close decision off Tua two years before, was on the comeback trail after narrowly escaping a prison sentence for kidnap and attempted murder.

But neither Grant nor Tua held their positions without fear of being challenged. Tua had so nearly come unstuck against Rahman, and Grant had looked decidedly pedestrian a fortnight after the Tyson v Botha fight, biffing away in a slovenly manner at a burly Syrian named Ahmad Abdin, before the latter found no air left in his lungs and retired at the end of the tenth round.

'Both Tua and Grant should be trying to substantiate their claims to greatness by fighting me,' said Rahman, dealing the cards again. 'It's a rhetorical question to ask if they are the next best out there. It's not justified at all, this hype that's got behind them. Grant was life and death with Obed. He's big and strong, but this power that they're projecting him as having – it's just not there. I don't see it. Where is it? Now, Ike, that's a different matter. Nobody has ever hit me as hard to the body as Ike did in sparring one day. But Grant? No. It's just not there.'

'Are you finding the wait frustrating?' I asked.

'Not at all,' said Rahman. 'This has been happening to me throughout my whole career, from the time I was preparing to fight George Foreman and then he pulled out. The thing with me now is that other heavyweights don't know what to expect from me. They don't know if they're gonna get knocked down, beaten up or just outboxed against me. They don't know what's gonna happen.'

★

The world's media were in town, but most of the press made only a cursory appearance at the Roseland for what was a show of modest meaning on the world stage and of limited entertainment value.

I arrived about an hour early and watched from the unlit sidelines as Cedric Kushner's promotional team set about checking everything was in order. A TV crew had set up camp on a temporary stage elevated at the back of the ballroom. The big dance hall was almost empty and icy cold. I tugged my jacket collar close to my neck and breathed warm air onto my hands.

Rahman arrived soon after, with Winky and Nelson, McGregor and Little Rock, and Little Rock's bouncy friend trailing behind them like a spacehopper gone amiss. Rahman noticed me from beneath his knitted ski hat and stretched out a huge hand to shake mine.

'Dom-in-ique!' he called out, and then vanished into the background, heading for his changing-room.

I wanted to buy a piping-hot mug of tea or coffee, but the bar only sold weak American lager and a tasteless orange juice concoction. I told the barman I'd like to pay way too much for the juice, but he ignored my sarcasm and took my four dollars without a flicker of a smile.

The undercard was an international carnival of the absurd and the abstract. A former American football running back struggled to get past a blown-up middleweight and was handed a gift draw. I looked at my press pack and saw that the underdog had been knocked out by Nigel Benn almost a decade ago.

There were fights between Americans and Puerto Ricans, and a girl dressed in rainbow sashes and with braided hair which belonged at a rock festival nearly stole the show. Angelo Dundee worked the corner of a dark-skinned Swedish heavyweight named Attila, and I wondered if Dundee – like Kevin Rooney – hoped for one more taste of the dream.

By the time Rahman and Rush were in the ring, their rival factions had already started a war of words in the audience. I looked across from the press section, more anxious than I would normally be in such circum-stances, seeing as Kim – by now my fiancée – was seated right in the middle of the two warring parties.

Rush's family and friends leaned from the Ballroom's balcony and hurled insults at Rahman's supporters. The men threw their hands out in anger and the women abused one another with shrieks of 'Bitch!' and 'Whore!'. Kim was sitting fairly still, grinning at the abusive swarms around her. She had felt nothing, when she was younger, of strolling from the East Village to the West at two in the morning, rather than catching a cab, just so she could chain-smoke her way home, so being the filling in a riot sandwich was not an altogether terrifying proposition to her.

Rush fought with a weirdly content look on his face – weird, because he soon discovered Rahman's physical strength was going to be too much for him. He back-pedalled for the first four rounds, his rusty-gold-coloured trunks shimmering in the dusky light of the ballroom, Rahman stalking him in solid black.

The entourages howled at each other during the one-minute intervals, and then at their man's opponent during each three-minute stanza of legalised combat. At times, Rahman looked uninterested, firing away at Rush with his power punches, but with only a modicum of composure and forethought.

Rush slapped at Rahman and cuffed at the scarred right side of his face.

'This is the heavyweight you think we should watch out for?' asked George, a British reporter in town for Lewis v Holyfield.

I shrugged, and watched Rahman pitch into Rush again. In the next round, he tore into his opponent in earnest, splitting the flesh above his left eye first and then his right, slicing him and dicing him, so that blood streamed out of the gaping incisions and onto the floor. Rush winced badly, and, in a moment of compassion, Rahman wavered and looked at the referee. The fight was called off, and dark oily teardrops dripped from Rush's eyelids. The referee guided the loser back to his corner, his trunks soiled by his own blood. The dark-red mess was everywhere – on Rahman's gloves, on the referee's shirt, on the cameramen at ringside.

Rahman leaned against one side of the ropes and raised a fist in the air as his fans cheered raucously and Rush's family gasped with concern. Rush was led away to be stitched up without anaesthetic, and when he re-appeared he had swathes of bandages wrapped tightly around his head, eyes and ears, like the Karate Kid.

Rush said Rahman was the strongest man he had ever faced in the ring. Rahman said it was no weakness to be compassionate, that he didn't need to be forced into a situation where, in order to win a fight, another human being had to be blinded. The damage Rush had sustained was immense. He wouldn't fight again for almost a year. I wondered how much glory there was left in the sport for him to enjoy.

'Come on,' said Claude, who was back in town for the Holyfield v Lewis fight. 'Let's go for something to eat.'

I moved over to Kim's seat, where she watched the Rahman family celebrations alongside her brother Luke, and I told her we were going. Rahman stepped past us, a T-shirt now glued to his body like clingfilm against his perspiration. He pursed his lips, leaned over us, and banged fists with his brothers and cousins, all of whom looked pretty formidable in their own right.

'So what did you think?' he asked me.

'Well, Rush was a difficult guy to look good against,' I replied.

'He was that,' said Rahman, as he walked away, followed by his family and cornermen. 'But I'm still there, Dom-in-ique! I'm still there!'

Kim and I walked with Claude and George, just bearing the offensive weather until we met up with Jack. Jack was a Vietnam Vet and like most of the people I had met in boxing, he didn't touch alcohol. Still, that didn't prevent us from trooping into Jimmy's Bar near Times Square. The Jimmy in question was Jimmy Glenn, a veteran New York fight figure who helped Old Timer in Monte Barrett's corner. His bar was narrow and packed, and men and women drank Sam Adams and Bass in handled pint mugs under posters advertising fights between Sugar Ray Leonard and Thomas Hearns, Muhammad Ali and Ken Norton, Roberto Duran and Esteban de Jesus.

Jack talked about a mythical 'pre-paid funeral expenses club' he had started, inducting heavyweight journeymen on the road to nowhere once a month. Rush was in line for a recommendation to join this undistinguished club. Claude asked the waitress for a glass of water and was told he had to buy a drink. He said he would pay for it, but she remained steadfastly stupid and said no. Jack called over Jimmy, and Jimmy fixed it.

I drank a beer and said I still felt Rahman was a threat to the winner of Holyfield and Lewis. Michael 'X' Bentt walked in and told Kim to watch out being involved with someone like me. I had another beer and said that Rahman would knock out David Tua or Michael Grant, if ever given the chance. George talked about all-time great fighters like Emile Griffith and Henry Armstrong. Claude got his glass of water. I had another pint and insisted Rahman was the best heavyweight in the world. Everyone else said it was time to get some food, and Kim looked mildly embarrassed.

We met up with one of Cedric Kushner's publicists, Eric, and sat at a table at the All-Star Café and ordered various sizes and flavours of burger.

'Rahman just reminds me of one of those big, strong, white heavy-weights,' said Eric, one of whose jobs it was to promote Rahman. 'He's big and strong, that's it. Let's be honest, he didn't look that good tonight. Someone like Ike would have walked right through Rush. Ike's an animal. A fucking animal.'

'And you don't see any animal instinct in Rahman?' I slurped, holding a bottle of beer to my lips.

'No. Do you?'

'Well, no, but I don't see it in any fighter the way it used to be prevalent in Tyson,' I countered. 'None of these heavyweights has that predatory instinct they used to need to reach the top. Take Kirk Johnson, for example.'

'Kirk Johnson? The guy's an animal!' mocked Eric.

'Sure,' I replied. 'As scary as a squirrel. Kirk "The Squirrel" Johnson. There's a nickname to send a shiver down an opponent's back.'

'Rahman's limited, Dom,' said Claude.

'Who are we talking about, that one we saw fight tonight?' George asked, as he prodded a fork at his Rancho-Bar-B-Q-Creosote-burger and wisely decided to investigate no further. 'Him? He was rubbish.'

'You should match Rahman with someone like Darroll Wilson,' I advised Eric. 'Someone like him would make Rahman look really good.'

'But why should you have to try and make him look good?' Claude argued. 'If he's as good as you think he is, why protect him?'

'I'm just saying, coming off a win like tonight, he needs a conclusive knockout win to get people's attention again.'

'You're thinking like a promoter,' said Claude.

'Oh dear,' I said. He was right. I was thinking like a promoter, and I was thinking like a person who was throwing all impartiality to the wind. It had been George who had said that a person could never remain impartial in this game, and I didn't want to prove him right.

Behind George and Eric, I watched the Swedish fighter Attila twist spaghetti and seafood onto his fork.

On my way back home to Hoboken, I leafed through a discarded copy of the *Daily News*. Only twenty-four hours to go. Don King held Holy-field's and Lewis's hands into the air on the back cover. Was this the closure that boxing fans had waited for since the heavyweight crown had been fractured? It was down to these two to unify the belts and stand tall as the king of boxing. Which would be the one to be crowned in glory, and which of the contenders would leave the canteen queue to emerge as the victor's next challenger?

CHAPTER TWENTY

King's Crowning Glory

'Aw, he's such a nice man, a real gentleman,' said the camper-van driver as she wound the vehicle up the drive towards the hotel resort. 'We jus' love having Lennox Lewis at Caesar's Brookdale. And all his people. Such a nice, friendly, polite crowd of people.'

There were only three weeks to go before the fight, and Lewis was bringing his sparring sessions to a close. The world wasn't exactly rabid with anticipation of the fight with Evander Holyfield. It was more relief, really, that at long last the average Joe on the street would be able to identify one world champion.

Holyfield was about to shut up camp in Houston and head for the colder environs of New York City. If the rumours were true, the weather on the east coast was going to do his virus little good. He had been conducting his prayer ceremonies in camp as normal, joining hands in a ring o' roses pattern with his trainers and conditioners and ballet instructors, only a chill had grabbed his chest and watered his eyes and his nose was sniffling a bit in front of the few reporters who made the trip to see him.

The whispers didn't reach the sports desks. Don King was still going strong, ranting about the unification of 'WBA-land' with 'IBF-world' and 'Planet-WBC', as though he were some kind of UN ambassador on a humanitarian mission to bring gods of war to the table together.

The tour of the big American cities had come to a close, with both Holyfield and Lewis stepping out of their meek and measured reputations and taking no prisoners in their verbal hostilities. Lewis had considered it an appropriate time to call Holyfield 'a hypocrite' again, citing his adversary's refusal to obey all Ten Commandments and refrain from committing adultery. Children born to Holyfield out of wedlock seemed to be popping up everywhere, and not for the first time. Holyfield's first wife had suffered the same experience as his current spouse, Janice Itson.

'He doesn't practise what he preaches,' Lewis had said. 'The man is a hypocrite. I don't mean anything by it, I just speak reality. That's what he is.'

Holyfield had not denied that his sleeping habits were anything but restrained, and announced that he would rather fall on his own sword than be damned by another man. 'We all sin at times,' he said. 'Let me be hung by my own words. [My marriage is] going through problems. I ain't never said I don't make mistakes.'

But Holyfield also broke away from his usually reserved attitude by taking a leaf from Muhammad Ali's book and predicting the round in which he would defeat his adversary. 'I hold to the truth,' he said. 'I believe by faith and not by sight. What I said, and I'll say it again, don't mean I have any less respect for Lennox Lewis than I had for any of my other opponents. Everything good that they've said about Lennox in the past is true. As good and as strong and brave as he is, it won't make no difference. I will still win, and it won't take anything away from what he has. I said it'll happen in the third round, and I'm saying it again now. You can choose to talk about it now, or you can choose to talk about it after the fight, but that's the fact of the matter. I will beat Lennox Lewis in the third round.'

Holyfield enjoyed a degree of solitude and anonymity about his training camps, but Lewis was the more private of the two, opting for the serenity of the Pocono Mountains in Pennsylvania over the vibrancy of Big Bear, California, or the candy-coloured surroundings of Miami Beach. The resort was not far from where Tim Witherspoon and his gang had been before the Levi Billups fight. It was surrounded with greenery and hillsides and quaint little streams running alongside its crazy-golf courses. Inside the hotel were heated indoor pools and honeymoon suites with heart-shaped beds and champagne-filled jacuzzis.

I saw Frank Maloney returning from a jog, dressed in his pale-blue French Connection gear and back-to-front golf cap. The camper-van slowed down and I jumped out to greet Maloney before he reached the Brookdale entrance.

We had some time to wait before Lewis was even scheduled to begin his sparring for the day, so the two of us grabbed a cup of tea in a fast-food restaurant and sat by the window, watching men and women jogging through the hills around us. Maloney dunked his teabag with pale fingers and opened the tiny little plastic containers of UHT milk.

'Actually, the only thing that irritates Lennox is press guys,' he said.

'Really?'

'No, I'm just kidding, don't put that in your story,' he laughed. 'It's just that it bothers him having to do so much PR work. It's a necessary part of this business, but if he could do away with it, he would. He'd rather just fight and leave the talking to me and Emanuel and Panos.'

'But he must see the necessity of it all,' I replied. 'Does he ever look at the way people responded to Frank Bruno back home, and wish they felt the same way about him?'

'No, no,' he said. 'The people loved Bruno because he was a loser. The British love losers and Lennox doesn't want to be loved for that reason. Look at what's happening now to Chris Eubank. When he was winning they hated him, and now that he's losing the whole time he's become the greatest thing that's ever happened. It's the mentality we've got. We don't have the American attitude that winning is the be all and end all of everything. The people who used to go to Frank Bruno fights are different from the ones who go to watch Lennox. The Bruno fans say, "Let's go and have a jolly good weekend and a few drinks in Las Vegas." The Lewis fans go to see him win.'

An hour later I was in the gym, watching Lewis stick jabs into the face of a journeyman named Chocolate. Lewis bent his knees and speared with his jab. Chocolate kept his legs rigid and tried to parry the attack with his gloves.

In front of the ring, rows of seats had been filled with a group of kids from a local orphanage. Lewis was being watched by one of his assistants, Harold 'The Shadow' Knight, while Emanuel Steward was talking to his latest protégé, a Norwegian former hoodlum named Rune. 'If he doesn't end up in prison first, he might be going places,' said Steward of his Scandinavian student.

During the break, Lewis opened his mouth for water, his blue gumshield clacking open. His dreadlocks were wet and long, creeping onto his shoulders from under his headguard. He skipped in time to the garage beats on the stereo, as the DJ chanted, 'Hit him with a left, Lennox, hit him with a right . . . an uppercut. Good luck, Lennox.'

'Gold medal winner at the Olympics, two-time heavyweight champion, it don't mean nothing,' said Steward, the undisputed king of hired guns in heavyweight boxing. 'This is the fight which will give Lennox the credibility he needs. You're only judged by your performances against big-name fighters in this game. And by big-name fighters, I mean the fighters whom the public believe are good – whether they really are or not doesn't matter. This is the first time Lennox has fought against the fighter America looks upon as the best.'

Steward loved to talk, and he didn't pretend otherwise. Holyfield's man, Don Turner, often feigned boredom and disinterest when in fact he had an ego the size of Atlanta. Steward was hardly modest, but he wasn't pretentious with it. Beyond the small element of needle which now existed between the two rival champions, there was little love lost between Steward and the Holyfield camp either. Holyfield had always had a problem with trainers' inflated sense of worth, reminding people that 'these guys are only as good as the men in their corner', and he had a point. It didn't take a genius to get a result with Evander Holyfield.

The acrimonious feelings between Holyfield and Steward stemmed from the time the two had worked together for a pair of fights in 1993. In the second, Steward had trained Holyfield to avenge his defeat to Riddick Bowe, with the Real Deal winning a passionately fought decision to hand 'Big Daddy' his first loss. When Holyfield had signed to meet Michael Moorer five months later, Steward had expected a percentage and Holyfield wanted to pay him a fixed sum. Steward was out, and Don Turner was brought in.

Turner wasn't overly keen on Steward either. Steward had enjoyed a glittering reputation in boxing for almost two decades, having transformed the Kronk gym in Detroit into one of the world's most celebrated and successful production factories of world champions. Turner had remained obscure for years until he had been hired by Larry Holmes to work his corner against Holyfield in 1992. Holyfield's wins over Tyson, in particular the eleventh-round knockout in 1996, had sent Turner's rates of pay sky-high, but he was still somewhat suspicious and resentful, seeing as many critics thought his questionable input in the Holyfield corner for the Moorer effort was a fairer indication of his ability than the success against Tyson.

'He's been telling Evander that Lennox will hit him, and that when he hits Lennox back, Lennox'll fall,' said Steward in his typically offhand manner, as though the children were playing up again, and what the hell, he'd just have to put up with it. 'They've overplayed this win over Tyson so much, but I know that Evander always knew in the back of his mind that Mike Tyson was a little kid at heart, and that if he ever roughed him up, Mike would just fall apart.

'Regardless of whether he won some of those big fights of his or not, the real Evander Holyfield is not the one who dealt with Tyson so easily,' he said, as the green light flickered on in a corner of the ring, and Lewis resumed his melting of Chocolate. 'Holyfield took some tremendous blows to the head against Riddick Bowe, even in that second fight. Who has he really beaten? We've talked about Tyson. Michael Moorer the second time around? Michael didn't even wanna fight – he told me his shoulder was all messed up, but they wanted him to go through with the fight anyway, so he did just to show that he had some heart.'

I alluded to the contrasting mental make-up of Holyfield and Lewis. Both were ice to Mike Tyson's fire, but Holyfield was the archetypal warrior, while Lewis was a tactician sometimes gripped by indifference. I wondered if the Briton's nonchalance drove Steward insane in the gym, knowing he preferred gung-ho aggression to placidity. Still, he had worked with enough heavyweights to have experienced all kinds of conundrum, and I didn't imagine Lewis's strategic nuances were nearly as problematic for him to cope with as Moorer's sudden conversion from a light-heavyweight assassin to a reluctant heavyweight boxer, or indeed Oliver McCall's teary-eyed fits.

'It's Lennox's real nature to be analytical and conservative,' Steward sighed. 'He's done it so many times in his fights, especially when he fought Phil Jackson. He knocked Jackson down early and then let him into the fight because he wanted to wait until everything was perfect. He should have beaten Lionel Butler in a round, but it went five. People talk about the Tommy Morrison fight being one of his best performances, but Morrison was finished by the second round and Lennox let it go to seven.'

'Winning at all costs is what counts the most,' said Maloney later on. 'If you're in a scrappy fight and win on points, that's fine by me. Winning is what people remember in this game. Maybe Lennox has got to look good in this fight with Holyfield, because if he just nicks it they'll say he struggled to beat a shot fighter. It's a sad position for him to be in.'

Lewis finished sparring and listened to Steward as his trainer removed the wraps from his hands. He smiled occasionally, his head bobbing up and down as he did so, his braided hair rocking in time with his laughter.

Outside, a light sprinkling of snow fell upon the pinewood forest. The sparring partners (Chocolate, Sajid Aziz, and a muscular Jamaican named Everton who had played the part of Holyfield in the HBO feature film *Don King: Only in America*, a movie based on Jack Newfield's biography of the Don) did their press-ups and drank water.

The quality sparring came from Maurice 'Mo Bettah' Harris and Jeremy Williams. Harris, a former drug-dealer from the streets of Newark, was lithe and mobile and superbly skilled. Williams, once a 'can't miss' prospect, was shorter and harder-hitting. Harris gave Lewis movement and skill, Williams tried to knock him down, slam-dunking him with some judo moves. Lewis had responded by hammering Williams in the balls and then hitting him on top of the head, and by the end of the afternoon Williams's eye was bruised and swollen.

'There's always a problem getting quality sparring for Lennox,' said his assistant, Harold Knight. 'Harris and Williams are the best. We asked Monte Barrett to come down but he wasn't interested, and Darroll only lasted two days.'

I smiled to myself. Both Barrett and Darroll Wilson had talked a lot about their prowess in the training camps of top fighters. Tyson had once wanted Barrett for sparring, too, but King and Horne and Holloway had prevented the hired help from bringing their own trainers and Barrett had refused.

'I had Riddick Bowe out twice,' Wilson had once told me. 'I'd love to fight him if he ever comes back. Lennox Lewis? I love sparring with Lennox. I like wiping that pretty little English accent of his off his lips.'

Another member of the Lewis camp had a moral dilemma when it came to scouting for more sparring talent. Iran Barkley, the bloated middleweight who belonged on Jack's 'Funeral Expense' squad, was desperate to earn some blood money. 'And he would have done it, too,' said the aide. 'He'd have given it his all. He wouldn't have quit, even if half his face was hanging off, because he needs the money to feed his kids. Honestly, there isn't a sweeter family man in boxing than Iran, but what was I supposed to do? Get him into camp to get beaten to hell by Lennox, or tell him I couldn't help put food on his table?'

Several hours later, when the darkness had fallen and Lewis had rested, his conditioner, Courtney Shand, drove me to a complex of cabins where the British fighter was staying. When we reached the champion's quarters, Shand knocked on the door and ushered me in. Lewis sat on a sofa and played chess with one of his friends.

Behind them was a king-size double bed. A fuzzy television screen displayed a kung-fu movie, but neither man was paying any attention. Lewis was in a fresh tracksuit with an FCUK ski hat on his head, pondering a move, pushing a pawn forward and signalling to his pal that the game had to wait a while.

He stood up and shook my hand, his dreadlocks bobbing around him. They reminded me of the beaded hairstyle favoured by the Predator during his jungle encounter with Arnold Schwarzenegger. Courtney disappeared and joined a friend next door.

Lewis gave me one of his sardonic smiles when I told him Maloney had said he was tired of meeting the press. 'Just another tribulation I have to go through,' he said, and offered me some gum. 'Sometimes I think they don't appreciate me because I won't dress up in a skirt like Frank Bruno did. I'm real, I'm me. I do things the way I want to do them, without making me look bad.'

I asked him if that was a criticism of Bruno, but he shook his head. 'No, it's just that Bruno does that because he's a lesbian.'

I looked at him uncertainly, and started to move on, but he suddenly jerked forward and looked at my tape-recorder. 'No, *thespian*, really – I meant to say I'm not a thespian!'

His friend guffawed, but Lewis looked passingly embarrassed. 'Really,' he said. 'I really meant to say "thespian". He's a thespian, and I'm not. I won't dress up in a skirt. I just won't do that kind of thing. People say that I'm pretty good at acting, though, but funnily enough I prefer to be behind the camera rather than in front of it. I like to orchestrate and set things up the way I want them to be. I just did some filming for the *Fantasy Island* TV series in Hawaii, and they gave me the best part in the script.'

He waited for me to take the bait, and I did. 'What was that, Lennox?'

'I played me,' he said, and laughed. 'I played myself!'

I didn't see myself as some kind of psychologist trying to smash his way through the exterior of Lewis's aloof persona, but I didn't think he was as devoid of personality or wit as his critics had described. I found him amusing and witty. He certainly wasn't dull, it was just that he looked at the crap going on around him and kept his tongue firmly in cheek, and saw little use in besmirching an opponent's reputation, or molesting a woman in a hotel room, or telling reporters to fuck themselves and their mothers.

If the American media were honest about it, they'd have admitted they loved the fact that Lewis had called into question Holyfield's moral integrity. They *oohed* and *aahed* about it, but they loved it. This was what they wanted. Lewis stirring it up. Lewis getting down and mean and nasty.

'This is not the Lennox Lewis of old!' King had bellowed at me. 'This is a new Lennox Lewis!'

'He's just a down-to-earth person,' Maloney had said between sips of weak tea. 'He just doesn't want to be seen collapsing outside nightclubs with a bottle of champagne in one hand and a beautiful blonde on the other. I honestly believe that when Lennox retires, he'll just want to disappear from the limelight.'

'Don King's saying you're a new Lennox Lewis,' I said, rolling the gum in my mouth. 'Holyfield's said he's going to knock you out whether he looks bad or not. Turner's said you'll be tough until you get hit, and that then you'll hit the canvas.'

'Have I got under their skin?' he asked me, his eyebrows leaping, as though this were all news to him. 'That's good if I have, but I didn't set out to do it intentionally. I just speak reality. Basically, my impression of Holyfield has remained the same ever since this fight was made. He's always struck me as a confident, arrogant, nice, religious, doesn't-practise-what-he-preaches kind of guy. I think that the things they've been saying about me are just all part of the normal hype you get in a big fight. I don't know why some people find me so offensive and criticise me the way they do, though. It makes me feel under-appreciated, the things the public and media sometimes say, but what Holyfield and other fighters say about me is all part of this game – all part of the politricks. Some people think I've got this snotty attitude, but I just don't know where they get that idea from. I suppose it's to do with my quiet confidence, but I'm just not loud and flamboyant like those other guys want to be. That's just not me.'

'And yet, your lack of loudness and flamboyance makes your detractors doubt your heart and your bravery,' I said.

'Sure,' he shrugged, reclining on the sofa and opening his eyes even wider. 'So I could be this warrior like Evander Holyfield, who gets his reputation by taking all those shots and getting into wars. But you know what, this sport is a game of intelligence to me, not a chance to show how brave I am by sticking my head into someone else's fists. In ten, twenty years' time, I'll still be able to know where I am when I get up in the morning.'

While the two fighters' definition of boxing was somewhat different, both Lewis and Holyfield shared the same theory when it came to the liberties taken by promoters. In the 1980s, the likes of Pinklon Thomas, Tim Witherspoon and Mike Tyson had naïvely assumed that the money would never end and that the political machinations were completely beyond their reach. Holyfield and Lewis, ten years on, both believed that they could control – to some extent – how much slack the puppet masters were given with their strings.

'I realise you're going to be used a certain amount in this business, but I've cut it down as much as possible,' said Lewis. 'I've got as much control of my career as I possibly could have. I've always tried not to be a pawn in this game – in the greater sense, I've always wanted to be a player. I'm in a game, and I'm in a game which has promoters like Don King, who will always want a bit of you and a bit of your opponent. They hold so many of the cards, but it's important sometimes not to take all this too seriously.'

The kung-fu movie crackled in the background, and the friend gazed at the two of us. Earlier in the day, American reporters had sniffled and sneezed their way through a Q&A session with Lewis, but no one had seemed very concerned about the fighter catching a cold. I wondered if he had heard the rumours about Holyfield catching the flu, but after blowing my own nose, I thought it prudent not to remind him of the possibility of such a thing happening to him.

'The Americans will always question me,' he said resignedly. 'But like I've said, I'd rather fight clever and keep my brain than fight brave and not be able to speak properly. I answer my critics in the ring. I would hope that by beating Evander Holyfield I will have answered all of the questions about me. I know that this is the most important fight of my career. This is a man in front of me whom I need to beat, and I know he's going to give me a certain challenge which I need to overcome. Perhaps I'll get the proper respect afterwards. You never know how you're going to be depicted, but I would hope that I'm paid respect after this win. Many boxers step into the ring, but there can only be one king.'

'There can only be one king?' I repeated. 'Is that your catchphrase for this fight?'

'That's right,' said Lewis. 'Only one king.'

'Because before the Shannon Briggs fight, it was "In a room full of men, I will be the last one standing".'

'And "I'm in it to win it"!' Lewis added with a chuckle. 'That applies to every fight, especially this one.'

★

The final week before the fight was chaotic and badly organised, and the media were growing fed up with being treated like naughty children by the PR whizzkids with the bouffant hairdos. Holyfield was scheduled to give a workout before the press at the Church Street gym near the World Trade Center but arrived late and opted to loosen up behind closed doors.

'This is takin' fuckin' forever!' protested a British reporter. 'Hurry up, or by the time we get in to see 'im he'll have had a few more kids!'

Two days before the fight, all of the fighters on the card gathered at the Garden's theatre arena for a final conference and the weigh-in for the main event. Don King held court and warbled on about each and every indivi- dual on the dais. Lewis and Holyfield sat smiling on opposite sides of the stage, the WBC champion in another FCUK number and a floppy felt hat, Holyfield in a dark-grey Nehru suit.

The next morning I made the mistake of joining a friend and some of his mates from the office for a 'quick pint' at an Irish bar next to the Garden. The undercard boxers weren't due to step onto the scales until later that afternoon, and, seeing as the lads had flown in for just four days, it seemed impolite not to see them for at least a couple of drinks before their return to rainy old England.

I wasn't going to the fight. It pissed me off too much to see good writers and committed sports journalists getting shoved to the very back of a massive arena like the Garden so that showbiz commentators who probably thought Tyson was still world champion could sit alongside Nicole Kidman and Catherine Zeta-Jones in the front-row seats.

No, as big as this fight was, I was happy to buy myself a takeaway dinner from the Thai Café in Brooklyn and watch the HBO broadcast alongside friends and family. I wouldn't have to sit behind some dollybird's seven-storey hairdo, I wouldn't have to listen to reporters with personal vendettas talk shit throughout the preliminaries, and I wouldn't have to watch various contingents of the 'Barmy Army' spread their buttock cheeks for the TV cameras.

'Still, you're a boxing writer, it seems crazy you won't be there,' said one of the lads, wiping the foam from his Guinness off his lips.

'I hope we can see what the fuck's going on in the ring,' said another.

'If I hear another flamin' Corrs song I'm leavin',' said the first one.

Someone bought a third round, as the waitress brought us plates of bangers and mash and chicken goujons and French fries with a variety of dips. The pub was dark and sweaty, and while it was decorated in green Christmas lights and plastic four-leaf clovers, and thick-set Irishmen pulled pints of creamy stout from brass pumps, the customers on this dank morning all wore Union Jack T-shirts and Lennox Lewis baseball hats, Kappa tracksuits and shirts with three lions on the breast.

The lads wanted to have a look at the undercard fighters weighing in. It didn't seem that great an idea until after the fifth round had been consumed. I was feeling a bit light-headed by now, and while the thought of bringing four beered-up Brits into a domain where I felt I had some kind of professional purpose would fill me with dread in a state of sobriety, right now getting them into the Garden and past the old codgers on the door seemed like a perfectly splendid idea.

I led Alex and the others through the staff entrance, but the three mates were halted by an elderly guard whom I had 'befriended' over the week.

'It's all right, they're with me,' I somehow managed to sputter, and to my astonishment the sentry reacted as though I were the President of the United States himself.

Upstairs, and inside the core of the Garden, I showed Alex where they should all sit themselves and returned a minute later with an armful of Diet Pepsi and bottled water in a vain effort to clear the fog from our heads and the sense of menace in our minds. We were all in high spirits by now, and this feeling of joy was only enhanced by the discovery that a Birmingham fighter with an unarguably spotty record was seated in the row before us alongside his wife and his trainer, Pat Cowdell. Howard Clarke was loving every minute of his stay in New York. With more losses than Barings Bank, and a career-high purse which may – *may* – have hit four figures, the Brummie light-middleweight had upset a favoured American in his last fight and was now being rewarded with a title challenge against the talented and unbeaten world champion, Fernando Vargas. Clarke, or 'Clarkey' as Alex and the lads decided to call him, couldn't stop smiling, sitting there in his leather Union Jack cap, his hair dyed gold, and the prospect of appearing on the same show as the undisputed heavyweight championship of the world.

Vargas sat at the other side of the room, wearing a baggy suit and spectacles which belied his viciousness, cradling his newborn baby in his arms. The baby's hair had been combed into the same style as his father's: shorn everywhere, save for a golden sprout of cockerel hair decorating his fringe.

When the two fighters stripped to their briefs and posed for the audience, all five of us went wild. 'Clarkey! Clarkey! Clarkey!' we all shouted. It didn't seem very professional on my part, and was to cause me a little embarrassment when I woke the next morning and reflected on the day's events through a dull, throbbing hangover. 'Clarkey! Clarkey!'

Vargas responded to our enthusiasm by cocking his head arrogantly towards us and cupping a hand around his ear. This incensed the others, who only chanted Clarke's name several decibels louder, and while I stopped my verbal volley of support for the doomed Midlander, I noticed rather sheepishly that my old pal the security guard was looking rather uncertainly in our direction.

Clarke and Cowdell, and particularly Mrs Clarke seemed delighted with this unexpected emergence of the Howard Clarke fan club, and I made myself feel a little better with my rather ill-conceived outburst of support for him by remembering that he had not a snowball's chance in hell of victory and that my sway from neutrality was hardly going to bother a young tiger like Vargas who had virtually ripped all fifteen of his previous opponents to shreds.

★

'It would have been better if he'd lost,' said Alex rather grumpily, sitting in his undeniably morose room in the Hotel Pennsylvania.

'Hotel Pennsylvania' was a rather grand-sounding name, and situated as it was directly opposite the Garden, you might have expected it to be quite an impressive establishment. Certainly it was formidable in size, but there it all ended, for the Pennsylvania was – and most likely still is – a monstrous creation perhaps only second to the Houston Metropolitan in my random search for America's grimmest of grim hostelries.

All of the undercard fighters had been booked in to the Pennsylvania, so for the passing fight fan – and there were thousands of them – the hotel lobby had turned into something of a convention for world champions and challengers.

Alex cracked open two cans of Miller and offered me one. 'You see, even if he'd lost, we'd at least have had something to really complain about. But we were all like, "That was it?" A bit fucking disappointing, really, and a long way to come for what was a pretty boring fight.'

'And what about the judges' decision?' I asked.

'To be honest, mate,' he replied miserably, 'we were fucking miles back. When it was all over, I had no idea who had won.'

The unification of the heavyweight championship had ended in a draw – in America of all places, where a result, one way or the other, was almost always guaranteed. The tabloid press, even the American tabloid press, had screamed 'Outrage' and 'Robbery' at their readers. Senate investigations were demanded, enquiries into the judges' backgrounds were ordered.

On the way to the ring, Lewis's flag-carrying escort had been challenged by a jobsworth suffering from brain drain. 'Fucking ridiculous,' snorted Alex, drinking his beer and shaking his head. 'Anyone seen with a Union Jack was told by the security guards to put it away, and if they refused, they were ejected from the arena. We were all treated like shit.'

But the HBO crew loved it, the atmosphere and the singing and taunting which the six thousand travelling 'Brits on the Piss' brought to the Garden. Holyfield had danced into the ring, his eyes closed, screaming his gospel songs in a kind of evangelical stupor.

'If Lennox Lewis had acted that way, he would have been put into a strait jacket,' commentator Larry Merchant would later say.

'You fat bastard! You fat bastard!' chanted the bellies in the bleachers, who then collectively enquired as to whether Don King had eaten all the pies. Before King had a chance to reply, it was unanimously decided that yes, indeed, he had eaten all the pies and that he was still very much a fat bastard.

From my view, seated in a Brooklyn apartment, with mad dogs running amok on the street outside, an irate fiancée cheering on Holyfield on one side of me, her brother shouting Lewis's name loudly on the other, the British fighter walked it. He jabbed and jabbed, fencing at Holyfield from long range and dropping in a right cross or a thunderous uppercut on occasion. At the end of the second round, Holyfield sat down in his corner and was heard clearly saying to his rather concerned trainers, 'This is it. He outta here, ain't gonna be no more rounds after this one.'

It was the third round, the round which God had apparently informed Holyfield that victory would be his. The American showed more aggression than he had displayed in the previous six minutes of combat, charging at a clearly pensive Lewis and eventually striking him with some powerful shots. Lewis was in a corner now, taking more than a few full-blooded whacks to the jaw, but the moment soon passed, and by the end of the round it was Holyfield's legs which were juddering under the impact of Lewis's blows.

The bell sounded, and Holyfield trudged forlornly back to his stool. Incredibly, it seemed as though he had not only placed complete confidence in the truth of God's 'message', but that he had no ulterior plan in case he and God had got their wires crossed. He sat slumped on his stool, demanded water be poured on the top of his head, and his trainers' faces soon betrayed clear signs of panic.

There were few highlights from then on, although Lewis hammered him in the fifth round and boxed with defensive expertise from then on. I gave Holyfield three rounds, and Lewis the remainder. I had seen numerous dodgy decisions during my short tenure in New York, but the outcome of this fight seemed about as clear cut as you could imagine.

Then the ring announcer, Jimmy Lennon, read the scorecards to the *glitterati* in the front rows and the pasty-faced Brits way up in the gods, and a stunned silence ensued. One of the judges, Eugenia Williams, gave it to Holyfield, 115–113. South Africa's Stanley Christodoulou had it for Lewis, 116–113. The first verdict seemed grotesque and even the second appeared to be too generous to Holyfield. Britain's Larry O'Connell had it 115–115. A draw.

There was a collective groan. Lewis looked as though someone had just tried to fool him into believing some kind of ludicrous fairy-tale, and Holyfield looked like he had been popped head-first into a cement mixer for half an hour.

'Did he even hit me with a jab?' asked Lewis.

'It's very simple,' said Holyfield. 'The people around the ring don't score the fight. The judges score the fight, and they scored it a draw. It's that simple.'

'We jus' gotta do it again!' bellowed King, and he was the only one smiling.

CHAPTER TWENTY-ONE

Incarceration

My two years in New York were nearly over. Somehow I had managed to find a one-way ticket to Heathrow for $150, and more and more of my time was being spent deciding exactly which paperbacks and drawers full of old magazines would be discarded and which would make it onto the flight back home.

Back in England, without buying an ugly dish with which to watch Sky Sports, I would be destined to tune into Shea Neary on ITV, delayed coverage of Southern Area super-bantamweight eliminators on BBC or topless transvestite wrestling on Channel 4. With the dish, I could watch Johnny Nelson lambast Benelux champions once a month but not Oscar De La Hoya v Felix Trinidad unless I was a 'Digital' customer. Oh, what joy to realise that some things about satellite TV in Britain never changed. The quality remained dire and on the odd occasion a jewel emerged from the dung pile the public had to fork out more cash to pay for an additional cable service.

No, every now and then, I had to admit, it was tempting to stay put in the States. And then it occurred to me how sad it would be to make such an important life decision – i.e. 'Where are my future wife and I going to spend our first married years together?' – solely based on whether or not I would be able to watch Bernard Hopkins v Antwun Echols on live television.

All of this questioning got me thinking about the decisions boxers made, especially those who had settled on choices which to an outsider seemed so clearly irrational. I wondered why some fighters – particularly heavyweights, and including numerous champions – risked it all for moments of complete insanity.

I was reminded of these bouts of madness shortly after the weekend of 20 March 1999. At the Emerald Queen Casino in Tacoma, Washington, just outside Seattle, a significant heavyweight double-header had taken place. In a rematch, Kirk Johnson and Alfred Cole had gone to war once again, and this time Johnson had deservedly won a decision.

The main event promised to be every bit as intriguing, with the elusive and intelligent Chris Byrd pitched in with the champion of heavyweight liabilities, Ike 'The President' Ibeabuchi. Byrd befuddled and confused Ibeabuchi for about three minutes before the muscular African had sat himself down on his stool at the end of the round and smiled a rather sadistic smile which said 'This guy can't hurt me one little bit'.

From then on, things became all very uncomfortable indeed for Byrd, who, despite his sharp reflexes and skills of evasion, simply could not stave off the relentless combinations coming his way. An enormous left uppercut eventually detonated on his jaw, sending him flopping to the canvas like a clubbed seal, and though he rose to his feet, slipped over again, stood up and sought to defend himself, the referee waved it all over with a second left in the fifth round.

The hulking Nigerian had surpassed Michael Grant's achievements and was now the most deserving contender to face the winner of the inevitable rematch between Holyfield and Lewis. Bearing in mind this plainly agreeable position in the world of heavyweight boxing, with the promise of millions of dollars heading for his bank account, and certainly not forgetting the fact that he had only twelve months earlier escaped a serious jail sentence for kidnap, you would have thought that Ike Ibeabuchi would have played it safe and refrained from any more of his disturbing behavioural outbursts.

One of Ibeabuchi's more harmless 'moments' had occurred a matter of hours before his showdown with Byrd. Byrd and his wife Tracy were taking a walk outside the Emerald Queen Casino when in the distance they noticed a lone figure staring up at the sky. It was Ibeabuchi, wearing a thick leather overcoat, cowboy boots and a heavy Stetson, apparently not bothered by the overwhelming heatwave which had earlier descended on the area.

I had heard a multitude of 'Ike stories', from the day he had been arrested for tearing off down the freeway with his ex-girlfriend's teenaged son in the back of a stolen car. Many of these would be best left untold; some, however, stand out, such as the occasion on which the fighter spent an entire day covering the windows and doors in his hotel room with masking tape in order to 'keep them out', Ibeabuchi's mother's insistence that he change hotels because someone had released 'demons' into the air-conditioning vents, and of an interesting shopping trip in Manhattan, which was recounted by an employee of Cedric Kushner's, Greg Juckett, to *The Ring* magazine.

It appeared that one afternoon in June 1999, Kushner had asked Juckett to 'babysit' Ibeabuchi for the day. Kushner had given three thousand dollars in cash to the fighter to spend in the New York shopping malls, and so the unlikely duo had traipsed from one store to another, until Ibeabuchi settled upon one particular clothes retailer and placed several jackets on the counter. When the shopping assistant had requested payment, Ibeabuchi asked Juckett if he could pay with a credit card. Juckett, perhaps with some doubts as to whether his head would remain attached to the rest of his body, had replied in the negative, and Ibeabuchi had responded simply by shrugging and departing quietly.

The following night, Ibeabuchi had sat at ringside in Madison Square Garden to watch Michael Grant batter Lou Savarese for a wide twelve-round decision, and then Lewis's sparring partner Maurice Harris slickly outbox the aggressive Jeremy Williams. The Harris v Williams fight had originally been intended to be Ibeabuchi v Williams, but Ibeabuchi had backed out after thumbing his nose at the $350,000 purse, and the fact that Grant was headlining in the main event when he felt it should have been him instead.

During a subsequent conversation with Larry Merchant, the HBO commentator revealed to me that he had personally telephoned Ibeabuchi on learning of the fighter's withdrawal to try to make him change his (unstable) mind. 'It's not something I usually do,' said Merchant, 'but I tried explaining to Ike that this was a perfect opportunity to steal the show – which he would have done – and put pressure on Grant or Lewis to fight him. I mean, he would have destroyed Williams in two or three rounds.'

Ibeabuchi paused for thought, and agreed that he would take the fight after all if Merchant could promise him $10 million for a fight with Lewis afterwards. Merchant wasn't too surprised by Ibeabuchi's demand, seeing as he had witnessed an even more extraordinary outburst during a previous meeting between HBO and Kushner. Kushner had thought it prudent to invite Ibeabuchi along for this power lunch, in an effort to impress HBO into signing the contender to an exclusive contract such as the one Grant enjoyed.

Ibeabuchi, not a standout in the field of diplomacy, had prodded a steak knife in the direction of all the bigwigs, and demanded that they stump up the cash right there and then for a $10 million showdown with Evander

Holyfield. After some polite coughing, it was pointed out rather delicately that $10 million was more than Lewis was being paid for fighting Holyfield, and that in any case Holyfield was Showtime's client, not HBO's. Needless to say, any plans to sign Ibeabuchi exclusively were put on hold.

All of which would have been pretty amusing, were it not for the fact that Ibeabuchi was arrested soon afterwards for sexually assaulting an escort girl called into his Las Vegas hotel room one night where he was staying as a guest of Don King. Bored and alone, Ibeabuchi had summoned the girl's services from his bedroom. On arrival, she had begun to perform a private lap-dance for the boxer, but his designs were obviously more far-reaching, and after a struggle which can only have been brief, given their relative sizes, the girl was pushed into a bathroom and assaulted. After the girl had made her escape, Ibeabuchi had barricaded himself into the room for as long as it took police officers to fire pepper spray under the door.

Ibeabuchi was brought to court for a preliminary hearing, where a judge set bail for a million dollars. Enraged, Ibeabuchi reportedly bit two police officers and hurled abuse at the magistrates. Soon after, it emerged that this had not been the first occasion on which allegations of sexual assault had been filed against him, only in the past the alleged victims had settled out of court.

I had met Ibeabuchi twice in the past and although he had neither throttled me nor claimed to be the reincarnation of a Prussian general from the Napoleonic wars, his grasp on reality at some stages seemed quite loose. In fact, so wired was the boxer that he really wasn't the perfect subject for the question I was asking myself – why did any fighter on the cusp of earning great riches choose to throw it all away in an act of grave stupidity? If you believed as I did that Ibeabuchi had great difficulty in distinguishing right from wrong, the answer in this case was that he never recognised the fact that he had made a choice in the first place. He just did what he did, and how dare anybody suggest that it was in any way improper?

Then there was Tyson, whose cringeworthy self-pity made him more embarrassing than intriguing to listen to these days. By now, Tyson languished in a Maryland prison cell, chucking television sets through windows after having his phone calls cut off by irate guards, but it still wasn't his fault he was behind bars again – no, somehow it was the fault of the two OAPs he had kneed in the groin for accidentally bumping into the back of his car one afternoon before his fight against Francois Botha.

And then there was Jo-El Scott, a heavyweight from Albany, upstate New York. In 1994 *The Ring* polled people involved in the sport to find out who they would most like to buy stock in. Oscar De La Hoya and Roy Jones came first and second respectively. Scott came third. One minute Scott was an undefeated, colourfully talented, exciting champion-to-be. The next, he was a cowardly, drunken, amoral felon who was convicted on numerous counts of statutory rape of girls as young as twelve years of age, and of reckless endangerment when he ran over an infant in a bid to escape police officers and failed to stop. The child was dragged for a hundred yards and suffered terrible facial injuries before becoming disentangled from the vehicle.

I didn't think that any of these actions should directly make boxing look bad, but the excuse-makers for the parties concerned did, especially those who sought to defend Ibeabuchi, who reasoned that the crime was less serious than it could have been because 'the girl in question worked for an escort service, and that speaks for itself'.

But the case which had seized my attention the most profoundly was that of Kassan Messiah, an angular heavyweight from New Jersey who had looked phenomenal in his first five pro fights under the alias Kassan Saxton, only to wind up serving a life sentence in a maximum-security prison for the contract killing of an insurance broker.

Why would a man commit a contract killing if it weren't for the fact that he needed the money? And why did Messiah, with the very real promise of making some serious money in boxing, opt to risk and ultimately lose it all, to murder another man for the mob?

It had all happened on 20 September 1994, when an insurance broker named Dennis Grasso was gunned down in the back room of his makeshift office in the upstate New York town of Dobbs Ferry. Any time the words 'New York' and 'homicide' were put together, images of graffiti-splattered Bronx subways and dingy Harlem back streets were conjured up, but Dobbs Ferry had more in common with a coastal village in Devon than with the tangle of metropolitan boroughs which stretched across the city they named twice. It was a million miles away from the skyscrapers and yellow cabs and demonstrators who besieged City Hall each week.

According to William Kane, Grasso's business partner and the sole witness to the crime, he and Grasso had been waiting for a business appointment between 7 and 7:15, when an unmasked man calmly stepped into their converted garage, demanded money with menaces, marched Grasso into another room, made him lie face down and then shot him dead. Having killed Grasso, the intruder then marched past Kane and out of the building altogether.

Almost three weeks later, Kassan Messiah was arrested at a rooming house in Ocean City, New Jersey. It took no time at all for him to be tried and convicted, even though so many of the witness's descriptions did not match. Messiah had won five fights in a row, four by knockout. He was already being touted in some quarters as a major prospect, and he had already experienced the result of living on the wrong side of the law, having spent nearly a decade in jail for manslaughter after a botched carjacking as a teenager.

The more I read about his case, on rolls of microfilm in small-town libraries, and from meeting his wife, Lorraine, in a bar in Newark, the more intrigued I became in Messiah's story. The biggest mystery to me was why a person should throw it all away by committing such a brutal act, though the fighter and his wife vehemently protested his innocence.

I made some light investigative enquiries by contacting the local police in Dobbs Ferry and the District Attorney from Westchester County who had prosecuted during Messiah's case, and if truth be told there was certainly the hint of something unsavoury going on behind the scenes. The first law officer at the scene of the crime could not be contacted, and the original statement given to him by Kane had gone missing very soon after Messiah's arrest.

Several black men had been seen acting strangely in Dobbs Ferry that day. It was a predominantly white neighbourhood, so African Americans were easily spotted. Messiah had claimed he was in Newark at the time of the assassination, but all of the people brought forward to legitimise his alibi were discovered either to have had criminal records of their own or relationships with people who had criminal records.

'In Kassan, they had somebody they could just get the case all wrapped up quickly with, because of his record. They figured they had their guy, because Kassan is basically a guy from the ghetto, whom they put in front of an all-white, middle-class, middle-aged jury. That's the way our judicial system works,' said Lorraine bitterly on the afternoon we met in Newark.

I had met Messiah in prison the week earlier. Green Haven Correctional Facility was a pretty intimidating sight to behold. After a forty-minute drive from the nearest train station, through the curves in the dark-green hills and past dense forestry, out into a clearing, I was greeted by a spectacularly monstrous flat stone structure. Several hundred yards long, its expanse interrupted only by a series of turrets equipped with searchlights and patrolling guards, it looked like a rebel base from *Star Wars*.

I signed myself in at a front desk, and produced my passport as identification. Two female guards, both bulkier than Bulgarian shot-putt champions, eyed me suspiciously and went through a painfully long list of items which were not permitted to be brought into the prison: cigarettes, glassware, firearms, home-baked cookies, fresh haddock, nibbed pens, cameras and hand-held recorders.

'You're not a reporter, are you?' one of them barked.

After convincing her I wasn't, I was led through an airport-style metal detector, had my hand stamped, and was then told to wait in front of the steel door before me. The door cranked open, my hand was checked under a fluorescent tube by another officer, and then once the steel barricade shut again, the next slowly grated open to allow me into the open air and towards another building.

The path led me from the outer perimeter and towards the visitors' block. Around me were walls topped with rolls of barbed wire. Another guard checked my papers before I was buzzed through into a long, gloomy corridor, which led into a canteen.

A feeling of claustrophobia clung to me. Though not overwhelmed by a sense of being physically threatened, I would perhaps have preferred that to the initial feeling of panic which threatened to grab me. The canteen reeked of solitude and despair and of sour, twisted regret, and this was with most of the inmates being surrounded by their family and loved ones.

I sat at an empty table and watched the prisoners hold hands with their wives and hug their children, and I wondered what kind of unspeakable acts some of them had committed to end up in a place like this.

Thirty minutes later, a gaunt figure appeared behind the guard's desk, and the guard pointed at me. Kassan Messiah was dressed in dark-green prison garb and black boots, and although he looked distinctly puzzled at this stranger who had come to visit him, he was happy to get a call from anyone who could make a brief change to his mundane routine.

For a man who claimed to have been wrongly incarcerated for almost five years, there was a remarkable sanity about Messiah. He spoke well and thought hard, and his mind had refused to dull and submit. The physical contrast with the way he had looked in his fighting days was striking, however. He had never been gargantuan like Lennox Lewis or Riddick Bowe; rather, he was from Evander Holyfield's mould – slight waist and broad shoulders which accentuated his statuesque, V-shaped upper body. Even so, his cheeks were now far shallower and his face sleek, as opposed to the healthier, toned features from five years before.

'The thing is, I watch what I eat,' he said. 'I go on fasts, not as a protest, but as a way of keeping myself strong mentally, like an act of self-discipline.'

'I can't record what you're saying because they wouldn't allow me to bring my tape-recorder in,' I said to him after a few minutes.

'You interested in writing about me?' he asked incredulously, ignoring what I had told him.

'Yeah, I've heard a lot about you,' I replied. 'I wanted to talk to you about where it all went wrong. Your old manager told me just to come straight here and see you.'

Messiah smiled widely, and asked me if I had a paper and a biro. I hadn't, because the shot-putters had taken them too, but he insisted he could work something out. He rose to his feet, talked to the guard on duty for a few seconds, and then reappeared by my side with an A4 pad and a blue Bic biro.

'You heard about my career?' he asked me delightedly. 'I've been count-ing every day as it goes by, thinking how much I'm missing out on the opportunity to resume my career. If I were released today, I'd go straight back to fighting. And if I'm released next year, I'll do the same thing. I'll keep on thinking about it until I'm physically unable to do so.'

'You just can't hold back time, though, can you?'

'No,' he replied, looking at his hands, the hands which a jury had decided had pulled the trigger and killed Dennis Grasso in cold blood. 'I know people say that being in prison can take a lot out of you, but I feel pre-served. I can still do it. I'm in the gym here every day. I've had fifty-eight amateur fights in prison, and I've won all of them.'

'Kevin Rooney said he used to bring some of his prospects here to spar with you.'

'That's right. He had a guy named Cisse Salif whom everyone thought was gonna be a bit special. I knocked him out twice, but they were only exhibition bouts. When I get outta here, I'll have to get together with someone like Kevin, someone who can generate some publicity, because I'm gonna have to be moved fast. Man, my pro career had only just started before all this happened. I was a thousand per cent confident in my ability to become champion of the world. I was confident that I could beat any-one, and I still am now. Ask any of the guys I've fought – they didn't wanna fight me, because they knew what was coming to them.'

Alone in his cell each night Messiah admitted that he pondered a clash with all the big names in the sport. To him, they were not imaginary matches, they were inevitable. Or so he prayed.

'Tyson and I would go to war, and it would be over early,' he said. 'We both have power, but I would out-think him. Lewis is bigger than me, but that would only make me more focused, keep on top of him, pressure him and concentrate on my accuracy. My dream was to fight Evander Holyfield, that would have been the ultimate fight for me. I would have knocked him out, too.'

'And now?'

'And now I look outside at what's happening, and I see my dream dwindling away.'

For a moment, I thought this was Messiah resigning himself to life behind bars – the sentence he was serving, and which would continue to run for as long as his succession of appeals continued to be dismissed with abandon – which didn't seem to go with his otherwise optimistic attitude.

'I'm talkin' about it slipping away because I don't think Holyfield's gonna be the man when I get outta here,' Messiah said. 'We ain't allowed to get pay-per-view in here, but we're allowed video tapes, and anyway, my wife said he got his butt kicked already by Lennox Lewis!'

We talked about life in prison, of the razor blades being smuggled in after being inserted into anuses, and of the three murders which had been committed behind the jail walls since his current prison term. Messiah talked about what could have happened that September night in Dobbs Ferry, his feeling that he had been set up by a pair of mysterious acquaintances, the volumes of law books he had been studying in order to build up knowledge and establish further grounds on which to appeal, even if the state-appointed lawyers who were supposed to be working for him were unfalteringly ineffective.

After an hour, he suggested we wandered around the outdoor exercise yard, where loved ones cuddled and groped on the grass, posed for Polaroid pictures, wept into each others' cheeks and stared vacantly at the hills which peered teasingly beyond the barbed-wire enclosures and watchtowers.

I had heard a story from one source that said if an inmate were popular, a crowd of his fellow jailbirds would form a cordon around him and his visiting partner in the courtyard so that the two could copulate without being seen. But this had little to do with Messiah's legal predicament or his boxing career, and even if I had wanted to verify this little vignette he would probably have been unimpressed about being asked. Still, it was a pretty dire future the man faced, and I wanted to know if, deep down, he accepted how crazy it would have been to trash a career which quite possibly could have paid him an assassin's fee several times over.

'It would have been a dumb choice to make, wouldn't it?'

'How do you mean?' Messiah replied, and stopped halfway around the yard, out of earshot of the guards, visitors or other prisoners.

'You were a professional fighter,' I continued. 'If you had accepted the job as a hitman – for what, a few thousand dollars? – you would have been pretty dumb to have accepted it. You were going somewhere with boxing, and now you're here and life doesn't look quite so exciting.'

'You're right,' he said. 'It would have been a dumb choice. A very dumb choice. But the mystery remains for me. I didn't do it. I don't know who did it, and I don't really care any more. But, come on, why would I use a car which I knew was registered under my mother-in-law's name? Why would I let a witness see my face, and then let him live?'

I remembered speaking to Messiah's former manager, Alan Gelb. 'Alan,' Messiah had protested down the telephone, on being granted his phone call after his arrest. 'If it had been me, the other guy would never have lived.'

Our time was up. Two hours had elapsed, and we shook hands. 'When I see you again,' Messiah said, 'you'll be watching me from ringside.'

I waited an hour for a taxi to come and collect me from Green Haven. The driver was the same woman who had taken me there from the train station. She was as friendly and chatty on this trip as she had been on the first one, and she happily stopped off at a gas station *en route* so that I could buy a paper and a drink for the journey back to New York.

'So what was he like?' she asked, looking at me through her rearview mirror, as the wagon bumped and rolled along a stony lane and past log cabins selling fishing equipment and coal.

'He was candid, an interesting guy,' I said.

'Did he do it?' she asked.

I shrugged. 'I don't know, I really don't. I suppose if I was forced to say, I'd guess he didn't pull the trigger but that he was involved somehow. But it wasn't really my intention to establish guilt or innocence. I just wanted to talk to him about his hopes and dreams – a different perspective on the world of heavyweight boxing.'

'And it's a crazy world, too, huh?' she said enthusiastically. 'What with Mike Tyson biting that guy's ear off and Muhammad Ali not being able to speak properly.'

'I guess so,' I said, feeling the tiredness creep into my eyes.

'My nephew's in jail, too,' she said.

'And what did he do?'

'Well, he didn't do anything, and that's the truth. He really is innocent.'

'So what didn't he do?' I persisted, though I rather wished I hadn't.

'He and a friend robbed a church one day,' she replied. 'Then the friend told my nephew to wait outside for a minute. The next day, they were both arrested. The friend had gone back into the church and strangled a nun.'

CHAPTER TWENTY-TWO

Hard Truths

The chill factor was growing steadily as New Yorkers rushed about the city during their lunch hour. Traffic cops tugged collars closely around their necks, delivery men held bags of sandwiches and steaming beakers of coffee guardedly to their chests, and rollerbladers navigated the roads with scarves wrapped snugly across their frosting lips.

In a café on Colombus Circle and 45th Street, Stan Hoffman stirred his tea and contemplated one of the most starkly profound aspects of his 'business'. He had been a boxing manager for almost twenty years, having made his money in the rock-music industry. He was now looking after Hasim Rahman's career, after yet more noises from the fighter himself that his displeasure towards his previous management was enticing him back in the direction of Don King.

Hoffman had started dealing with fighters in 1980, guiding the careers of a light-welterweight named Joe Louis Manley, and a promising heavyweight, James Broad. Manley won a world title, lost it to British fireman Terry Marsh inside a circus tent in Basildon, and now made good money in insurance broking. Broad lived up to his surname and ate himself out of title contention. Bloated by a voracious appetite for alcohol as well as food, he now struggled to survive with a debilitating liver disorder.

And so to the dilemma. In this painful, beautiful sport, this cruel business of prize-fighting where the noble trod alongside the wretched and where the best were so frequently stalled in their progress to reach the top, how did someone keep his or her personal feelings separate from their professional ones? In this sport, where the majority of its participants, officials and all other extravagantly colourful characters knew each other more than fleetingly, and where one man could be legally maimed or destroyed by another, how did the players keep their emotions in check?

'I can only answer that question by giving examples,' said Hoffman, pressing the flavour out of his teabag with a spoon, and scratching at his white, straggly beard. 'Hasim is fighting Oleg Maskaev on Saturday night. Maskaev and I have been really friendly together for years now. He trains at Gleason's, and I've been in and out of there all my life. I've seen his little daughter grow up, and I count his trainer, Bob Jackson, as a very close and dear friend of mine. But all of that has nothing to do with anything. From the moment you sign to make a fight, the other guy becomes the enemy. We are all in the business of boxing. If my son is on the other side of the ring, my fighter must still beat him. I love my son to death, but if he's on the other side of the ring, I will do everything that I can to make sure my guy beats him. That's how seriously this business has to be taken.'

'It's interesting that you're going straight into this bout with Maskaev,' I said, 'rather than spoon-feeding Hasim for a couple of fights as you get to know him better.'

'I realise that, but this fight's gonna move us up considerably,' said Hoffman. 'I've been pressuring the IBF but as usual they're vacillating. If they move Rahman up afterwards they're worried they'll get sued by David Tua's people, and if they don't move him up, they'd better start getting worried about being sued by me!'

'As if they didn't have enough problems of their own, poor things,' I added sarcastically, because the IBF were now under investigation by the FBI, and Bob Lee and his allegedly cocaine-snorting cohorts were none too pleased at having their accounts and annual reports under close scrutiny. Yes, the Bureau had fucked up in trying to nail King and his empire not once, not twice, but three times, but with this lesser opponent they looked as though they were heading towards a successful prosecution at last.

All three of the world's major governing bodies – the WBC, WBA and IBF – were widely believed to be corrupt, it was just that the IBF were easier targets because they were the only ones based on US territory. There was also the none too small matter of Lee and several of his lieutenants being caught on tape admitting to selling high rankings for fighters in return for bulky brown envelopes at conventions in exotic locations such as Aruba, Bangkok and San Diego, as well as the unwittingly taped confessions that Thanksgiving Day presents from 'Fuzzy' (Don King) and 'The Fat Man' (Cedric Kushner) had arrived in the post.

I arranged to meet HBO's Lou Di Bella in his disarmingly informal office in the Grace building, just off Times Square. A lot of people in boxing couldn't have cared two hoots about allegations of corruption and organisational malpractice, but Di Bella (official title, senior vice-president of sports; real title, most powerful money-man in boxing) cared a great deal.

'This is a corrupt, sick sport,' he said disdainfully, as the telephone rang by his side persistently. 'This is a sport governed by people who are looking for the betterment of themselves, rather than for the betterment of the sport. The way fighters are ranked? It's a joke. This fight – Rahman v Maskaev – is a quality heavyweight fight. I can't tell you what the clown organisations are going to do with the winner, but I can say that whoever it is will be on my radar screen as far as a title shot is concerned.'

'But you've had your fair share of headaches with Rahman in the past,' I said. 'He's pulled out of fights after letting Don King whisper in his ear, then there were back injuries, then . . .'

'Sure, but these really aren't the biggest headaches I have to deal with,' said Di Bella. 'I don't think you can get a much more competitive match than this one on Saturday night. This kind of fight emphasises once again what I've been trying to do at HBO for some time now – which is to de-emphasise to the fighters the need to wear these belts given to them by a tinpot organisation. I do not require that a fighter wears one of those plastic belts in order to get an HBO fight.'

'Which is a shame,' I suggested, 'because the sport's history is intrinsically linked to the wearing of belts.'

'Well, we are in the business here at HBO of major events and major entertainment. That means major fights, entertaining fights. Our priority is not to establish the belts as something that is important in this day and age, and the organisations are the only ones to blame for that.'

Thirty minutes later, our conversation came to an end. 'By the way,' said Di Bella, shuffling through the piles of paper around his sofa. 'I think there's gonna be an upset on Saturday night.'

★

There were three days to go. I was back in my favourite place in the world, Atlantic City. The fighters had arrived on the Tuesday, Maskaev driving in from Staten Island, Rahman catching a flight from Baltimore after having trained in Phoenix for six weeks.

Maskaev, a big Russian, whose head, Larry Merchant said, reminded him of a horse, was usually to be seen wandering around with his chain-smoking manager, and the rotund and pleasant-mannered Bob Jackson. The three of them sported navy shellsuits advertising the manager's pick-up truck firm, but other than that their presence was low-key. Maskaev was shy and for the most part uncommunicative, owing to a lack of confidence in his stumbling English, but the manager, Steve Trunov, was quite witty, if also lacking in grammatical prowess.

'He vill vin easily,' Trunov said to me, between gasps for breath, after stubbing out his fifth cigarillo of the morning. 'Oleg Mash-ka-ev will be revelation Saturday night.' He looked and sounded like a James Bond villain.

Rahman and his team came striding into the press-room on the Wednesday afternoon, and the fighter greeted me with another drawling 'Dom-in-ique', one hand shaking mine, the other clasping me tightly on the shoulder.

'How you been, Dom-in-ique?'

'Good, thanks,' I said. 'How about you?'

'Great, I'm just great,' he replied, pulling his leather jacket off and sitting at a table behind me, alongside his younger brother Ibn, who was barely out of his teenage years and looked big enough to knock down buildings.

'So here's another chance for you to show who's the best prospect in the world,' I said.

'Best *contender*,' he corrected me. 'But you're right – ain't no one gonna remember David Tua after they see what I do on Saturday against Maskaev.'

'But he's a tough, durable guy,' I said, 'and he gave Tua hell a couple of years ago. You really think you can look that good against him?'

'Sure! Why – what do you think?'

'I think you'll win, but I think it'll be hard and gruelling, and it'll probably go into the late rounds.'

'We'll see,' said Rahman.

'You're in for a surprise,' Ibn said to me. 'Are you gonna be at the fight?'

'I will be.'

'Then I wanna see you straight afterwards and hear what you have to say then.'

'Yeah, you can come to the post-fight party and we'll speak again, Dom-in-ique!' Rahman said happily.

'So you think there'll be no problems?' I asked.

'No problems,' said Rahman. 'Actually, maybe one problem. And that'll be when I have to hold all my people back and say, "Whoah, there now, everyone, stand back and let the man count to ten first," then y'all can come and celebrate with me.'

'That's pretty cocky. Are you sure you're not underestimating him?'

'I don't underestimate anybody.'

'Yet you've already described Maskaev's style as –'

'Horizontal.'

'Exactly.'

'And my style's vertical.'

'You should be in comedy,' I said.

'I don't underestimate Maskaev at all,' Rahman insisted. 'But you should have seen me in training camp. I've been sparring better than ever before. I've been sharpening up on some things which a lot of people don't even believe I can do.'

'Such as?'

'No, no, Dom-in-ique. You wait and see on Saturday night. How long you say it's gonna go?'

'Eight rounds.'

'Eight rounds?' Rahman said, arching his eyebrows and smirking. 'We'll see.'

'You can't knock him out in a round,' I said.

'We'll see,' Rahman repeated.

I checked myself into a ground-floor room at Bally's, who were hosting the show, unpacked my luggage and showered. The itinerary for the week included press conferences, weigh-ins, medicals and HBO one-on-one interviews with the four main event fighters – Rahman, Maskaev, Lennox Lewis's sparring partner Maurice Harris, and a six-foot-six slugger from Detroit named Derrick Jefferson.

Atlantic City was still horrible but the hotel rooms along the boardwalk were blessedly comfortable and inexpensive. If you were really hard up you could stay in one of the motels further inland for about twenty-five dollars a night, but being somewhat old-fashioned, I liked to sleep easy, knowing I had a reasonable chance of waking up in the morning to discover that a) my room had not been burgled, b) I had running water in the bathroom, and c) I had woken up in the morning.

Still, even though my room was spacious and relaxing, the water scaldingly hot and the giant TV set capable of transmitting over a hundred channels, it had also become Dullsville after a couple of hours, and so I decided to wander about thirty feet across the casino floor to the bar. I joined Stan Hoffman, Chuck McGregor and Steve Nelson for a glass of orange juice.

Hoffman kept referring to the shady characters he could call on if someone ever stepped on his toes, Chuck spoke confidently of a Rahman victory on Saturday night, and Nelson talked about a former fighter of his getting caught in bed with a state trooper's wife, and of the time he unwittingly chatted up George Best's fiancée at Annabel's on a trip to London.

Rahman, Ibn and their father joined us after twenty minutes, and all three, devout Muslims that they were, ordered fruit juices.

On the surface, Rahman's family and management team dealt with each other civilly, but there was an undercurrent of distrust between some of them, and I guessed that had he been forced into admitting it, Rahman himself would have owned up to some discord.

I sat opposite Rahman, his brother and father flanking him, both taking a deep interest in the questions I was about to ask him.

'You've got your family around you more than you ever have done in the past,' I said.

'And who says that can't be so?' Rahman asked, defensively.

'Not me,' I said.

'Sometimes the people who can give you the best career advice are the ones who have been around you all your life,' the fighter added.

'So you've seen what happened to so many of the others in the past?'

'I've seen what's happened.'

'So how much control do you have over your own destiny, compared to them?'

'I have much more say than they ever did,' said Rahman, clasping his hands together and looking at me still a little bit suspiciously. 'The money is even greater now than when they were fighting. I believe that many of today's fighters have learned from their mistakes. This is not a twenty-year business, so a fighter needs to do the right things with his money as soon as he gets into this sport.'

'And what are they?'

'You take what you have, and you spend it accordingly,' Rahman drawled. 'You realise that it's not gonna be coming in twenty years from now. Don't go out there and live a lifestyle you can't keep up.'

'And so you've made preparations for the day when boxing's all over for you?'

'Definitely. I've always had a plan. Insh'allah, I've been blessed to go about doing things the way I should. I'm surrounded by people with good educational backgrounds advising me, and I believe I'm in good hands.'

I thought about Rahman's admission earlier in the year that $30 million would always be preferable to a world title, and I thought of Lennox Lewis smiling benignly as he contemplated the furore which surrounded his championship fight with Holyfield.

'Lennox Lewis says it's important not to always be so serious about this sport. Is it possible to take this all too seriously?'

'I would say that if boxing was all a fighter based his life on, then that would be dangerous,' said Rahman. 'Like everyone else, though, he has to show dedication to his job. But this is not a sport to me. This is a business, it's a job, and I deal with it accordingly. Boxing doesn't come first in my life – it comes a distant third after my religion and my family – but I have to perform well at work in order to provide for my family and take care of my children.'

'Stan says there's no problem keeping the personal side of it all separate from the business. Is that the same way for you?'

'While I'm in the ring, I'm trying to win the fight,' said Rahman, hunched over now and challenging me with his eyes to test him. He was not only sensitive to the allusion that his family was not equipped to take a role in his career, but also to the prejudice held by some that a boxer could not conduct a conversation which demanded little more than an analysis of what he would like to do to each prospective opponent. 'I mean, I'll try my hardest to knock the guy out as early as possible and so put us both at the least risk possible. When the fight's over, that's it. You don't have to be my enemy. If he hurts me, I won't hold it against him. What happens in the fight happens. But when that last round's over, it's all finished.

'I believe that no matter what I tell you, Allah, God, already has a plan for this fight. I believe that Maskaev and I are just gonna go in there and go through the motions – whatever they may be. If it is meant for me to lose this fight, then I will lose this fight, but I truly believe that I cannot lose.'

'Are you going as far as saying that God will side with one fighter against another?'

'I wouldn't say that Allah would side with me. I don't know that, and besides I can't say what Allah is gonna do. I do believe that Allah will be with me when I'm fighting, and that gives me strength right there. I'm not trying to turn this all into some kind of side-show like some fighters do, or claim that I speak to God, or that God's told me I'm never gonna lose. All I'm saying is that I pray for Allah to watch over me, and I believe he does.'

We talked for almost two hours that evening, and even though I still felt that Rahman was made of championship material, I felt I had to challenge the three of them on their sincere belief that Maskaev would be easily dismissed, and that 'The Rock' was already proven as Lewis's most dangerous challenger in the world. Soon though, we all tired of the verbal jousting and decided it was time to head back to our respective rooms.

Rahman smiled broadly and said, 'All the things I heard before getting into professional boxing have turned out to be true. This is the only sport where the lions are afraid of the rats.'

The following morning, I joined him in the health spa, as he and his father cruised through some sit-ups, while Chuck kept a fairly cursory count as he talked about his upbringing in Chicago. Chuck's father had promoted wrestlers, including 'Gorgeous George' – the man whose schtick was copied by a young Cassius Clay. Chuck had joined the Chicago police force and served for nine years before the death of his parents, a messy divorce and a battle with the drink sent him packing to Phoenix, where he had trained fighters ever since.

Chuck tucked a cap firmly over his short curls of greying hair, and rested a friendly hand on my shoulder while the Rahmans sweated and complained in the background.

'I can't stop, Chuck, I can't stop!' yelped Rahman, pushing himself faster and faster through the exercise.

'People are always asking me how fighters today compare with those from the past, and it's very simple,' Chuck began to explain. 'Today's athletes are bigger, stronger, faster and technically better, but one thing they don't have is the mental strength, because the rewards come too quickly for them.

'When I was growing up, I spent a lot of time in the Chicago gyms with men who would complete twelve-hour shifts at the steel-mills, shower and change, take the hour-long bus trip to the gym, work out, shower again, and then go home for their dinner. That's how dedicated and proud they were. That way of life would be unthinkable for most fighters today.'

By midday, the principal parties had all converged on a conference room. The fighters, the managers, the commissioners and the hotel reps were all dressed in their smartest outfits as they took it in turn to address their audience of scribes and TV executives.

It was clear that Rahman was seen to be the favourite in the main event. The press credentials issued advertised both his and Maskaev's names, but carried the image of the American fighter only. Kushner, who promoted both the muscular man from Baltimore and the heavy-jawed Russian, perhaps unintentionally let slip his alignment when he announced that after the fight Rahman would emerge as the best young heavyweight in the world.

Maskaev spoke stiltedly about his self-belief, his new-found faith in Jesus and thanked all the right people before resuming his seat.

'Vee have vot vee vont,' rasped Trunov. 'Zees is going to be like Shtalingrad in 1942 – no prisoners taken. Oleg Maskaev is going to surprise you all. Sorry my English. Thank you.'

Trunov sat down, sounding very much like a man in need of some fresh air. Maskaev's trainer, Jackson, enjoyed his two minutes in front of a microphone, and said it was no wonder he and Kushner were never invited to the same party together.

Rahman seemed relaxed and assured when it was his turn, but his final statement declared a belief that the Russians had seriously underestimated him, which Trunov interpreted as a strange thing for a supposed favourite to profess, remarking to me later that day, 'He fucking scared to fucking death . . .'

It was the usual mundane entertainment at boxing press conferences, but a moment of flickering sensitivity went by generally unnoticed. As the two fighters were pulled together for publicity shots, Maskaev smiled resignedly and whispered to his opponent, 'It's nothing personal, you know?'

Rahman looked momentarily embarrassed, smiled ruefully and glanced down at the floor. 'No, man,' he said softly, 'we just gotta do what we gotta do.'

★

Anyone who has been to Atlantic City will know that most of the hotels provide two different kinds of dining experience. Most guests choose the filthy canteen where you pay $12.95 to eat as much as you can bear; these are normally given absurdly misleading titles like 'The Sultan's Banqueting Room' or 'The King's Festival Hall'. Alternatively, there are the five-star dining-rooms which list *filet mignon*, lobster terrine and roast goose with a plum-and-armagnac sauce on their menu. Unfortunately, a meal at one of the latter establishments will set you back considerably more than $12.95.

On the evening of the press conference, I ventured out onto the bitterly cold boardwalk, paid for a Big Mac and fries from the nearest McDonald's, took this dubious meal back to the comfort of my hotel room, and soon after felt sick. Thankfully, I recovered in time to pay the Rahmans a visit in their suite on the fourteenth floor of the Bally's Tower. The three of them were relaxing, playing cards and brushing up on their Arabic.

The patriarch of the family produced some sheets of paper, held his arm across the English translations and asked Hasim to pronounce each of the Arabic words, with Ibn looking on approvingly. Rahman recited the words 'Messenger', 'Greatest' and 'Prophet' in the language of his faith.

Ibn and their father corrected him occasionally, congratulated him occasionally. The father had become a Muslim when Hasim had already completed his education, and so back when Hasim was starting out in an amateur boxing programme, Ibn was sent to a seminary in Canada to study Islamic philosophy and read the Qur'an.

Seldom in the past had Rahman alluded to his religious beliefs. In fact, on the only occasion I had brought it up – during our second meeting, in Houston – he had stared at me with a rather uncomfortable, deadpan expression on his face which led me to believe he would prefer to talk about something else. Now, over two years later, Islam had become his priority in life.

I asked them all about how they felt towards Western – particularly American – attitudes towards Islam, and though Ibn and his father were the most vociferous in their views, Hasim was also forthright and opinionated. 'Most people's view of Islam is ignorant,' he protested. 'The media create stereotypes and the public believe them. To most people, there is no difference between Elijah Muhammad, Malcolm X and Louis Farrakhan . . . to the average person, they're all the same, and that's plain ignorance. Religion defines people, not the other way around. When you hear of a bomb going off in the Middle East, or an aeroplane being hijacked, you hear, "The Muslims did this." But when a crime is committed by a white American or a British person, do they describe them first as Christians?'

'Fair enough,' I said.

The wave of heart-felt sentiment was now coming from all directions as Ibn and their father highlighted more perceived hypocrisies and double standards. 'What is your religion?' the father asked me.

'Catholic.'

'Well, please don't take offence to this . . .'

'Go on.'

'When you hear about Catholicism, you are not constantly reminded of priests abusing children.'

'I don't know about here, but there have been a few cases in Britain recently when the tabloid press hounded some priests about those kinds of things.'

'Well, over here, the press highlight what they want their readers to believe, and talking about abuse in the Catholic Church is not one of those things. Look, I accept that Catholicism does not promote child abuse, but why can't people see that Islam does not promote terrorism?'

'I suppose you've got too many prominent Muslims committing actions which haven't exactly endeared them to the Western press,' I replied.

'Like?'

'Like Colonel Qadaffi, Saddam Hussein . . .'

'Actions define a Muslim,' said Rahman, shaking his head. 'Colonel Qadaffi, among most Muslims, would not be considered a good Muslim. Look at David Koresh – did you look up to him as a good Christian?'

'Point taken,' I agreed. 'So who are the good ambassadors for Islam that you look up to? Muhammad Ali?'

'I really can't speak much for Muhammad Ali, because I really haven't studied too much about what he has done for Islam,' replied Rahman. 'I would say in sports, it would have to be Hakeem Olajuwon, because he looks after his community and conducts himself in the correct manner.'

'And maybe one day you'll be able to stand beside him in a similar manner,' I suggested.

Rahman liked the idea. He nodded thoughtfully and rubbed his chin with the palm of a hand. 'Like I said, Islam is my priority in life right now. Islam, my family and my community.'

'I have a girlfriend back in London who has studied Arabic and Islam,' I mentioned off-hand.

'I thought you said you were married,' interrupted Rahman's father.

'I am. She's a girl, and she's a friend. She's a girlfriend.'

'You can't say that kind of thing in America unless you mean she's your mistress.'

'But you can in England.'

'Where are we now?'

'America.'

'Exactly. When in America . . .'

'What are you first – an American or a Muslim?' I asked.

'A Muslim, of course,' said the father. 'And if you want to know why, you can come and see for yourself tomorrow morning.'

'We're going to the Masjid at eleven o'clock,' said Rahman. 'Come with us. It won't be an intrusion. You can come along and see for yourself.'

★

The next morning, I met the Rahmans in their hotel room again, and waited while a crowd of worshippers in skullcaps and long white shirts gathered by the door and talked to the fighter. Among them was a squat, bearded man with a receding hairline and stumpy legs.

Dwight Muhammad Qawi had reigned as both light-heavyweight and cruiserweight champion of the world, and during his time had fought Michael Spinks, Evander Holyfield and George Foreman. He had been called Dwight Braxton before converting to Islam while in jail and then hammering another Muslim, Matthew Saad Muhammad, for the WBC light-heavyweight crown in 1981.

'My comeback's over,' he muttered in disgust and to no one in particular. 'They robbed me again, so that's it. I'm tired of this crap, man. I was hoping to get one last big fight and then they go and treat me like that. I've been in this game for too long to have people take advantage of me like that.'

'What kind of big fight were you hoping for?' I asked, anticipating his response would be another one of the macabre 'Seniors Tour'-type bouts, which were cropping up everywhere.

'One of the big two, man: Lennox or Holyfield. They're the only guys who can get me motivated now.'

I looked at Qawi and it was all I could do not to shake my head in disbelief. The thing was, no fighter from yesteryear I had ever come across, ever truly believed that it was all over. Beneath the diplomatic resignation which had followed his loss to Shannon Briggs in 1997, George Foreman still claimed the champions were too scared to fight him. Larry Holmes had told me that Lewis had admitted to him in person that he would never manage to get past the Holmes left jab.

'Maybe he was trying to humour you, Larry,' I had suggested.

'Well, that's a helluva way to try and humour a man who was world heavyweight champion for seven years,' Holmes had sniffed.

But at least Foreman and Holmes had proved that they were partially equipped to give a good account of themselves as they approached their fiftieth birthdays. Qawi, however, was small and rotund; he'd never been a natural heavyweight; he had been smashed to defeat in the fourth round of his rematch with Holyfield in 1988; and in his last fight he had been outboxed by a lardy boy from Chicago named Tony La Rosa who was routinely butchered each time he stepped up in class to fight even the over-the-hill likes of Buster Douglas and Razor Ruddock.

We drove to the end of Atlantic Avenue to the local mosque – a tatty old building with tarnished brickwork and unwashed windows. Rahman and his entourage led the way inside, removed their shoes and sat down in prayer as the resident Imam exhorted Islamic values into a microphone.

Initially, the proprietors were none too happy with the presence of a non-believer, but after receiving several distinctly uncertain and unhappy glances from some of the congregation, I was allowed to watch and listen from the sidelines, alongside a Jewish photographer who felt twice as uncomfortable, I'm sure, as the majority did of our close proximity to them.

Hasim and Ibn sat cross-legged at the back of the room on a dark, tired carpet and facing the corner where the Imam, in a flowing white robe, conducted what sounded to me more like a spiritual rally than the peaceful country church sermons I was used to listening to at Easter and during Midnight Mass.

Most of the congregation were of Asian or Middle East extraction, and none recognised the well-built black American or his family and companions as being part of the heavyweight carnival about to commence the following evening.

There was fire in the Imam's voice, but thankfully he contained it enough not to whip his audience into a frenzy. Instead, Rahman and his fellow believers nodded their heads in understanding, listened intently and on occasion rose to their feet without any urging and made brief prayers with hands cupped open.

Did they marry their wives for their beauty, their money, their family status or for their religion, the Imam wanted to know.

'When you leave your house and go to work each day, does your best friend come knocking at your door? And if he does, does your wife tell him that you are not at home? Then, does she ask him in for a cup of tea? A cup of tea! No, this is not the Islamic way. The men stay with the men, and the women stay with the women. But do not be mistaken. A Muslim who treats his wife in a manner that says he is the boss and he can do with her as he pleases, because the Qur'an says so, is not a Muslim. This is not the Muslim way.'

The Imam was unrelenting, unyielding. He barely paused for breath, and he always sounded angry.

'Do you bring your child up to be an American or a Muslim?' he asked. 'Do you call him Mikey and let him close the door to his bedroom without interrupting him and asking him why? He says he wants his privacy, and so you agree, and then one day you do go into his room, and he is sitting beside some joints rolled up on his table! Is this the right way? This is not the Muslim way.'

An hour later, the Rahmans decided it was time to leave for the HBO one-on-one interviews back at Bally's. Rahman was not bothered about their punctuality, tired as he was of the growing sense that professional boxers now had to pander to the cable channel's every whim.

'That thing about Larry Merchant calling Ike Ibeabuchi at his home, there's no way he should be able to do that. It's none of his business.'

'Just to make a call?'

'HBO don't make calls like that. They should go through the manager or the promoter first,' said Rahman emphatically. 'He calls my home like that – *bing* – I slam the receiver down. "Sorry, what's that you say, Larry? No, can't hear you. Oh, hang on there a moment . . . *bing!*" An' I hang up. That's it.'

'Well, don't go telling him I told you that during your post-fight interview. You might get HBO pissed off with me and it won't help my work much . . .'

'Oh, don't you worry – their bans don't last long,' laughed Rahman. 'How many times has Di Bella banned me now? Two, three times? They always come back to you in the end, when they need you.'

By the time we returned to the hotel, the rest of Rahman's family had arrived. More brothers – all of whom looked perfectly capable of taking on Maskaev themselves – cousins, sisters-in-law, and Rahman's wife Crystal, and their son Little Rock.

After the interviews, all the fighters congregated in the conference room for the weigh-in, and, more importantly (because heavyweight weigh-ins were just cosmetic affairs, designed to entertain the media as much as anything else) the obligatory examinations by the local physician.

Crystal was young and elegant, sitting between her in-laws while her husband stripped to his shorts and had his pulse and heart rate taken by the doctor. Maskaev wandered past her with a colleague but she did not turn around, nor look away from where her husband was standing.

I approached Rahman after he had come off the scales. The time was closing in now. There were no nerves nor any clear signs of stress, but the expression in his eyes had become more concentrated, and all of the fighters were growing quiet and remote.

'I wanted to ask your wife a question,' I said.

He frowned and glared at me uncertainly. 'Why's that?'

'Just wanted to ask her how she feels at this stage of the week.'

'I don't know about that,' he said pessimistically. 'No, you don't need to speak to my wife. You can ask me how she feels right now.'

'Not quite the same, though, is it?'

'I've never let any reporter speak to my wife. It's like the man said this morning – the men stick with the men, the women stick with the women.

You can ask my brother or my father any questions you like, but my wife has to be left alone.'

★

There is often something bewildering and sickening and uniquely stimulating about a fight. I felt it now, only two hours before Rahman and Maskaev were expected to start raining blows on each other, as I sat inside the convention centre and shivered in the cold.

The Latinos had an expression for a knockout, which when translated meant 'the little death'. I thought they could take that one step further – a loss of any kind in professional boxing was like a little death. So much was on the line when a fighter entered the ring. Defeat could set him back for years. He couldn't look forward to a quick second chance at the same opponent, as a player on the tennis tour or a football team in the Premier League might be able to do.

The technicians were still laying reams of cable around the ring. The lights were being tested, releasing beams through purple, red, green and blue filters. The arena was cold. Outside, the flat, dark expanse of the Atlantic looked ghostly and forbidding.

At the back of the hall, two paramedics sat purposefully beside a stretcher and resuscitation unit. The preliminaries began, and the seats started to fill. The suave VIPs and their artificially enhanced dates made their grand arrivals. Rival heavyweight contenders turned up with their wives or their posses, seeking to study and analyse and pose. Journalists wandered down from the press-room with their laptops and cans of Coke.

A four-round fighter was beaten badly, his eyes forced into a deathly vacuum, his lips smudged a bloody orange as though he had been sucking on an ice-lolly. The tension was rising. The pit of my stomach had begun to churn softly, the eager anticipation curdled by a nagging sense of nausea.

In a divided locker-room deep in the bowels of the convention centre, Rahman sat by a table, waiting for the time to dress for war, pushing Marvin Gaye cassettes into a small stereo system and chatting aimlessly with a hot-shot lighter weight contender and the contender's pals.

Behind them all stood Nelson and Chuck, leaning against a wall quietly. Hoffman was there, too, decked out in black garb, looking like some kind of Transylvanian gargoyle. Two burly commissioners with bald heads and bored expressions stood by, insuring no foul play was committed along the lines of horseshoes in gloves or needles in arms.

'Where's Winky?' I asked Ibn.

'Winky's not welcome any more,' came the reply. 'The drinking, the gambling, the fighting. It was no good for Hasim to be surrounded by that. That's what Dad and I are here for now, to keep Hasim surrounded by the right people. Winky wasn't a Muslim.'

'So you've got to be Muslim to be with Hasim now?'

'No, you don't have to be,' said Ibn, 'but it helps.'

A camera crew wandered in and asked all non-participants to leave the room while they did some filming. Rahman undressed and started to shadow-box for the camera, but the hot-shot and his friends were reluctant to leave their seats and, on being prodded in the back by the white commissioner, their tempers boiled.

'Get the fuck off me, man. Yo', get ya fuckin' hands off me, man!'

'C'mon, bro,' said the black official calmly, 'you know better than that.'

Somewhat placated, the youths started to trudge out of the locker-room, with Rahman throwing uppercuts and jabs at the air, and Crystal standing nervously outside the door, biting her nails and staring at her husband.

'Are you his wife?' asked the official, as the youths disappeared, calling out warnings that he would one day get his 'fuckin' jaw broke'.

Crystal nodded, but declined the man's offer for her to come inside the locker-room and wait. She kept staring at her husband. She said, unconvincingly, that she was fine.

Behind a curtain Maurice Harris donned a scarlet-and-blue robe after receiving the call for him to come to the ring. I wondered how similar the feelings were between a fighter called to the ring and those of a dead man walking.

I squeezed back into the locker-room, where the recording of Rahman's warm-ups had ended, and where the fighter himself now stood stoically in the middle of the room, in his shorts and boots, gazing impassively at his reflection in the mirror at the other end of the room. He seemed oblivious to the rest of us. The waiting time was nearly over, but his own thoughts and fears cocooned him now.

Obed Sullivan slapped my shoulder, and then wished his old adversary luck. I told him I thought this was gracious of him, but he smiled and confided that deep down he did not care who won or lost that night, and that he had wished the same fortune for Maskaev, that he had told Maskaev only a minute beforehand to target Rahman's body for that was Rahman's weakness.

'Goodbye, Hasim,' I said quietly, shaking his ungloved right hand. He looked at me and there was the faintest sign of a nod. 'I hope God sees you both through this safely,' I added, but he had gone away again, staring at himself, or through himself, and I doubted he could hear any sound at all.

★

Harris v Jefferson was dazzlingly exciting and shockingly brutal. From the comfort of a living-room sofa, and through the medium of television, boxing was considerably sanitised. In the flesh, it was uncompromising, a warped mixture of finesse and savage artistry.

'I'm prepared to do whatever it takes to win,' Derrick Jefferson had told me two weeks earlier. 'I'm prepared to die if I have to.'

'If that's what it takes,' Maurice Harris had concurred. 'There's nowhere else for me to go in this life. This is the only thing I know.'

The two of them knocked each other down a total of five times, blasting each other into states of virtual unconsciousness, and they bled so profusely that some of the ringside photographers looked as though someone had brushed paint across their foreheads. In the sixth round, Harris was poleaxed by a blindly thrown left hook. He tried to regain his feet, but the muscles in his neck heaved violently as he tried to raise his head and the referee rescued him from what may well have been a killer blow.

Jefferson was interviewed, the TV executives slapped each other with tacky high-fives, and Harris was carted off to God only knew where, as Russian folk music filled the arena and Maskaev appeared in the ring in a midnight-blue robe.

When Rahman finally appeared at the back of the arena, he stood still, held his arms out before him, smiling to himself as the *thump-thump-crash* of 'We Will Rock You' started up again. He marched to the ring in time to the music and skipped close past the poker-faced Maskaev after climbing through the ropes. In the distance, I watched Little Rock jump up and down excitedly, and I watched the haze veil Crystal's face.

The fight was earnest and gruelling. Both men jabbed hard and frequently, and while the Russian was the more limited of the two, his face was a picture of patience. Rahman wanted the spectacular knockout – he had said as much to me in the bar a few nights earlier – but he was having difficulty connecting cleanly and early with his bombing right hand.

Maskaev stalked persistently and fired classic one-two combinations. It was nothing fancy, but his rhythm was offsetting Rahman's attacks and Rahman was sweeping out and missing, and he was getting caught with counter blows.

We were already into the third round, and so far there had been no signs of Rahman's much-vaunted improvement. Both men were beginning to suffer, clubbed as they were by each other's weapons of choice – Maskaev, the jab and the hook; Rahman, the too often nullified right hand.

A grey bruise spread like an amoeba across Maskaev's cheekbone and right eye, and Rahman's lower lip was slashed, blood dribbling onto the pale blue canvas.

The crowd screamed out their support and advice for both men, but it was only Maskaev who was paying close attention to the people who mattered – his cornermen. Every three minutes, the two fighters threw themselves down upon their stools and gazed at each other through the water which fell from the sponges being squeezed above their heads.

The skills, the movement and the natural flair of each man was being steadily ground out of him, and the fight was becoming a battle of attrition. Any fancy work was over. It was now down to who hit the other more often and who could stand up to the punishment longer – the very basest instinct of what it meant to be a successful prize-fighter.

A right hand punctured Maskaev's defences at the end of the seventh round but the Russian was unperturbed, and I sensed gloomily that Rahman's confidence was sagging. He was caught against the ropes at the start of the eighth, beaten ferociously about the body and head. His legs dipped as he leant back and then propelled himself forward in an attempt to try and grab his tormentor around the waist. The crowd rose to their feet.

Rahman was turned and pursued into another set of ropes, his mouth agape. Maskaev's features had been battered and worn, too, and the judges had Rahman marginally in front. Rahman still wanted the knockout, and so he dipped his shoulders, preparing to launch the right hand again. Maskaev anticipated the move and strode in quickly with a booming right of his own. The combination of the Russian's shot and Rahman's advance with a strike of his own produced terrible results for Rahman. The Russian's right hand landed flush, forcing a sickening vertical sway of his opponent's head. Rahman crumbled and fell, his body sent through the ropes so that he struck the ground surrounding the ring head first. His legs followed, dragging a computer down with them, which furthered his trauma by landing on his knees. Rahman was out cold for several seconds as the doctor and the commentators rushed to his aid. His eyes turned white and then a glimmer of consciousness returned.

The referee counted above him. The boxer had twenty seconds – given the circumstances – to regain his feet and get back into the ring, but the doctor was having none of it. Chaos broke out. A chair was flung from several rows back and landed squarely on the back of a ringside official's head. Fights broke out, punches were thrown, jackets were ripped. Wide-eyed innocents darted for cover as wannabe gangstas surged forward, fooling bystanders with cries of 'Security! Security!'.

Rahman's family charged forward in a desperate bid to be by his side as he was tended to by the medics, but they were confronted by a confused pack of hired muscle in yellow T-shirts who tried to repel them. I watched Ibn leap over two rows of seats to get to his brother, and I stood on my seat to catch a better view of Rahman through the mayhem, wondering in horror whether his neck had been broken by his fall upon the concrete. Then I thought of Crystal and Little Rock, but they were lost in the sea of violence before me.

It was ugly and it was compelling. The rioting took about ten minutes to quell, and when it was over I was relieved to see Rahman rise to his feet and cautiously climb back into the ring to await the official announcement that he had lost by eighth-round knockout. He looked dismayed – angry even. Dreams had been broken and recriminations would follow, I was sure. For Hasim Rahman, the hard work would have to begin all over again. The aura of invincibility – only partially threatened by the controversial loss to David Tua – was gone. He would have to battle now to remain a contender, as another loss would take him not just further away from world championships and that $30 million purse, but into the realms of the journeyman, the opponent.

Thirty minutes later, he was back in his changing-room, surrounded by his buddies who kept smacking him on the back, telling him it was no big deal, that he would be right back in the picture in no time at all. Rahman wasn't buying it. He quietly told Hoffman that he had made mistakes in training and that he had deserved this rude awakening. He had taken Maskaev lightly.

'I never thought this would ever happen to me,' he said when the noise had died down. 'I never believed that this would happen to me. I thought I could never be knocked out. Please, I need some time to myself. I need to think about things. I need some space.'

Gradually the room cleared until only Hasim, his family and Hoffman remained. 'I'll call you when I get back home,' Rahman said to Hoffman. 'We'll talk more then.' And then Hoffman departed too.

It was approaching 2 a.m. and the convention centre had almost emptied. Rahman showered and changed, his body sore and bruised, his lips torn and crusting. The exhaustion crept into his limbs, but his head pounded more with the disappointment of defeat.

With his wife and young son, he stepped out into the misty early-morning air beside the main entrance to Bally's and asked an attendant to bring him his vehicle. Little Rock sat in the back, and Crystal sat by his side as Rahman drove all the way back to Baltimore, talking and thinking the whole way there, and wondering where this painful but addictive business of his was going to take them all.

CHAPTER TWENTY-THREE

A Place in History

A week after Rahman's defeat to Oleg Maskaev, Lennox Lewis won the undisputed heavyweight championship of the world by earning a decision over Evander Holyfield at the Mandalay Bay Casino in Las Vegas.

Holyfield raised his game and Lewis took more risks. The combination made for a better fight than their first duel at Madison Square Garden eight months previously, and Lewis was a worthy winner. Even so, Holyfield's improvements flattered to deceive and there were some who considered the result as much of a travesty as the one before. Whether you believed this was the case or not, most felt the two men were both weary old war-horses by now and vulnerable to the challenges of the young heavyweights around the corner.

All this made it somewhat surprising when Lewis opted to defend his unified crown for the first time against an undefeated, well-regarded contender like Michael Grant, rather than John Ruiz, a moderate boxer with unspectacular credentials. Still, as had been documented countless times in the past, modest credentials were certainly no major hindrance if you were a heavyweight promoted by Don King. And so it was that Ruiz was not only the premier contender in the myopic eyes of the WBC, but also the WBA, after their previous mandatory candidate Henry Akinwande once again tested positive for hepatitis B.

The WBC announced that they were prepared to give Lewis some leeway and allow him to take on Grant before Ruiz was accommodated. King took his case to a court in Philadelphia, which decided that Lewis should be stripped of the WBA belt for not honouring a written agreement prior to the Holyfield rematch that whoever won would take on the WBA's number-one contender next.

Lewis pre-empted the WBA and relinquished their title, and King quickly made plans for a June date between Ruiz and Holyfield for the 'vacant' WBA championship. Despite this puerile performance, it was clear that much of the WBA's power — as well as that of the other sanctioning bodies — was seeping through their fingers with each and every nonsensical twist and turn they made.

Lewis was urged by many quarters to free himself of all title belts and simply defend what most of the world recognised as being the 'real' heavy-weight championship. He refrained, and went into the Madison Square Garden arena on 29 April with the WBC, IBF and more recently formed IBO belts as proof — as if it were needed — that Grant was challenging the legitimate king of the jungle.

I flew from Gatwick to Newark airport three nights before the title fight. HBO were hyping the show with the label 'Too Big', as though the combined height and weight of both men contributed in any way to the notion that it was going to be a great fight. Giant posters of Lewis and Grant standing with fists cocked against the Manhattan skyline while lightning bolts zigzagged behind them greeted commuters as they exited the Lincoln tunnel, walked through Times Square and headed for the Garden.

I thought Grant was going to win. On his best day, Lewis was in my opinion the most outstanding heavyweight since a twenty-year-old Mike Tyson; but the champion seemed too cocksure about Grant's inexperience and supposed lack of natural ability, and I felt that Grant had the kind of style which would have enabled him to walk Lewis down with a relentless jab, take him into the late rounds, test his stamina severely and ultimately stop the champion with a few minutes left to go.

I wanted to be wrong. I liked both men a great deal, but whereas Grant had so often been lavished with undue praise for mediocre performances, Lewis had consistently been chastised no matter what the outcome of his contests by the vitriolic tabloids.

Even so, I made a strange prediction which came true two nights before the Lewis v Grant fight, and it made me even more certain that my analysis was going to be proven correct. Lewis's old opponent Shannon Briggs was hoping for another quick, meaningless win at the Hammerstein Ballrooms in midtown Manhattan on the Thursday night, against a small heavyweight named Sedreck Fields. Fields had nine wins and nine losses, and had been hammered in his previous fight by Maskaev. He had won a couple of marking-time contests in Belgium and France shortly beforehand, but each time he had stepped up the level of opponent he faced, he normally lost a lopsided decision. That's what Briggs and his handlers must have felt.

I suspected otherwise. All of Fields's defeats had come against reasonable opposition, and only twice had he been stopped inside the distance – once against Maskaev, who was no mug by any stretch of the imagination, and once early in his carer, a fate which befalls many fighters before they work out whether this is the kind of business they truly want to be in.

Also, Fields was considered to have some kind of worth by those in the know, because he had frequently been employed by Holyfield as a sparring partner, and on the night he and Briggs fought, the journeyman had Holyfield's trainer Don Turner assisting in his corner as a short-notice favour.

Briggs turned up looking like an electric-blue warlock, bullied Fields for a round or two and then got himself left-hooked all the way to a points loss which sent him as far away from the world championship orbit as possible – and probably heading towards the WBA's next mandatory position, knowing how insanely their rankings system worked.

The Hammerstein show was another of Cedric Kushner's *Heavyweight Explosion* cards, part of a new monthly format which also incorporated loud rap music, dancing girls of such dubious appearance that one reporter questioned whether they were Ru Paul's sisters, and an excruciating female MC, who wandered around the place asking people if they were having a good time, and could they 'give it up' for a motley collection of B-list celebrities. It was sordid but healthy fun, and as about as far removed from political correctness as anyone in New York dared to venture.

It had been almost nine months since I had last seen Monte Barrett, but I couldn't miss him at the Hammerstein, wandering around in a tracksuit as fiercely red as a Grenadier's tunic, some huge logo scrawled across the front, and a beanie hat on his head. He was on his mobile phone as the result of the Briggs fight was announced, pacing beside the iron rails which separated the press from the crowds at ringside. The MC was imploring the audience to sing along to the rap music, and the dancers were squeezing baby lotion over their bodies. A six-foot-six-inch white girl clambered into the ring and smacked about a black girl who was half her size. Some girls in Everlast T-shirts and cycling shorts performed a synchronised dance routine.

'This isn't crazy,' sighed a man to my right.

A Golden Gloves champion amateurishly clobbered a Cuban exile for a few rounds, and neither looked more embarrassingly inept than the other.

'Now we know,' said Jack Obermayer, seated to my left, 'Golden Gloves fighters can't fight any more. Look at what boxing is coming to.'

I was too busy reading a local newspaper story on Jack to see what he was referring to. 'There's no money in boxing writing,' he had told the reporter. 'This is a labour of love.' I read on. 'You haven't made it in this business until Jack gives you a nickname,' Nigel Collins of *The Ring* had informed the paper.

'Hey, Jack,' I said. 'You've never given me a nickname.'

'Oh,' said Jack. 'You're the "Fresh-Faced White Boy!"'

★

I was back where I had started. Gleason's Gym. Before I wandered across the street to watch Barrett train, I grabbed a coffee at a diner, where the case of Elian Gonzales was being discussed on the radio while two over-weight cops played 'Maximum Force' on an old arcade machine, pumping imaginary bullets not only into the masked terrorists, but also the graphic images of their female hostages.

A lot had gone on during the intervening years. There was no Russian entourage at Gleason's this time, but one of the young kids who had watched their champion work out that blistering summer's day was now champion of the world himself, while his father had been brought on board to strengthen Barrett's coaching team.

It was late, and Zab and Yoel Judah stood perched next to one of the rings as Barrett thudded his hands into pads and then performed tiny smile-shaped patterns as he bobbed from under one side of a piece of string to another, his hands making little circular movements against the sides of his face as he did so, as though he were scrubbing his chin with a flannel.

Yoel was a former kickboxing champion who looked about fifteen years younger than he actually was. Zab was the finest fighter of his seven sons, and now held the IBF light-welterweight title. As youngsters, the Judah brothers had all strained to get into the gym. Yoel had made them work hard at school, and rewarded them with further work with the boxing gloves. Bad grades meant no trip to the gym. It was a father's way of keeping his children's options open if the violence of boxing soon ground the dreams out of them.

Shortly after I had last seen Barrett, he had lost for the first time. I had seen the fight on video, but it had not left me with the same hollow feeling as Rahman's loss to Maskaev had done. Rahman's defeat had been absolute and momentarily terrifying. There was enough of a margin of error about Barrett's decision loss to Lance 'Mount' Whitaker not to feel that his career was over.

When their fight had been signed I had considered Whitaker to be the perfect foil for Barrett's slick skills and mobility. I had always considered Whitaker to be a big, lumbering ox with little finesse and even less originality. But, after a sprightly start, Barrett had run out of gas by the fifth round and his blows were bouncing harmlessly off Whitaker's forehead whenever they connected. Barrett had swept the opening four rounds, Whitaker the next four. It was a twelve-round fight for something called the WBC Continental Americas title, which Barrett was defending. The next couple of rounds were evenly contested, then Barrett's work-rate accelerated and he seemed to have grabbed victory at the last moment.

The tide changed again while the remaining seconds dwindled, and with them Barrett's hopes seemed to evaporate. Whitaker poured on the aggression and Barrett gave ground, and then a second or two before the bell, Whitaker cracked him with a huge overhand right which sliced a vertical cut down the centre of Barrett's forehead and sent him skipping, semi-conscious, into his corner. The bell rang. I had it even, but the biggest highlight of the fight had been captured by Whitaker.

One of the judges gave it to Barrett, but the other two thought Whitaker had done enough, and Barrett had lost.

A week later I called Barrett's manager, Joe De Guardia. 'He's a little depressed right now,' said De Guardia. 'It could have gone either way, but he's upset with himself for not doing as well as he knows he could have done.'

I left it a few days before I rang Barrett. 'I was my own worst enemy,' he said. 'This won't affect me at all.'

But what about his firmly held belief that he could never lose? I didn't want to put it to him in a way which would have sounded cocky or condescending, but so strongly had he once insisted that defeat was unthinkable that I wondered whether he would now unravel psychologically.

'I beat myself,' he said quickly. 'I didn't lose to anyone else.'

Watching him in Gleason's then, eight months later, I wondered whether this reasoning was just another part of the clichéd logic a fighter comforted himself with when things were not going according to plan. But Barrett had since made a successful comeback after taking four months off while his wife was ill. He had appeared in the main event of two Hammerstein shows on the trot, taking a decision from a square-built pug named Derrick Banks and then knocking out the sometimes dangerous Samoan Jimmy Thunder in what many had described as the best performance of his career.

'I've been making his defence a lot stronger,' Judah told me. 'And I've made his balance better, too. He can punch and he's got a great chin – not that he's gonna get hit – no way. It's all about leverage, that was his problem. Before he came to me, his defence was his legs, he relied on them too much, but I've been slowing him down and showing him how to use his arms and shoulders, slipping and rolling, the kind of moves he needs when his legs slow down.'

When Barrett's training for the night was over, we left Gleason's and rested beside his new car, drinking Gatorade and talking about what had changed in his life since the day I had met a 10–0 fighter in the furthest reaches of Brooklyn.

'I always knew there would be good and bad in this game – you know how it is – but as I got more experienced, I became more mature,' he said with a smile, his lips expressing each word fully, his body leaning against the car as the skies darkened behind him and the illuminations of the skyline reflected off the water and the looming presence of Brooklyn Bridge. 'I learned a lot about the business of boxing, and I learned it quickly because I had to. It's made me a stronger person overall. I have to keep clean and focused, because this is the livelihood that I have chosen for me and my family. I've tried to be idealistic in a lot of things, but these days I'm just trying to be more conscious of my role as a father, and of all the decisions that I make with my career which might affect that. I was impatient in the beginning. I think, like any young heavyweight, I wanted to be on TV, wanted to fight often, get people to know me . . . you know, you want everything to come within seconds of deciding you want it. But I learned that things which are worth while take time to build.'

The previous evening, Grant had failed miserably against Lewis. He had come into the ring staring at the ceiling, praying to God and muttering unheard incantations. Lewis had sauntered, as usual, to the Clint Eastwood beat of the ice-calm gunslinger. Grant had gulped air thirstily and seemed on the verge of hyperventilating.

Lewis had scorched Grant in two rounds. At the end of the press conference which had followed, Grant had recognised me as he passed by and headed towards the side exit and his waiting limo. 'Nick!' he had called out, turning his head to smile at me as his entourage hurried him along. 'How you doin', Domi-Nick?' And then he was gone, unable to walk in a straight line as he hobbled away in pain, his words grinding inside his mouth.

'I felt sorry for Michael,' said Monte, as I recounted this tale to him. 'He let his anxieties get to him. He was overcome with emotion, anxiety and fear. He should have forgotten about being a born-again Christian – God is with you, you should just accept that and then get on with the job. You have to have confidence and faith in yourself. Instead, his anxieties got the better of him, and he just rushed out with his hands down. You just can't do that against a guy like Lennox Lewis. He'll take you out, and that's what happened. I get anxious with the business side, but not the part when it comes to the actual fighting. I had and still have a lot of high hopes for myself, despite losing to Whitaker. You know what? I've got twenty-three wins and one give-away! He was stronger than I expected, but I just didn't do what I was supposed to do. I didn't listen to my corner and I paid the price, even though I thought I won. Since then I've become more durable, more open-minded and more hungry, so my destiny must have been to lose that fight so I could become this way. The loss could have made me or broken me. It's made me.'

I remembered Barrett once describing to me his dislike for Rahman, after the two had exchanged words during a gym workout. Hasim had been surprised when I had mentioned the incident, barely recalling any ill-feeling between the two and telling me that he was truly sorry if any offence had been taken on the other fighter's part. Whatever had been the case, it still rankled 2GUNZ several years on, and he wasn't about to cut Rahman any slack when I asked him to compare the consequences of his loss to Whitaker to the one Rahman had suffered against Maskaev the previous November.

'But he's Hasim, and I'm Monte,' said Barrett indignantly. 'There are no similarities there. For one, he was always overrated. I respect every boxer, but he was overrated. He never had as much ability as me, and he still doesn't. Monte doesn't get stopped. No way do he and I belong in the same boat. He's been stopped twice now.'

'So had you been stopped against Whitaker, the damage would have been much longer-lasting?' I asked.

'I don't even think about getting stopped,' Barrett replied, looking a little insulted. 'Nobody's gonna stop me. The only way I get stopped is if I quit, and I ain't never gonna quit.'

The other boxers in the gym had filtered away into the night by now, and the doors to the building were being locked up. The car's engine was warm and purring beside us. On paper, Barrett had rebounded from the Whitaker defeat, and he sensed now that he was only two or three fights away from getting the chance to combat the same demons which had engulfed Michael Grant during the walk to the ring to box Lennox Lewis.

'I'm a matchmaker's dream,' he said. 'Any day now, and I'm gonna take one of those top guys by surprise. I'm calm about it all, about what's going to happen to me tomorrow and the day after. We all go through fear and anxiety, but you deal with it. It's easy for me to control my emotions, because it has to be. This is my destiny.'

★

I was back in Easton now, walking and talking with Larry Holmes. Perhaps I was becoming too sentimental about boxing for my own good. Perhaps I had to learn to become more detached and aloof from it all, like Lennox Lewis, who had said that sometimes you had to remember not to take this all so seriously; or to Monte Barrett, who had said it meant nothing personal and that he and his opponent could catch a movie together the following night; or to Hasim Rahman, who said the glory and the belts didn't matter at all as long as he kept putting money in the bank.

They were all edging nearer to what they kept referring to as their 'destiny'. Lewis was counting down the days until his pay-day with Mike Tyson; Barrett was sensing an opportunity to fight in some form of championship eliminator which would then leapfrog him into the big picture; Rahman was taking to running on deep sands to increase his 'resistance', and admitting that 'one more defeat, and it's over'.

And then there was Tim Witherspoon, still fighting and still getting his body broken and beaten by opponents just so he could get his telephone reconnected, or take everyone out for another Chinese takeaway. The last time I spoke to his manager, Tom Moran, they had all just returned from a long spell in Antigua, where the old heavyweight had wound up getting a draw against an opponent who would have been lucky to have lasted a few minutes with him in his prime.

'But the way Tim sees it,' said Tom, 'is if they're gonna keep paying him to fight guys who can't hurt him, why not?'

Walking beside Holmes, I relayed Moran's thoughts through my mind. 'Don't you find it sad to see someone like Tim getting beaten up at his age? Don't you see why people wince at the thought of fifty-year-old Larry Holmes trying to get a fight with Lennox Lewis?' I asked, as Holmes and I paced slowly from one of his many office blocks to another.

During the last week of my stay in New York I had met Renaldo Snipes, a former opponent of Holmes, at an Italian restaurant in the Bronx. Snipes was gruff and bore a huge chip on his shoulder, and he had frowned beneath thick, Denis Healey eyebrows when I brought up his alleged association with local mobsters.

Drinking bottles of beer and eating seafood linguini, he had begun our meeting by insisting angrily that his fighting days were over, and that he would never fight again. And then, three beers later, and supplied by me with the knowledge that Holmes and 'Bonecrusher' Smith and Wither-spoon fought on, he had sighed, looked at me coldly and muttered, 'I'm gonna come back, and for one reason only – the people are demanding to see Renaldo Snipes again, because nobody else out there can fight.'

'It's only sad if we're doin' it for $30,000, $40,000,' Holmes replied. 'It ain't sad if we doin' it for $250,000. How can that be sad?'

'Because you're taking away from your achievements of the past,' I said. 'History might not treat you so kindly. Look at Tim – he won the world title from Greg Page in 1984, and just the other day the two of them fight on your undercard and Tim gets beaten up in eight rounds.'

'History,' murmured Holmes, admiring his buildings from afar. 'Let me tell you something about history. We all live for the moment. We have to live and we have to survive. When it's time to die, you die, an' there ain't nothing you can do about it, and it ain't no different for heavyweight champions. It all ends for us the same way it ends for everyone else. Why should we all care about history, when the day we die we ain't never gonna see what was written about us anyway?'

'You never know,' I suggested.

'Well, my friend, if you ever find out otherwise, you jus' make sure you give me a call and let me know,' said Holmes.

I was still feeling uncomfortable about the way in which Rahman's career had been derailed, and with the personal torment I had felt since being drawn so much more deeply than I had ever imagined was possible into the insanity of boxing.

But then Holmes started laughing, and I did too, and cheered now by his frankness and honesty, I started to remember why the sport had meant so much to me for so long, and why – despite its ruthless dark side – its charisma and purity would surely keep me along for the ride for many years to come.